W9-COY-629

Queensbury, NY 12804

LEGAL ASPECTS *of* ELDER CARE

MARSHALL B. KAPP, JD, MPH, FCLM
Garwin Distinguished Professor of Law and Medicine
Southern Illinois University School of Law and School of Medicine
Carbondale, Illinois

JONES AND BARTLETT PUBLISHERS
Sudbury, Massachusetts
BOSTON   TORONTO   LONDON   SINGAPORE

World Headquarters

Jones and Bartlett Publishers
40 Tall Pine Drive
Sudbury, MA 01776
978-443-5000
info@jbpub.com
www.jbpub.com

Jones and Bartlett Publishers
Canada
6339 Ormindale Way
Mississauga, Ontario L5V 1J2
Canada

Jones and Bartlett Publishers
International
Barb House, Barb Mews
London W6 7PA
United Kingdom

Jones and Bartlett's books and products are available through most bookstores and online booksellers. To contact Jones and Bartlett Publishers directly, call 800-832-0034, fax 978-443-8000, or visit our website www.jbpub.com.

Substantial discounts on bulk quantities of Jones and Bartlett's publications are available to corporations, professional associations, and other qualified organizations. For details and specific discount information, contact the special sales department at Jones and Bartlett via the above contact information or send an email to specialsales@jbpub.com.

This publication is designed to provide accurate and authoritative information in regard to the Subject Matter covered. It is sold with the understanding that the publisher is not engaged in rendering legal, accounting, or other professional service. If legal advice or other expert assistance is required, the service of a competent professional person should be sought.

Production Credits
Publisher: Michael Brown
Associate Editor: Katey Birtcher
Editorial Assistant: Catie Heverling
Production Editor: Katherine Macdonald
Production Assistant: Roya Millard
Marketing Manager: Sophie Fleck
Manufacturing and Inventory Control Supervisor: Amy Bacus
Composition: Newgen Publishing & Data Services
Cover Design: Scott Moden
Printing and Binding: Malloy, Inc.
Cover Printing: Malloy, Inc.

Library of Congress Cataloging-in-Publication Data
Kapp, Marshall B.
 Legal aspects of elder care / Marshall B. Kapp.
   p. cm.
 Includes bibliographical references and index.
 ISBN-13: 978-0-7637-5632-1 (cloth)
 ISBN-10: 0-7637-5632-6 (cloth)
  1. Old people–Legal status, laws, etc.–United States. I. Title.
  [DNLM: 1. Aged–United States.   2. Health Services for the Aged–legislation & jurisprudence–United States.   3. Geriatrics–legislation & jurisprudence–United States. 4. Public Policy–United States.   WT 33 AA1 K17L 2010]
KF390.A4K37 2010
346.7301'3—dc22
                                        2009000034
6048

Printed in the United States of America
13 12 11 10 09   10 9 8 7 6 5 4 3 2 1

Table of Contents

Preface

Caring for older individuals is a significant component of professional life for providers of health and human services in the United States today. Planning, providing, and evaluating geriatric care raises a wide variety of legal issues for health and human services practitioners and those who advocate for, develop, and enforce the public policies within which services are delivered. Therefore one would expect educators of present and future service and public policy professionals in the aging arena to integrate a substantial amount of teaching about legal issues into the course content for those professionals, and indeed we are seeing some substantial movement in this direction in undergraduate, graduate, and continuing professional education programs aimed at the student audience just described.

However, a major obstacle to the effective, aggressive integration of legal content into the aging curriculum is the absence of good, targeted pedagogical material aimed specifically at teaching health and human services and public policy professionals about the legal aspects of geriatric care. This book aims to fill that gap by supplying an organized collection of materials that can be used for educational purposes at various levels and by instructors with or without prior legal teaching expertise and experience.

I hope this text will be useful for lecture courses, seminars, and tutorials at various levels for students in the fields of public policy and administration, social work, nursing, sociology, psychology, health and human services administration, philosophy (including ethics), medicine, and criminal justice, among others, who are interested in aging. Each chapter provides excerpts (to the extent they are relevant and available) from selected statutes and regulations, judicial opinions, and the legal and healthcare journal literature, as well as commentary on these materials, discussion questions and hypothetical cases, and suggestions of other information sources for the teacher and student. My goal is to inform and sensitize those who will deal professionally with older persons about some of the current and potentially emerging legal issues they may encounter in providing services to older persons and to help them deal intelligently with legal issues and the responsibilities they impose.

A Note on Legal Citations and Legal Sources

This book includes legal citations for statutes and regulations, judicial decisions, and published articles. The law has its own unique method for citing these sources of authority.

Legal citations for statutes and regulations generally take the form of Volume, Name of Publication (abbreviated), Section or Part, and Year. Thus, for example, 42 U.S.C. §1395 (1999) (the Medicare statute) is found at Volume 42 of the United States Code, Section 1395, with the most recent publication of that Section in 1999. In some situations, such as citation to the Federal Register or Congressional Record, the page number rather than section number is given.

Citations to judicial opinions in litigated cases take the form of name of case, volume, name of official reporter system (abbreviated), first page of opinion plus page(s) of material specifically quoted or referred to, and year. For state court cases, there usually is a parallel citation to the state Reporter system. For example, *Kapp v. The World*, 333 A.2d 450, 400 N.J. 100 (1998) refers to a case that can be found in Volume 333 (Second Series), beginning at page 450 of the Atlantic Reporter system or Volume 400, beginning at page 100 of the New Jersey Reporter system. For federal cases, F. Supp. refers to the Federal Supplement Reporter system (which contains opinions of the federal district, or trial level, courts); F., F.2d, or F.3d refers to opinions by Federal Circuit Courts of Appeal; and U.S. or S.Ct. refers to opinions by the United States Supreme Court.

Legal citations to published articles ordinarily take the form of Author, article title, volume of journal, name of journal (abbreviated), beginning page and page number(s) of material specifically quoted or referred to, and date. A reference to Marshall B. Kapp, *A Brilliant Idea*, 125 Harvard L. Rev. 400 (2007) thus could be found in Volume 125 of the Harvard Law Review beginning at page 400 and published in 2007.

For further information about legal citation forms, consult the latest edition of *The Bluebook: A Uniform System of Citation*, published by the

Harvard Law Review Association in Cambridge, MA. *The Bluebook* is now in its 18th edition.

Copies of any of the legal sources cited throughout this text may be obtained by instructors and students for free. Hard copies of all federal and state statutes and regulations, as well as federal case reports and case reports from one's particular state (and often from other states as well), may be found at local law libraries (located in law schools and federal and county courthouses) and most decent-sized public and college libraries. Federal laws may also be obtained by contacting one's congressional representative, and state laws may be obtained from one's state representative. Law libraries are the best place to find law review/law journal articles; articles usually may be ordered through a college's interlibrary loan system.

Statutes and regulations also are easily obtainable on the World Wide Web. Federal judicial opinions are available for free at www.uscourts.gov/link and www.Alt.Law.org. Materials from individual states generally are available at www.state.[abbreviation of specific state].us. Another valuable web portal for obtaining primary legal materials is www.findlaw.com. Valuable government links include www.gpo.gov/su_docs (for Code of Federal Regulations and Federal Register), www.gao.gov (for reports of the Government Accountability Office), www.cms.gov (for materials of the Centers for Medicare and Medicaid Services, including the Medicare and Medicaid laws and interpretations), and www.medicare.gov (Medicare materials).

General websites of interest to teachers and students of law and aging include www.aclm.org, www.uslaw.com, www.nih.gov/sigs/bioethics, www.law.uh.edu/healthlaw, and www.healthlawyers.org. To research questions relating to law and aging in countries besides the United States, begin with *International Elder Law Research: A Bibliography*, 2 J. Internat'l Aging, L. & Pol'y 143–166 (2007).

About the Author

Marshall B. Kapp is the Garwin Distinguished Professor of Law and Medicine in the School of Law at Southern Illinois University-Carbondale. He holds a joint faculty appointment in the Department of Medical Humanities at the SIU School of Medicine. He is Professor Emeritus at Wright State University School of Medicine, where he taught and directed the Office of Geriatric Medicine and Gerontology from 1980 through 2003. He was a member of the adjunct faculty during that time at the University of Dayton School of Law, where he taught a course on Law and Aging. In 2003, the Gerontological Society of America presented Kapp with its Donald P. Kent Award.

Abbreviations Used in This Text

See generally Acronyms in Aging: Organizations, Agencies, Programs, and Laws, www.aarp.org/research/reference/agingtrends/aresearch-import-881.html

Activities of daily living (ADLs)
Administration on Aging (AoA)
Adult Protective Services (APS)
Adverse drug events (ADEs)
Age Discrimination in Employment Act (ADEA)
Agency for Healthcare Research and Quality (AHRQ)
Alzheimer's disease (AD)
Alzheimer's Home Screening Test (AHST)
American Association of Homes and Services for the Aging (AAHSA)
American Medical Association (AMA)
Americans with Disabilities Act (ADA)
Area Agencies on Aging (AAA)
Artificial nutrition and hydration (ANH)
Assisted Living Federation of America (ALFA)
Association of American Medical Colleges (AAMC)
Attorney General (AG)
Cardiopulmonary resuscitation (CPR)
Centers for Medicare and Medicaid Services (CMS)
Certified nurse assistants (CNAs)
Chronic obstructive pulmonary disease (COPD)
Clinical Laboratory Improvement Act (CLIA)
Contract Research Organization (CRO)
Compliance Program Guidance (CPG)
Congestive heart failure (CHF)
Continuing care retirement community (CCRC)
Controlled Substances Act (CSA)

Department of Health and Human Services (DHHS)
Department of Health, Education and Welfare (DHEW)
Department of Housing and Urban Development (HUD)
Department of Justice (DoJ)
Department of Motor Vehicles (DMV)
Do not resuscitate (DNR)
Driver rehabilitation specialist (DRS)
Drug Enforcement Agency (DEA)
Durable power of attorney (DPOA)
Emergency medical service (EMS)
Emergency Medical Treatment and Active Labor Act (EMTALA)
Employee Retirement Income Security Act (ERISA)
End-of-life (EOL)
End-stage renal disease (ESRD)
Equal Employment Opportunity Commission (EEOC)
Fair Housing Amendments Act (FHAA)
Fair Labor Standards Act (FLSA)
Family and Medical Leave Act (FMLA)
Federal Bureau of Investigation (FBI)
Federal Insurance Contributions Act (FICA)
Federal Trade Commission (FTC)
Federation of State Medical Boards (FSMB)
Fiscal year (FY)
Food and Drug Administration (FDA)
Food, Drug, and Cosmetic Act (FDCA)
Health Insurance Portability and Accountability Act (HIPAA)
Home- and community-based long-term care (HCBLTC)
Home- and community-based services (HCBS)
Home Health Advance Beneficiary Notice (HHABN)
Home health agency (HHA)
Home health care (HHC)
Institutional ethics committee (IEC)
Institutional review board (IRB)
International Federation on Ageing (IFA)
Least restrictive alternative (LRA)
Licensed practical nurse (LPN)
Life-sustaining medical treatments (LSMTs)

Long-term care (LTC)
Managed care organization (MCO)
Mini-Mental State Examination (MMSE)
Minimum Data Set (MDS)
National Academy of Elder Law Attorneys (NAELA)
National Bioethics Advisory Commission (NBAC)
National Highway Traffic Safety Administration (NHTSA)
National Research Council (NRC)
Nursing Home Quality Initiative (NHQI)
Office of Inspector General (OIG)
Old Age, Survivors and Disability Insurance (OASDI)
Older Americans Act (OAA)
Omnibus Budget Reconciliation Act (OBRA)
On-Line Survey and Certification Assessment Reporting (OSCAR)
Oregon Death With Dignity Act (ODWDA)
Patient Self-Determination Act (PSDA)
Persistent vegetative state (PVS)
Personal Responsibility and Work Opportunity Reconciliation Act (PRA)
Power of Attorney (POA)
Preferred provider organization (PPO)
Quality Improvement Organization (QIO)
Resident Assessment Instrument (RAI)
Registered nurse (RN)
State Units on Aging (SUAs)
Study to Understand Prognoses and Preferences for Outcomes and Risks of Treatment (SUPPORT)
Supplemental Security Income (SSI)
Uniform Determination of Death Act (UDDA)
Uniform Guardianship and Protective Proceedings Act (UGPPA)
Utilization review (UR)

Acknowledgments

Gratitude is expressed to the Garwin Family Foundation for its support of the Chair held by the author, which permitted him the opportunity to work on this book.

Copyright holders of the following works graciously permitted portions of them to be included in this book:

Marshall B. Kapp, *Aging and the Law* originally appeared in Robert Binstock et al., eds., *Handbook of Aging and the Social Sciences* (6th ed.) (2006) (Elsevier).

Marshall B. Kapp, *Social Values and Older Persons: The Role of the Law* originally appeared in Vol. 7, No. 1 (2005) of Marquette Elder Advisor's Law Review, reprinted by permission of Marquette Elder Advisor's Law Review.

Marshall B. Kapp, *Family Caregivers' Legal Concerns* originally appeared in Vol. 27, No. 4 (Winter 2003–04) of Generations: Journal of the American Society on Aging, © 2004 American Society on Aging.

Marshall B. Kapp, *Ethics and Medical Decision Making* originally appeared in James E. Birren, ed., *Encyclopedia of Gerontology* (2nd ed.) (2006) (Elsevier).

Marshall B. Kapp, *The Business Case for Medical Informed Consent* originally appeared in Vol. 19 (2007) of International Journal of Risk & Safety in Medicine, © Author.

Marshall B. Kapp, *Informed Consent Implications of Diagnostic Evaluations for Dementia* originally appeared in Vol. 21, No. 1 (Jan./Feb. 2006) of American Journal of Alzheimer's Disease and Other Dementias, reprinted by permission of Sage Publications, Inc.

Marshall B. Kapp, *Legal Liability Anxieties in the ICU* originally appeared in J. Randall Curtis & Gordon D. Rubenfeld, eds., *Managing Death in the Intensive Care Unit: The Transition from Cure to Comfort* (2001). Reprinted by permission of Oxford University Press, Inc.

Marshall B. Kapp, *Regulating the Foregoing of Artificial Nutrition and Hydration: First, Do Some Harm* originally appeared in Vol. 50, No. 3 (March 2002) of Journal of the American Geriatrics Society, reprinted by permission of the American Geriatrics Society.

Marshall B. Kapp, *Editorial, The U.S. Supreme Court Decision on Assisted Suicide and the Prescription of Pain Medication: Limit the Celebration* originally appeared in Vol. 2, No. 2 (March/April 2006) of Journal of Opioid Management, reprinted by permission of Taylor and Francis.

Marshall B. Kapp, *Old Folks on the Slippery Slope: Elderly Patients and Physician-Assisted Suicide* originally appeared in Vol. 35, No. 1 (1996) of Duquesne Law Review, reprinted by permission of Duquesne Law Review.

Marshall B. Kapp, *Economic Influences on End-of-Life Care: Empirical Evidence and Ethical Speculation* originally appeared in Vol. 25, No. 3 (April 2001) of Death Studies, reprinted by permission of Taylor & Francis.

Marshall B. Kapp, *Reforming Guardianship Reform: Reflections on Disagreements, Deficits, and Responsibilities* originally appeared in Vol. 31, No. 3 (Spring 2002) of Stetson Law Review, reprinted by permission of Stetson Law Review.

Marshall B. Kapp, *Consumer Direction in Long-Term Care: A Taxonomy of Legal Issues*, Vol. 24, No. 3 (Fall 2000) of Generations: Journal of the American Society on Aging, © 2000 American Society on Aging.

Marshall B. Kapp, *Altering the Home Care Agency/Client Relationship: Notice Requirements* originally appeared in Vol. 5, No. 3 (Fall 2004) of Care Management Journals: Journal of Long-Term Home Health Care, reprinted by permission of Springer Publishing.

Marshall B. Kapp, *Consumer-Driven Long Term Care: Shaping the Government's Role* originally appeared in Vol. 8, No. 2 (Spring 2007) of Marquette Elder Advisor's Law Review, reprinted by permission of Marquette Elder Advisor's Law Review.

Marshall B. Kapp, *Nursing Home Reform Act* originally appeared in Elizabeth Capezuti et al., eds., *Encyclopedia of Elder Care* (2nd ed.) (2007), reprinted by permission of Springer Publishing Company.

Marshall B. Kapp, *Improving the Quality of Nursing Homes: Introduction to a Symposium on the Role of Regulation* originally appeared in Vol. 26, No. 1 (March 2005) of Journal of Legal Medicine, reprinted by permission of Taylor and Francis.

Marshall B. Kapp, *Resident Safety and Medical Errors in Nursing Homes: Reporting and Disclosure in a Culture of Mutual Distrust* originally appeared in Vol. 24, No. 1 (March 2003) of Journal of Legal Medicine, reprinted by permission of Taylor and Francis.

Marshall B. Kapp, *"At Least Mom Will Be Safe There": The Role of Resident Safety in Nursing Home Quality* originally appeared in Vol. 12, No. 3 (2003) of Quality and Safety in Health Care, reprinted by permission of BMJ Publishing Group.

Marshall B. Kapp, *Making Patient Safety and a "Homelike" Environment Compatible: A Challenge for Long Term Care Regulations* originally appeared in Vol. 12, No. 1 (2005) of Widener Law Review, reprinted by permission of Widener Law Review.

Marshall B. Kapp, *Resistance to Nursing Home Restraints Reduction Revisited: Introduction to a Symposium* originally appeared in Vol. 20, No. 3 (Summer 2008) of Journal of Aging & Social Policy, reprinted by permission of Haworth Press. Article copies available from Haworth Document Delivery System, getinfo@haworthpressinc.com.

Marshall B. Kapp, *The Nursing Home Crisis: Views from a Trustee in the Nonprofit Sector* originally appeared in Vol. 4, No. 2 (2002) of Journal of Health Care Law & Policy, reprinted by permission of the Journal of Health Care Law & Policy.

Marshall B. Kapp, *Medicaid Planning, Estate Recovery, and Alternatives for Long-Term Care Financing: Identifying the Ethical Issues* originally appeared in Vol. 7, No. 2 (Summer 2006) of Care Management Journals: Journal of Long-Term Home Health Care, reprinted by permission of Springer Publishing Company.

Marshall B. Kapp, *Confidentiality* originally appeared in Sana Loue & Martha Sajatovic, eds., *Encyclopedia of Aging and Public Health* (2008), reprinted with kind permission of Springer Science and Business Media.

Marshall B. Kapp, *Regulating Hematology/Oncology Research Involving Human Participants* originally appeared in Vol. 16, No. 6 (December 2002) of Hematology Oncology Clinics of North America, reprinted by permission of Elsevier.

Marshall B. Kapp, *Protecting Human Participants in Long-Term Care Research: The Role of State Law and Policy* originally appeared in Vol. 16, No. 3 (2004) of Journal of Aging & Social Policy, reprinted by permission of Haworth Press. Article copies available from Haworth Document Delivery System, getinfo@haworthpressinc.com.

Marshall B. Kapp, Book Review of *Elder Mistreatment: Abuse, Neglect, and Exploitation in an Aging America* originally appeared in Vol. 5, No. 1 (Fall 2003) of Marquette Elder Advisor's Law Review, reprinted by permission of Marquette Elder Advisor's Law Review.

Marshall B. Kapp, *Should Home Screening Tests for Alzheimer's Disease Be Regulated?* originally appeared in Vol. 43, No. 3 (June 2003) of The Gerontologist, reproduced by permission of the Gerontological Society of America.

Marshall B. Kapp, *Health Care Rationing Affecting Older Persons: Rejected in Principle but Implemented in Fact*, originally appeared in Vol. 14, No. 2 (2002) of Journal of Aging & Social Policy, reprinted by permission of Haworth Press. Article copies available from Haworth Document Delivery System, getinfo@haworthpressinc.com.

CHAPTER 1

Introduction

This Introduction examines some of the fundamental questions that are explored in more specific contexts in the following chapters of this book, including what is "the law" and what does it have to do—both positively and negatively—with older Americans, their families, the professional health care and human service providers and institutions who care for older persons, and the public policymakers and advocates who establish the legal boundaries within which such care takes place?

LAW AS A SOCIAL TOOL (TABLE 1.1)

Law is a social process that embodies and symbolizes important public attitudes while at the same time influencing various actions by society. In light of these fundamental social roles, law and the legal system exert an enormous impact on the everyday lives of older persons and those who care for and about them.

Types of Law

The "law" is not one monolithic entity but instead is composed of several distinguishable but interwoven strands. Constitutional law emanates from the written documents that serve as the basic blueprints for the national government and the various states and localities. A constitution, and judicial interpretations of its provisions, spells out the powers and limits of a government as it relates to its citizens. The federal Constitution's Bill of Rights (the first 10 Amendments) and the Fourteenth Amendment, which extended most of those rights to the state level, explicitly protect

Table 1.1   Types, Sources, and Functions of the Law

Types of law
    Constitutional
    Statutory/legislative
    Regulatory/administrative
    Common law
Sources of law
    Federal government
        Constitution Article I Taxing and Spending Power
        Constitution Article I Power to Regulate Interstate and Foreign
            Commerce
    State government
        Police power
        Parens patriae power
Functions of the law
    Delineate groups' relative social status
    Prevent or mitigate potentially harmful behavior
    Create and finance social programs
    Control production and distribution of resources
    Set and enforce minimum standards of quality
    Establish personal rights

individuals against unwanted official intrusions by limiting the authority of the federal and state governments in important respects. For example, the Fourteenth Amendment's guaranty of equal protection of the laws probably would prohibit a state from enforcing a law that attempted to single out only persons above a specified age for periodic driving reexaminations as a mandatory condition of licensure.

Statutory or legislative law consists of enactments by elected federal, state, and local legislatures operating under constitutional authority. Political ideology and pragmatic considerations greatly influence how elected officials use their constitutional powers to legislate social policy. Among the numerous federal statutes of direct significance to older persons are the Social Security Act provisions on retirement and disability, Medicare and Medicaid health insurance, the Older Americans Act (OAA), various Omnibus Budget Reconciliation Acts (OBRAs), the Age Discrimination in Employment Act (ADEA), the Americans with Disabilities Act (ADA), the Age Discrimination Act, the Employee Retirement Income Security

Act, and the Patient Self-Determination Act. Relevant state statutes would include, among many others, those concerning guardianship, advance medical directives, and special treatment of property taxes for older landowners. Older persons are also more likely to be affected by local ordinances concerning fire safety in businesses and dwellings (including assisted living facilities and nursing homes) and minimum age restrictions on who may occupy units in particular types of rental communities.

Often, legislatures pass broadly written statutes (for instance, the creation of a prescription drug subsidy for older persons in the Medicare Modernization Act of 2003). The authority to fill in the crucial specific details pertaining to the implementation and enforcement of such a broad program usually is delegated to administrative (regulatory) agencies that are part of the executive branch of government, such as the federal Department of Health and Human Services or state health or welfare departments. Every public program benefitting older persons is governed pervasively by rules or regulations that have been promulgated as part of the formal administrative lawmaking process.

Finally, common law refers to principles developed by the courts, pursuant to an evolutionary process of case-by-case adjudication, to resolve disputes and guide future conduct in situations where there are no applicable constitutional, statutory, or regulatory provisions. Contemporary laws relating, for example, to medical malpractice mainly come from the common law (although both substantive and procedural principles may subsequently have been modified by, or codified in, statutes).

Sources of Legal Authority

Congress' power to legislate (and, hence, federal administrative agencies' delegated authority to regulate) in areas affecting older persons emanates from two main provisions in Article I of the U.S. Constitution. One section grants Congress the power to collect revenues through taxation and to spend those revenues to promote the general welfare. The Social Security retirement and disability programs, Medicare, and Medicaid are illustrations of government's power to bestow benefits on a specific group while at the same time imposing binding legal obligations on both program beneficiaries and their service providers. The U.S. Supreme Court has specifically rejected legal attacks on Congress' authority to enact the Social Security Act, which is a form of tax (income withholding) program.

Another section of Article I empowers Congress to control interstate and foreign commerce. The ADA and ADEA, for instance, both impose legal duties on employers and service vendors who are engaged (and almost all of them today are so engaged) in some element of interstate commerce.

State legislatures and administrative agencies attain the authority to enact statutes and publish regulations affecting older persons through two inherent governmental powers: police and *parens patriae*. The police power is the state's innate authority to act to protect and promote the general health, safety, welfare, and morals of the community. Laws authorizing involuntary commitment of mentally ill individuals who pose a serious danger to others (e.g., a demented person who subjects his neighborhood to an imminent fire hazard by leaving his stove turned on constantly) are examples of the police power in action. By contrast, *parens patriae* (literally, "father of the country") is the state's innate authority to benevolently protect people who are unable, because of disability, to fend for themselves adequately; guardianship laws, for instance, are justified on this theory.

Functions of the Law

The law as a social tool serves a number of important purposes. First, legal definitions that create distinct groups solely on the basis of their members' chronological age are a clear means of establishing and delineating relative social status. The law can affect the social status of the elderly, either positively or negatively, by requiring others to treat them either equally or preferentially.

Second, the law may seek to prevent or mitigate potentially harmful behavior, for example by requiring automobile seatbelt use or mandating periodic vision examinations for drivers. Similarly, federal regulations require local institutional review boards to evaluate and approve or disapprove (or order the modification of) risk-to-benefit ratios created within biomedical and behavioral research protocols involving human subjects exposed to an undue possibility of harm. An example of such a subject group would be persons with Alzheimer's disease whose desperate families may be willing to consent to almost any experimental intervention carrying even the most remote possibility of benefit.

Third, law is a tool for creating and financing social programs, many of which are either targeted intentionally toward older persons or incidentally but disproportionately affect the elderly. Medicare and the various health and social services funded under the OAA are examples of this facet of the law.

Fourth, law is an instrument for controlling the production and distribution of particular resources; licensure statutes for professionals and businesses, as well as legislation establishing and funding specific professional education programs, illustrate this role. So, too, do certificate of need laws, which require a satisfactory prior demonstration of public need for a particular health facility (for instance, a nursing home) before the facility may be built or expanded.

Fifth, laws try to ensure that consumers receive services that satisfy minimum standards of quality. Quality control is one of the chief rationales for the professional liability or malpractice tort system currently in place. It is also a justification for licensure and certification laws, such as the parts of OBRA 1987 that set new minimum quality standards for nursing homes and home health agencies receiving federal dollars for their services. Political considerations frequently influence the ways in which quality assurance laws get (or fail to get) implemented and enforced in practice. This is illustrated both by the consistent cooperation between consumer advocacy organizations, federal and state enforcement agencies, and the plaintiffs' personal injury bar on one side and the aggressive political lobbying efforts of the health care industry, especially the nursing home trade associations, on the other.

Finally, law is an instrument for establishing personal rights. Legal rights may be of two general types. Liberties, or negative rights, consist of an individual's shield against unwanted external interference. For instance, a physician is legally prohibited from performing surgery without the informed consent of the patient (or the patient's surrogate) because the patient owns a liberty right or freedom concerning the integrity of her own body. OBRA 1987 and its implementing regulations contain entire sections devoted to the rights of nursing home residents (e.g., rights to privacy, religious practice, and communication) against unwanted intrusions by nursing facilities or their personnel. Conversely, positive rights, or claims, entitle an individual to demand some affirmative benefit from someone else. Social Security, Medicare, and Medicaid create entitlements for designated older persons. So, too, do provisions requiring reasonable accommodations (that is, affirmative action, not just equal treatment) from employers or businesses serving disabled persons under the ADA.

LEGAL STATUS OF OLDER PERSONS

As noted earlier, one function of the law is to assign social status to individuals based on their membership in particular age groups. A major question confronting lawmakers, as the ones who are responsible for formulating and implementing specific public policy choices, is the extent to which laws and policies should differ for people of different ages. Should laws affecting older people reflect the philosophy that (1) the elderly are just like the rest of the population, so that they ought to be assured equal treatment and protection against discrimination, or, alternatively, the view that (2) the elderly as an identifiable group are unique in some relevant manner that compels, or at least justifies, special (i.e., preferential) treatment as compared with everyone else? Both advocates for older persons and lawmakers have been inconsistent on this matter, justifying their actions on both sets of arguments, depending on the particular issue context. The first model of aging and the law embraces liberty or negative rights: the right of the older individual to be protected against unwanted outside interference or unequal treatment. The latter position results in the legislative creation or judicial recognition of entitlements (claims) for the provision of specific benefits that may be enforced by the individual, solely because of his or her membership in a specific age category, against others in the public or private spheres.

Equality and Nondiscrimination

The principles of equal or nondiscriminatory treatment are contained in many laws that may affect various aspects of older persons' lives. Prominent examples include the Age Discrimination Act, ADEA, ADA, state and local ordinances forbidding housing discrimination against the aged, and the removal of age references from most state guardianship statutes pertaining to adults.

The most straightforward illustration of law in this category is the federal Age Discrimination Act passed in 1975. This Act, codified at

42 U.S.C. § 6102, provides the following: "No person in the United States shall, on the basis of age, be excluded from participation in, be denied the benefits of, or be subjected to discrimination under, any program or activity receiving federal financial assistance."

(The ADEA and ADA are discussed in Chapter 10.)

Special Needs and Preferential Treatment

In contrast to the foregoing nondiscrimination laws pertaining to the elderly is a set of laws that, paradoxically, treat older persons collectively as a group that is significantly different from, and presumptively disadvantaged in comparison with, the younger portion of the population. These latter laws represent the development, through legal processes, of programs that provide special, preferential benefits to which older persons are entitled by virtue of achieving a specified chronological age, usually plus satisfying some other qualification such as having a specific work history or present financial need. The movement toward group claims or entitlements, predicated on the presumption of unique needs resulting from old age, has been quite successful. It is exemplified by laws establishing the Social Security retirement system and other public pension programs, Medicare, Supplemental Security Income, social services (including legal services) under the OAA, government housing subsidies for the elderly, and expedited hearings for older litigants in civil lawsuits.

Title 2 of the Social Security Act (42 U.S.C. §§ 401–433 2004), entitled Old Age, Survivors and Disability Insurance, establishes retirement benefit payments for retirees aged 62 and older (the benefit amount increases the longer one waits to claim the benefit) who contributed to the Social Security trust fund by way of Federal Insurance Contribution Act (FICA) payroll taxes during their years of employment. In the same vein are legislatively established public pension programs, using advanced years as one eligibility criterion, for railroad retirees, state and local government retirees, military retirees, and veterans.

Another example of Congress' authority to collect revenues and then spend them to benefit the elderly as a group is Title 18 of the Social Security Act, created in 1965 as the Medicare program (42 U.S.C. §§ 1395 et seq.). Medicare has evolved through legislative amendment, most recently the 2003 Medicare Prescription Drug, Improvement, and

Modernization Act of 2003, Public Law No. 108–173. Medicare actually is a combination of several federal entitlements (Medicare Parts A, B, C, and D) that subsidize the cost of hospital, hospice, and physician services and outpatient prescription drugs, and to a much lesser extent nursing facility and home health care, rendered to persons aged 65 and older who either have worked and paid FICA taxes for at least 40 calendar quarters or are spouses of persons who have paid FICA taxes for at least 40 quarters. Services may be provided by private or public health care providers. The permanently and totally disabled who qualify for the Social Security Disability Insurance program and persons with end-stage renal disease also are eligible for Medicare.

Passage of the Medicare legislation as a centerpiece of President Lyndon Johnson's Great Society initiative was predicated on a congressional judgment (quite well founded at the time) that older persons, purely by virtue of membership in the elderly cohort, were likely to need public financial assistance to secure meaningful access to acceptable quality medical services. Put differently, advanced age was used in the Medicare legislation as a workable proxy for the inability of many older people to obtain group health insurance (and the lower rates thereby available) once they had terminated employment and were subject to be targeted for expensive individualized premiums, as well as extensive examinations for preexisting conditions. What really was created by Congress and President Johnson, as the recent politics of Medicare expansion has made undeniable, was a vast new middle class entitlement program. This result is not inconsistent with the intent of the original architects of Medicare to use the 1965 legislation as a strategic, incremental first step toward eventual national health insurance, although it is at this point incomplete.

Title 16 of the Social Security Act (42 U.S.C. § 1381) established the federal Supplemental Security Income (SSI) program in 1972, replacing a variety of "old age assistance" means-tested programs that were administered by the states under very minimal federal guidelines. Under the SSI legislation, monthly cash payments are provided to any eligible aged, blind, or disabled persons whose income and assets fall below predetermined amounts. To qualify as an aged person under SSI, an individual must be at least 65 years old.

The SSI program is an excellent illustration of the legal doctrine of federalism, or the appropriate distribution of authority between the federal (national) government and the various states. The Tenth Amendment of the U.S. Constitution states the following: "The powers not delegated to the United States by the Constitution, nor prohibited by it to the states, are reserved to the states respectively, or to the people." Welfare traditionally was a subject reserved for state action. SSI was an exercise of Congress' taxing and spending authority to superimpose national welfare standards on the states by essentially paying states to adopt congressionally set standards, because preexisting state provisions and standards varied hugely among the states and were perceived by national policymakers to be deficient in many cases.

The OAA (42 U.S.C. § 3001), enacted in 1965 and subsequently amended during several reauthorization processes, provides federal funds to an extensive nationwide network of State Units on Aging and local Area Agencies on Aging. In turn, these state and local entities pass these funds on to a network of thousands of providers of a variety of social services to older persons, including legal and long-term care ombudsman counseling and representation. Eligibility for most OAA-funded social services is restricted to people aged 60 and older and their spouses, on the theory that membership in that age group can accurately and fairly serve as a substitute for assessing individual need. Consequently, OAA programs do not require participants to prove financial need on an individual basis. In harmony with this philosophy, federal OAA funds are distributed to State Units on Aging largely on the basis of each state's proportion of the national population 60 years and older. Yet, numerous targeting requirements that do not directly affect an individual's eligibility for services have been included in amendments to the OAA passed since the late 1970s. For example, intrastate funding formulas developed by each state, through which State Units on Aging distribute funds to Area Agencies on Aging, are required by the OAA to favor those local areas that are more heavily populated by low-income and minority elderly, as well as older persons with the greatest need for services. Similarly, providers of OAA-funded services must target low-income and minority elderly, as well as those with the greatest need for their services.

Lawmakers also have assumed that at least a portion of the elderly population requires direct public financial subsidization concerning housing arrangements. Hence, Congress has legislated a variety of rent subsidy and home-owner assistance programs that use age as one criterion for eligibility. Furthermore, many federal and state housing assistance programs that are age neutral on their faces, in effect indirectly benefit older persons disproportionately because those persons meet financial means-tested eligibility criteria.

State statutes in some jurisdictions (e.g., California) afford older persons preferred status when they appear as plaintiffs in civil litigation by expediting their cases for trial on the court's docket. These statutes are predicated on the presumption that, absent special treatment, older persons as a group may be in danger of being disadvantaged by having their lawsuits outlive them. In many states the advanced age of a crime victim is considered an aggravating factor in determining the severity of the offense and the proper punishment.

The assumption in public benefits programs that age should be treated as an automatic proxy for negative characteristics such as poverty, dependency, vulnerability, illness, and disability has been questioned, both recently and decades ago. As noted by Robert Binstock, the "compassionate ageism" that undergirded the creation of today's age-based programs actually "set the stage for tabloid thinking about older persons by obscuring the individual and subgroup differences among them." Richard Kalish referred to the equation of old age with failure, and hence a need for public beneficence, as "the New Ageism." (Richard A. Kalish, "The New Ageism and the Failure Models—A Polemic," 19[4] Gerontologist 398–402 [1979])

DOES THE LAW ACCOMPLISH ITS GOALS?

A large body of law, which might be termed "geriatric jurisprudence," has been created with the praiseworthy intention of benefitting the older persons toward whose lives these laws are aimed. Insufficient follow-up attention, however, has been directed to investigating whether this intention is always satisfied in actual practice, that is, whether laws that are supposed to improve the quality of older persons' lives really work to achieve that goal. Only recently have scholars begun to use the analytic lens of therapeutic jurisprudence to explore the ways in which the law in practice (as opposed to theory) can exert positive or negative effects on real older people in a variety of tangible contexts, including long-term care regulation, end-of-life medical care, protection of human research subjects, guardianship and other interventions for the mentally incapacitated aged, and others. Research to date on this question indicates that the effectiveness of the law in these areas is decidedly mixed. The research points to some successes, some failures, and many uncertainties.

To cite but one of many possible examples, most state guardianship statutes have been amended in the last two decades to ensure that proposed wards in guardianship proceedings are ensured the right of representation by legal counsel. Yet, elder law experts have noted a lack of any empirical evidence that appointment of counsel actually has increased the effectiveness of guardianship proceedings (however effectiveness may be measured).

LOOKING TO THE FUTURE

A variety of challenging legal questions relating to older persons and the social relevance of age and aging are likely to confront individuals, corporations, public and private agencies, and society as a whole in the coming years. Some of these questions undoubtedly will concern the impact of continued technological advances on medical decision making. Some will revolve around the continued dilemma of balancing the autonomy and safety concerns of older persons, especially as new kinds of acute and long-term care delivery settings keep developing and more people live to a point at which their own decisional capacity becomes impaired. Issues relating to the participation of older persons in the workplace and the consumer marketplace raise a panoply of possible legal concerns. Changing family roles—for example, increasing numbers of grandparents as primary caregivers for their grandchildren—will necessitate the development of innovative legal responses. Perhaps most profoundly, the growing consciousness among government, private entities, and the general public that financial and human resources to support the health care and retirement income needs of a rapidly aging population are finite, and in many senses shrinking, will challenge lawmakers and the legal system to satisfactorily balance the legitimate, but no doubt sometimes competing, interests of individual elders and other components of our society.

DISCUSSION QUESTIONS

1. What characterization of the elderly should be reflected in the law? Should laws affecting older people reflect the philosophy that (1) the elderly are just like the rest of the population, so that they ought to be assured equal treatment and protection against discrimination, or, alternatively, the view that (2) the elderly as an identifiable group are unique in some relevant manner that compels, or at least justifies, special (i.e., preferential) treatment as compared with everyone else? *See* Marshall B. Kapp, Age-specific public programs, *Encyclopedia of Ageism* (pp. 30–32) (Erdman B. Palmore, Laurence Branch & Diana K. Harris, eds.), Binghamton, NY: Haworth Press (2005).

2. The text above discusses the constitutional principle of federalism. Should government concern and intervention regarding the health and welfare of older persons take place mainly at the national, state, or local level?

3. When "compassionate ageism" and the "new ageism" equate aging with failure and need, to what extent are these concepts accurate? In other words, to what extent are vulnerability and dependency real, serious problems for older persons, their caregivers, or society, such that these characteristics ought to be incorporated into public policy relating to the aged?

For better or worse, the law and legal processes, as powerful reflections, protectors, and shapers of social values, play a central role in the lives of older persons and those who care for and about them. A central question is whether in formulating, interpreting, and enforcing the law, chronological age ought to be treated by legislatures, regulators, and the judiciary as a material, indeed an important, or even determinative, consideration, or by contrast as a factor that should best be rejected and ignored as irrelevant or even harmful.

A good summary of the OAA is found at *The Basics: Older Americans Act*, National Health Policy Forum (Apr. 21, 2008), *available at* www .nhpf.org/pdfs_basics/Basics_OlderAmericansAct_4-21-08.pdf. For a description of the structure and functioning of the aging services "network" established by the OAA, see *The Aging Services Network: Accomplishments and Challenges in Serving a Growing Elderly Population*, National Health Policy Forum (Apr. 11, 2008), *available at* www.nhpf.org/pdfs_bp/BP _AgingServicesNetwork_04-11-08.pdf.

THE LAW AND SOCIAL VALUES

We must begin by distinguishing law from the related areas of public policy and ethics. To a large extent this distinction is artificial. Almost two centuries ago, Alexis de Tocqueville, the great French observer of American society, noted after traveling through this country that "[t]here is hardly a political question in the United States that does not sooner or later turn into a judicial one."

Nevertheless, and to grossly oversimplify, in a public policy assessment we are asking whether a possible government action, according to a variety of measures, is a good or bad idea and whether it is something that society would be wise to do. Ethics pose normative questions about what we ought to do from the perspective of moral rightness and wrongness. Law (in the form of federal, state, and local constitutional provisions, statutes, administrative rules and regulations, and common law judicial precedent) is the instrument through which we establish the boundaries or parameters within which meaningful discussions about public policy and ethics may take place and then be carried out in a principled manner.

In examining law as a boundary setter or guidepost for the consideration of policy initiatives and ethical dilemmas, there are three key questions. First, what affirmative, positive duties or responsibilities do we impose and enforce on government and/or private actors? When do we *require* that someone act in a particular manner? Second, when there is no legal *duty* to act, what *powers* do we nonetheless afford government and private actors to act if they *choose* to act? Finally, and perhaps most significantly, what legal *restraints* or limits does the law place on the powers of governmental and private actors to protect the liberty and property interests of the individuals who are affected by the actions of governmental or private actors? How do we legally balance and mediate the conflict that sometimes emerges between public power, on one hand, and private rights, on the other?

Some matters of good public policy and ethical consensus, such as ensuring adequate health care for everyone regardless of age or personal financial means, are not embodied in the law. Conversely, some legal provisions are not totally consistent with wise social policy or the prevailing ethical consensus. Most of the time, however, in a functioning democracy, the law *does* embody sound, morally defensible public policy choices.

A paradox of freedom is that its protection and perpetuation depend on the shared security provided by a strong, functional legal system and a populace committed to it. True freedom depends on our ability to rely on the legal system for protecting the right to contract with others, safeguarding of personal liberties and property interests, delineating clearly the relationship between individual and social responsibilities, and punishing wrongdoers to incapacitate and deter them from future misdeeds. These functions of the legal system all affect the well-being of older persons and, not incidentally, comprise the basic content of the required first-year curriculum in every American law school.

In performing its role of civilizing society, the law reflects, promotes, and helps to shape social norms or values. First, the law *reflects* and embodies prevailing social attitudes by codifying or enshrining them with a formal, official, and enforceable status. Medicare, for example, exists because Congress has enshrined the prevailing social consensus about the value of health security for older persons in a detailed set of obligations, powers, and entitlements. Some people get impatient with the law when it lags behind the solidification of social and ethical consensus on a particular issue. Stem cell research and cloning are good examples; both are areas where many commentators have expressed concern that we presently do not have adequate laws in place to deal comprehensively with rapidly changing and controversial scientific possibilities. However, the very fact that both the science and accompanying social attitudes about the conduct and use of that science are in a highly dynamic state argue for caution in rushing to enact law in these and similar areas before a firm social consensus on the basic value questions has been achieved.

Second, the law *promotes* social values by enforcing its provisions, ultimately through the use of force if necessary. If one decides to disobey the law, he or she does so at peril to his or her own physical and economic well-being. The availability of enforceable sanctions is one of the law's distinguishing characteristics; philosophers may try to convince us to behave in certain ways, but ultimately they cannot fine or put us in jail. This is precisely why it is the legal system to which we turn in those unfortunate circumstances when less intrusive alternatives fail and push necessarily comes to shove.

Third, the law helps to *shape* social values by acting as a grand educator—albeit not infrequently one with a heavy and intrusive fist. Sometimes people who are forced, under penalty of law, to behave in particular ways undergo a reluctant attitude transformation as a result; in spite of themselves, they internalize the norms undergirding a specific law. For instance, the OBRA 1987 implemented regulations forcing nursing homes to radically change their practices regarding the use of physical and chemical restraints on their residents. In the early days of OBRA, great consternation and teeth-gnashing prevailed throughout the nursing home industry about the anticipated disastrous impact of this law on facilities and unrestrained residents. In fact, although early compliance often was begrudging, clinical practice regarding the use of restraints has changed enormously for the better, and nursing home professionals have learned that, when properly done, the reduction or elimination of restraints in most cases can and should be accomplished to benefit everyone concerned. Hospitals, in turn, have learned from the long-term care experience and altered their restraint practices as well.

CONTENT OF THE LAW AND THE ROLE OF AGE

The discussion thus far has dealt chiefly with the *functions* or *jobs* of the law. To fulfill these multiple functions, laws require *content*. Laws need to be *about* something. One fundamental issue is how, if at all, the law's content ought to reflect the phenomenon of age. In shaping and enforcing laws, to what extent is age *material*, that is, potentially making a meaningful difference in the outcome? To what extent may we object that age is irrelevant?

DISCUSSION QUESTIONS

1. Do you believe that lawmakers, including judges, ought to take chronological age into consideration in making, interpreting, and enforcing the law? What relevant difference does age make for either an individual or a whole group? *See* Howard C. Eglit, *Elders on Trial: Age and Ageism in the American Legal System*, Gainesville, FL: University Press of Florida (2004).
2. Do you agree that, most of the time, the law embodies sound, ethically defensible public policy relating to older persons? Can you give examples of exceptions to this statement?
3. Can you give other examples (besides the one of restraint use in nursing homes) of situations in which the law has actually been able to change people's attitudes?

For older individuals and their families establishing a comfortable, ongoing working relationship with a qualified attorney—akin to the ideal relationship forged between patient and primary care physician—is essential. Elder law has become a recognized specialty. Among places to seek out recommendations for an appropriate attorney are one's physician (especially if the physician has a large geriatric practice), the social worker at health facilities or agencies with which the caregiver has contact, the local area agency on aging, local organizations such as the Alzheimer's or Parkinson's disease associations, and, most prominently, other caregivers who are in similar situations and have successfully found legal counsel. Most local bar associations operate lawyer referral services; if this resource is used, the caregiver should ask specifically for the names of attorneys who specialize in elder law. The National Academy of Elder Law Attorneys (NAELA) maintains a geographical roster of certified elder law specialists as well as state affiliates. Selecting an attorney who has achieved NAELA certification and membership in the state affiliate should be highly encouraged when a family caregiver is searching for legal counsel.

DISCUSSION QUESTIONS

How will you prepare yourself to assist older patients/clients and their families to locate and secure the professional services of qualified legal counsel in their vicinity? For assistance, *see* National Academy of Elder Law Attorneys, www.naela.org; American Bar Association Commission on Law and Aging, www.abanet.org/aging; American Association of Retired Persons (AARP), www.aarp.org/research/legal-advocacy; and National Senior Citizens Law Center, www.nsclc.org.

NOTES

Sections of this chapter were originally published in Marshall B. Kapp, *Social Values and Older Persons: The Role of the Law*, 7 Marquette Elder's Advisor 69–81 (Fall 2005); Marshall B. Kapp, *Family Caregivers' Legal Concerns*, XXVII(4) Generations 49–55 (Winter 2003–04); and Marshall B. Kapp, Aging and the Law, *Handbook of Aging and the Social Sciences* (6th ed., pp. 419–435) (Robert Binstock et al. eds.), Burlington, MA: Academic Press (2006).

CHAPTER 2

The Right to Make Decisions: Informed Consent and Refusal

Older individuals, most often in collaboration with their family members and friends, face a variety of important decisions at various points in their lives. These decisions concern multiple matters, such as financial planning and management, insurance, place and partners of residence, driving, activities, and the details of supportive services. Frequently, older persons are confronted with complicated medical decisions that arise in response to acute or chronic ailments. The process of medical decision making raises ethical (as well as legal) considerations for the older person *qua* patient, relatives, friends, and health care providers.

The ethical and legal implications of medical decision making overlap but are not identical. They overlap both in the sense that ethical principles underlie legal doctrines (that is, we do legislate ethics all the time) and in the sense that the law generally sets the boundaries or parameters within which ethical decision making, based on a balancing of normative principles of right and wrong, must take place.

To a significant extent, the ethical (as well as legal) implications of medical decision making are generic, in the sense that they apply to adults of all ages. Principles and rules developed to deal with medical decision making for younger adults apply with full force to older persons, who do not lose their ethical standing just because they have achieved older age. However, the patient's advanced years may in some instances raise issues that demand particular attention by the involved parties.

INFORMED CONSENT

An exploration of the ethical ramifications of medical decision making for all adult patients must begin with the doctrine of informed consent. Informed consent lies at the core of medical ethics today and in many ways has heralded the modern era in medical ethics. The informed consent concept originates with the principle of autonomy (self-determination, especially regarding the integrity of one's own body) and envisions a shared, interactive, decision-making process involving both the health care provider and the patient as full participants.

Informed consent is not a recently created idea. Plato referred to the requirement of informed consent to distinguish between the treatment of slaves and freemen. The informed consent concept was opposed by Hippocrates (in favor of physician-knows-best paternalism toward patients). Interest in the concept was renewed in 17th century European political philosophy, but opposition to it by the American Medical Association led to its dormancy in the American medical context until well into the 20th century. Today, there is broad agreement in the United States that, in the arena of clinical medicine, informed consent is a concept essential to the American commitment to individual rights and an evenhanded relationship between patients and health care providers. In addition to its foundation in autonomy, the informed consent doctrine has been justified by reference to the ethical principles of authenticity (letting the patient be true to his or her own values), privacy (the right to be left alone), beneficence (doing good for others), and nonmaleficence ("First, do no harm.").

It is important to note that commitment to the informed consent doctrine and its ethical predicates is not universal. In numerous other cultures, the process of medical decision making is driven by other opposing values, such as medical paternalism or a belief that families, rather than individual patients, ought to make the decisions. Professional caregivers in the United States must be sensitive to these cultural considerations, which may be particularly strong for older, especially immigrant, patients and their families.

Content of Informed Consent

In their legal formulation, the substantive components of the informed consent doctrine have evolved on a case-by-case basis as a matter of individual state common (judge-made) law. Additionally, most states have enacted statutes and/or promulgated regulations enumerating their jurisdiction's specific details regarding informed consent, for clinical care generally and/or within particular settings such as nursing facilities or public mental institutions.

The doctrine of informed consent applies to diagnostic and therapeutic medical interventions and to research-related activities involving a patient's participation (see Chapter 8). For a patient's decision about a medical intervention to be considered ethically and legally valid, three interrelated but separate elements must be present (see Table 2.1). First, the patient's participation in the decision-making process and the final decision regarding intervention must be voluntary, that is, not unduly dictated by force, fraud, duress, or other real or threatened ulterior forms of constraint or coercion. Second, the patient's agreement must be properly informed. Before proceeding, the health care professional is obligated to disclose sufficient information about the proposed intervention to empower the patient to make a knowledgeable, intelligent consent or refusal. The third essential element of legally valid consent is that the patient is presently cognitively and emotionally able to understand and manipulate pertinent information in order to make effective choices concerning personal medical care.

In terms of the informed component of the informed consent doctrine, there are two competing standards for determining how much information about a proposed medical intervention must be shared with the patient beforehand. The medical custom or reasonable professional standard

Table 2.1 Elements of Informed Consent

1. Voluntariness
2. Informed (knowing, intelligent)
3. Capable decision maker

asks what information a reasonable, prudent physician would disclose to a patient under similar circumstances. By contrast, the more recently developed materiality/patient orientation standard asks what information might make a difference (that is, might be material) in the decision-making reasoning of a reasonable, average patient in similar circumstances.

The philosophical rationale, promoted by patients' rights advocates, for the progression in informed consent doctrine in close to a majority of jurisdictions from a reasonable physician to a patient-oriented standard of information disclosure is the belief that the latter approach better promotes the ethical ideal of patient autonomy, whereas the former approach reinforces the negative practice of physician paternalism that tends to impinge on patient autonomy. There is a fundamental distinction between the two approaches. Physicians make treatment decisions based on their calculations of likely patient benefit, as affected by the particular personal characteristics of the patient being treated. Patients, by contrast, focus on the personal consequences of a decision, especially the risks and costs associated with various ways of addressing their health problem. Under the autonomy principle, the factors most important to the patient must guide the decision calculus.

Under either the materiality or reasonable physician standard, the basic elements of information disclosure included within the health care provider's fiduciary or trust obligations to the patient clearly include the following: diagnosis or nature of the problem; nature and purposes (that is, expected benefits) of the proposed intervention; reasonably foreseeable risks associated with the intervention, specifically, their likelihood of happening and potential severity if they do materialize; reasonable alternatives and their benefits and risks; and (because there is a recognized right of informed refusal) the probable risks and benefits of not undergoing the proposed intervention.

There are other informational items that some ethical commentators and courts have argued should be included as a necessary part of the informed consent process: complementary and alternative medicine alternatives, which are increasingly popular with older individuals; the cost implications of the proposed intervention for the patient (an item of importance, especially to many older persons); the particular provider's personal experience and success rate with the specific intervention recommended; other provider-specific information; the provider's financial incentives arguably impacting the patient's care; the level of uncertainty in the medical community regarding the particular intervention; and the role, if any, that defensive medicine considerations are playing in the health care provider's treatment proposal (see Table 2.2).

When informed consent to particular medical interventions is indicated by the spoken or written words of the patient (or the patient's legally authorized surrogate, as discussed in Chapter 4), the consent is characterized as express. However, there are many situations in which the patient's permission does not need to be put in words but instead may be implied from the totality of the circumstances. This occurs when, through actions, the patient signifies a wish (or at least a willingness) to receive the specific intervention by voluntarily submitting to it in a way that the health care professional can reasonably rely on to conclude that the intervention has been authorized. Implied consent is appropriate for most routine, nonrisky, noninvasive kinds of medical interventions. It is not an exception to the general informed consent doctrine; it is just a different (created by behavior instead of words) form of permission.

Express consent is more appropriate when the proposed medical intervention is intrusive and/or significantly riskier than ordinary, everyday life. With very few exceptions created by particular state statutes for certain kinds of interventions (such as testing for the HIV virus or AIDS), express consent in the form of spoken words by the patient is quite

Table 2.2 Elements of Information Disclosure

Diagnosis/nature of the problem
Expected benefits of the intervention
Reasonably foreseeable risks
Reasonable alternatives
Risks and benefits of refusal
Complementary and alternative alternatives?
Cost implications?
Provider-specific information, including personal experience?
Provider's financial incentives?
Level of uncertainty about the intervention?
Role of defensive medicine considerations influencing the provider's
  recommendations?

ethically and legally adequate, as long as it is voluntarily and competently given on the basis of sufficient information. For particularly intrusive or risky interventions, the health care provider may choose to document the patient's consent by requesting that the patient sign a separate piece of paper labeled a consent form, in addition to making a progress entry in the patient's medical record. Voluntary accreditation standards with which the provider complies, such as those of the Joint Commission on the Accreditation of Healthcare Organizations, may require the use of separate written consent forms for particular categories of medical interventions.

DISCUSSION QUESTIONS

1. Does the concept of informed consent make sense in the context of aging services? Can older people really make their own choices about important life matters? Wouldn't it be in older persons' best interests if knowledgeable caring professionals made the choices for them? *See* Vernee N. Belcher et al., *Views of Older Adults on Patient Participation in Medication-Related Decision Making,* 21 J. Gen. Intern. Med. 298–303 (2006).

2. Even if the informed consent doctrine makes sense in theory, what are some of the practical problems likely to arise as we try to apply informed consent to older persons in actual practice? What kinds of decision aids may be useful in helping older persons to make informed choices about their own medical care? *See* Erin Mathieu et al., *Informed Choice in Mammography Screening: A Randomized Trial of a Decision Aid for 70-Year-Old Women,* 167 Arch. Intern. Med. 2039–2046 (2007); Margaret Holmes-Rovner et al., *Are Patient Decision Aids the Best Way to Improve Clinical Decision Making?* 27 Med. Decision Making 599–608 (2007).

3. How do you, and how should you, deal in practice with situations involving patients from foreign cultures who do not wish (or whose families do not want them) to make their own decisions about important matters?

4. In practice, is there really a difference between the two standards of information disclosure: (1) the customary practice or professional-oriented approach versus (2) the materiality or patient-oriented approach? How would the standard in effect change the way that the professional caregiver would approach the informed consent process with a patient/client?

5. Should service providers be required to inform their older patients/clients about complementary and alternative medicine alternatives, the cost implications of the patient's decisions, provider-specific information including personal experience, any financial incentives on the part of the provider that might influence the advice being given, the level of uncertainty in the professional community regarding the intervention being suggested, or the extent to which the provider's recommendation might be influenced by the provider's legal risk management concerns? Is this information routinely shared? If not, why not?

6. Why should a patient/client be told about the potential risks and benefits of deciding not to follow the service provider's recommendations? What is the downside of not so informing the patient/client who declines the recommended intervention? *See* Richard F. Wagner, Jr. et al., *Informed Consent and Informed Refusal,* 21(6) Dermatol. Surg. 555–559 (1995).

RISK MANAGEMENT IMPLICATIONS

Besides the ethical justifications for the informed consent doctrine previously explained, there are also important legal risk management reasons that geriatric service providers must pay attention to the decision-making rights of their patients/clients. Health care providers are on notice that failure to comply with the requisite components of the informed consent doctrine before engaging in specific medical interventions with a patient may expose them to the risk of being held liable for damages in a civil medical malpractice action brought by or on behalf of the patient whose right to give or withhold permission for the proposed medical intervention was violated.

For a long time, physicians and other health care providers have been instructed that engaging in a robust informed consent (or, more accurately, informed choice) process with their patients serves a valuable legal risk management function, both by reducing the likelihood of malpractice claims being brought on the basis of insufficiencies in the communications/consent process and reducing the likelihood of adverse outcomes in those civil actions that do get filed. First, there is substantial empirical evidence that open, honest, respectful discussion of treatment alternatives, including always the option of nontreatment, enhances the quality of trust within the professional–patient relationship, with trust acting as a strong deterrent to the bringing of malpractice claims against providers irrespective of the injuries suffered by patients.

Moreover, observational studies consistently link inadequate professional–patient communication about proposed treatments with poor rates of patient adherence to such aspects of the ostensibly agreed on treatment plan as taking medications as prescribed, doing rehabilitation exercises, or restricting activities as part of the rehabilitation process. Poor patient adherence resulting from the patient's failure to enthusiastically embrace the treatment goal often jeopardizes the successful achievement of clinical results anticipated as a result of the medical intervention; the resulting patient disappointment with an unsatisfactory, even harmful, outcome from the intervention may increase the possibility of a subsequent lawsuit being initiated against the provider for negligence in professional performance. Conversely, patients who feel satisfied with the informed consent process are more likely to contribute through self-care to a favorable clinical outcome and thereby greatly reduce the probability of any subsequent legal action.

Additionally, there is evidence that a working informed consent process can improve patient safety by enlisting and empowering the patient as a full partner in helping to prevent medical errors from occurring. When errors in the clinical arena are prevented, so too are negative outcomes and hence the probability of malpractice actions based on negative clinical results is diminished.

Finally, and obviously, documentation that the health care professional has engaged in a process of properly educating patients and/or their surrogates about reasonable treatment choices serves as an essential part of the defense against any civil actions that the patient does initiate against the provider when a bad outcome happens. Documentation demonstrating reasonable conduct by the provider during the informed consent process can assist with the provider's defense against claims brought either for negligence in performance of the medical intervention or for negligence in carrying out the informed consent process itself.

DISCUSSION QUESTIONS

1. Do you believe that risk management concerns actually influence service provider behavior regarding the informed consent process? What legally "defensive" behaviors do providers engage in because of concern about potential liability for acting without proper patient/client consent?

2. Do you believe the statement that "a working informed consent process can improve patient safety by enlisting and empowering the patient as a full partner in helping to prevent medical errors from occurring" is applicable to the geriatric context? To what extent can older patients/clients be involved effectively in contributing to the safety of their own care?

Exercises

Case 1

Mr. L is an 80-year-old man who has developed difficulty in swallowing (dysphagia). He is not very concerned about his symptoms, but his granddaughter is worried and convinces him to undergo a thorough medical examination. The exam reveals a mediastinal mass impinging on the esophagus. A biopsy is recommended. If the mass is found to be cancerous, immediate major surgery, including laryngectomy and tracheostomy, would be needed to avoid obstruction. Radiation and chemotherapy might produce palliation but probably would not produce a cure. Even with aggressive treatment, obstruction could be delayed for a while but not indefinitely. Mr. L otherwise is in good health and is alert, oriented, and mentally intact. He lives in an apartment near his adult granddaughter, on whom he relies for transportation. He has not asked many specific questions about his current situation, because he does not want to impose on the physician's time for lengthy explanations, but Mr. L has not executed a durable power of attorney for health care document. The granddaughter has requested that the physician not tell Mr. L the diagnosis because of fear that Mr. L would not tolerate either the diagnosis or the disfiguring operation very well. She states that her grandfather has a history of depression. The granddaughter further argues that Mr. L's symptoms are so mild he may not need the surgery and, in any event, at his age an invasive plan of care would not be appropriate.

Should Mr. L be told his diagnosis and prognosis? Why or why not? Can a decision be made to withhold this information from Mr. L based on his granddaughter's warning about his emotional state? Has Mr. L implicitly delegated his decision-making authority to his granddaughter?

Case 2

Mrs. P is a 65-year-old married woman who just retired after teaching high school math for 30 years. She has always been a very active and energetic person in her professional, family, and community lives.

Mrs. P was admitted recently to the hospital for evaluation of abdominal pain and dysfunctional uterine bleeding. She was diagnosed with a malignant mass, which her physician strongly recommends be surgically removed immediately. She has no other serious health problems.

However, Mrs. P is scheduled to leave next week on a long-planned, and already paid for, trip with a group of fellow new retirees to remote parts of Africa for a 4-week safari. She says she is fully aware that delaying the surgery may have a serious negative impact on the ultimate outcome, but she is afraid that postponing the eagerly anticipated trip would really mean forgoing the opportunity forever. She says she will take medicine with her to control pain and that she can return to her Boston home and health care team if an emergency develops.

Mrs. P's husband has always been deferential to his wife's wishes, but now he balks. He believes his wife is not "thinking straight" about her situation. He says she has become "like a different person" on this subject. He implores the physician and her nurses to "really lean on" Mrs. P to convince her to undergo the surgery immediately.

What should the physicians and nurses do to make sure that Mrs. P is making a truly informed, voluntary, and competent decision? Do they have a duty to convince her to follow their advice? How far can they go in "leaning on" Mrs. P? If Mrs. P insists on going on the safari, what legal options are available to her husband and to the involved health care professionals? Should the husband and the health care professionals pursue their legal options? Why or why not?

The Business Case

There is an additional reason geriatric service providers should pay close attention to the matter of informed consent: the "business case" for it. Despite the powerful ethical and indisputable risk management arguments for implementation of a rigorous informed consent process in the health care arena, many physicians persist in ethically and legally suboptimal behavior in this context. Repeated studies consistently document that physicians routinely share with patients less information about treatment options than patients indicate they would want to know. Deficiencies in the informed consent process, besides representing transgressions of fundamental bioethical principles, are inadvisable from a legal risk management perspective. Suboptimal provider conduct in this context unnecessarily exposes the provider to possible malpractice litigation and liability. Nonetheless, the ethical and risk management arguments appear to be insufficient to change the informed consent practices of many physicians and other health care providers. Consequently, a new additional argument for more conscientious implementation of the informed consent doctrine in clinical practice needs to be asserted: the business case for informed consent.

Primarily out of frustration with the demonstrated failures of centralized health planning, command-and-control microregulation, and managed care approaches to bring about a health care system in which high quality is reasonably accessible to everyone at an affordable price, large-scale experiments in consumer direction have taken center stage. The health care environment in the United States has grown increasingly economically competitive in the last few years, as providers are forced to vie for patients (and the private and third-party payment dollars that accompany them) in the marketplace. Health care purchasing decisions, in both the acute and long-term care realms, have become, for a large percentage of the American population, more and more a matter of consumer choice and direction. Although the notion of public "report cards" for health care providers has attracted some skeptics, an enormous amount of comparative data about providers' credentials, costs, and clinical outcomes is being made available to the general population today, via the Internet and in hard copy form, for consumers' health care shopping purposes. Once consumers are armed with purchasing power and appropriate information, they are likely to actually behave as consumers and demand that health care providers deliver high-quality services at reasonable prices and under additional conditions agreeable to the buyer, such as demonstrating respect for the patient's right to make informed medical decisions. Health care professionals will need to learn how to compete for the finite pool of patients on the basis of price, but also on the basis of other factors—such as a positive attitude on the provider's part about the patient's decision-making autonomy—that are attractive to an increasingly sophisticated, discriminating shopping public.

A health care provider's willingness and ability to explain the various ramifications of complicated medical interventions is a very influential criterion for many patients in choosing among providers competing for the patient's business. Indications of positive performance in this sphere has great potential value in terms of a provider's marketability to consumers who are constantly becoming more sophisticated and savvy about evaluating and distinguishing among competing providers. Thus, as a matter of sound business sense, health care providers have a self-interest in presenting as positive an image of attention to the informed consent process as possible to the health care–purchasing consumer population.

There are several sources of data to which consumers might look, and hence to which provider attention should be paid, to form an impression about how well a specific provider does in facilitating meaningful informed choice about medical alternatives among its patients. Certainly, patients contemplating the selection of a health care provider may give some (or more than some) credence to word-of-mouth experiences and perceptions shared among friends about their own interactions with particular providers; creating and maintaining a positive image for attention to the informed consent process is beneficial to providers trying to keep or expand patient volume (their active "book of business"). If present or former patients consistently undergo negative experiences in getting providers to explain their medical choices to them, word of that dissatisfaction tends to spread quickly within communities. It also is conceivable that in the future, just as government agencies and private organizations now collect and publish data submitted by health care providers either under legal mandate or voluntarily on such matters as service costs and patient outcomes, data will be compiled and disseminated about providers' track records in fulfilling the requirements of informed consent.

Doing better at informing patients about material aspects of their care— aspects that might affect the decisions they need to make—simultaneously

DISCUSSION QUESTIONS

1. Why do you believe it is that "the ethical and risk management arguments appear to be insufficient to change the informed consent practices of many physicians and other health care providers"?
2. Do you agree that attention to informed consent is in the best interests of health and human services providers, economically and otherwise? Is this really an "arena in which the legal, ethical, and economic incentives are closely aligned" for providers? Is this more true when older consumers are involved, or less true? Do older consumers really care about the informed consent practices of service providers? Do geriatric service providers really have to compete for a "book of business"?
3. How can health and human service providers best convey to consumers a positive image of respect for the consumer's informed consent rights?

serves patients' interests in actively and autonomously participating in decisions about their own medical care, on one hand, and providers' interests in maximizing patient care revenues by attracting more patients in an increasingly competitive health care marketplace, on the other. This is one arena in which the legal, ethical, and economic incentives are closely aligned.

DECISION-MAKING CAPACITY

An essential element of valid informed consent is sufficient cognitive and emotional capacity on the part of the person making decisions to make a claim of autonomous decision making legitimate. However, some older persons lack enough capacity to understand and manipulate relevant information so as to make effective choices concerning medical care and other personal matters to act truly autonomously. "The determination of whether patients are competent is critical in striking a proper balance between respecting the autonomy of patients who are capable of making informed decisions and protecting those with cognitive impairment." Paul S. Appelbaum, *Assessment of Patients' Competence to Consent to Treatment,* 357 N. Engl. J. Med. 1834–1840 (2007). Legally relevant criteria for decision-making capacity include a person's present ability to (1) communicate (indicate) any preferred choice, (2) understand (grasp the fundamental meaning of) the relevant information, (3) appreciate (acknowledge) the medical situation and the likely consequences of particular treatment options, and (4) reason about (engage in a rational process of using the relevant information) intervention or nonintervention possibilities. *See* James M. Lai & Jason Karlawish, *Assessing the Capacity to Make Everyday Decisions: A Guide for Clinicians and an Agenda for Future Research,* 15 Am. J. Geriatr. Psychiatry 101–111 (2007).

Figuring out how to obtain informed consent to perform an evaluation that needs to be done for the purpose of ascertaining whether the process of informed consent even makes any sense for a particular older individual in the first place presents a legal and ethical challenge for geriatric health and human service providers.

The informed consent doctrine should apply to the situation of clinical interventions intended to evaluate particular patients for the potential presence of various forms of dementia, including Alzheimer's disease. A thorough evaluation for dementia is extensive and multifaceted. Some aspects of the evaluation, such as general physical observation of the person coupled with an in-person interview, are sufficiently routine, nonintrusive, and low risk that the absence of overt, expressed objection by the individual being observed ought to qualify as implied consent. By contrast, though, other components of a truly comprehensive dementia evaluation entail the formal administration of structured instruments, the conduct of radiological studies (e.g., computed tomographies), and other elements intrusive and/or risky enough that implied consent would not be adequate. Even the obtaining and review of the patient's medical records that were generated by other providers requires authorization, under both common law confidentiality principles and federal (and, in some instances, state) statutes and regulations intended to safeguard patient privacy.

Whether implied or express, ethically and legally valid consent requires the presence of information, voluntariness, and decisional capacity.

What this means tangibly in the context of a dementia evaluation is that the person for whom an evaluation is proposed must agree to undergo this diagnostic intervention. Such consent must be tendered only on a voluntary basis and predicated on sufficient information. Additionally, however, consent to participate in the evaluation process can only be given by an individual with sufficient cognitive and emotional wherewithal to ensure that the permission represents a truly autonomous statement of the individual's authentic, unambiguous wishes.

Therein, of course, precisely lies the ethical and legal Catch-22 dilemma. How can we ensure that persons for whom there exists sufficient suspicion of dementia to trigger a professional evaluation are not, in fact, so cognitively or emotionally impaired that they have become incapable of personally making an autonomous choice about whether or not to undergo the complex dementia diagnosis procedure?

In practice, of course, we frequently deal with this conundrum by honoring the patient's theoretical right to make the ultimate choice more in the breach than in the observance, by in many cases relying on permission tendered by a family member on behalf of the person to be evaluated rather than asking the affected individual personally. Indeed, the propriety of this type of surrogate consent, even when the surrogate has no legal authority in this regard whatsoever, often is simply taken for granted by the parties proposing the dementia evaluation or responding to a family's request that a dementia evaluation of their loved one be done. This efficient approach to the challenge of informed consent for dementia evaluation has an obvious and strong practical appeal, but it represents a trade-off that carries significant negative implications for (deficits in) respecting the dignity and autonomy (self-determination) of the person for whom dementia evaluation is proposed.

We could continue to cope with the Catch-22 of consent for dementia evaluation by relying as we traditionally have on informal surrogate requests for evaluations, coupled with the absence of active, assertive objections by the person to be evaluated—in other words, we can keep "bumbling through" rather than invoking involvement of the formal legal system. This is the path of least resistance and perhaps the most ethically sensible one in situations where there are no obvious conflicts of interest and all parties appear to be working to protect and promote the best interests and, to the extent feasible, the autonomy of the individual in whom dementia is suspected. Although (absent confirming legislation, durable power of attorney, or a court order) reliance on family members or friends for consent to evaluation lacks any formal legal imprimatur and forgoes the due process protections afforded by a more legalistic way of carrying out business, the relative ease, speed, and economy of this approach are valuable virtues.

Many written instruments for assessing decisional capacity have been developed, but the touchstone is still the Mini-Mental State Examination (MMSE) (see Table 2.3).

Table 2.3   Questions and Tasks Adapted From the Mini-Mental State Examination

---

Orientation
What is the (year) (season) (date) (day) (month)?
Where are we (state) (county) (town or city) (hospital) (floor)?

Registration
Evaluator names three common objects, and then asks the person being
  evaluated to repeat all three.

Attention and Calculation
Count backward from 100 by sevens (serial sevens backward).
Alternatively, spell "world" backward.

Recall
What were the three common objects named during registration earlier?

Language
Name a "pencil" and a "watch."
Repeat the following: "No ifs, ands, and buts."
Follow a three-stage command: Take a paper in your right hand, fold it in half,
  and put it on the floor.
Read and obey the following:
    Close your eyes.
    Write a sentence.
Copy the design I am showing you.

Data from Marshal F. Folstein et al., *"Mini-Mental State": A Practical Method for Grading the Cognitive State of Patients for the Clinician*, 12 J. Psychiatr. Res. 196–198 (1975); J. R. Cockrell & Marshal F. Folstein, *Mini-Mental State Examination*, 24 Psychopharm. Bull. 689–692 (1988).

DISCUSSION QUESTIONS

1. What sorts of symptoms or behaviors should trigger an evaluation of a patient's/client's mental capacity to give or withhold informed consent to some intervention? Does the nature of the proposed intervention matter? Should all requests by a family for a dementia evaluation of their loved one lead to an actual evaluation? What other mental disabilities, besides dementia, may impair an older person's cognitive and emotional capacity to make autonomous decisions?

2. From a practical standpoint, how would you deal with this Catch-22 situation: How would you balance the need to respect the older person's right to make autonomous choices, on one hand, against the imperative to protect the individual against foreseeable, preventable harm stemming from that person's bad, irrational choices about medical treatment or other important life matters?

Exercises

Mr. H is a 68-year-old man with hypertension and chronic renal failure. He was admitted to a hospital where he gave consent to and underwent a series of diagnostic tests, including a contrast study. He was diagnosed with end-stage renal disease (ESRD); despite treatment with a full complement of medications, his high blood pressure and hyperkalemia are not properly controlled. Mr. H needs long-term hemodialysis to survive and to avoid serious symptoms of ESRD related to fluid overload. When the physician broached this subject with him, Mr. H flatly refused to consent to the dialysis, announcing that he does not want "any mechanical stuff on my body." Mr. H has a history of alcohol abuse but appears on examination to be alert and knows his whereabouts. Nonetheless, the nurses indicate he periodically seems "confused" and his MMSE is only 20 out of a possible 30 points.

Does Mr. H have decisional capacity? Is the capacity to decide about diagnostic tests the same thing as the capacity to decide about dialysis? What weight should be given to Mr. H's score on the MMSE in assessing his capacity to decide about the initiation of dialysis? Is it necessary to seek a psychiatric consult? What weight should be given to the psychiatrist's opinion? Who is best qualified to evaluate Mr. H's decisional capacity in this situation? If Mr. H lacks decisional capacity, what should be done?

Many states have enacted legislation that addresses surrogate decision making for individuals who cannot make autonomous medical decisions for themselves. The Illinois statute is representative. 755 ILCS 40/25 provides as follows:

(a) When a patient lacks decisional capacity, the health care provider must make a reasonable inquiry as to the availability and authority of a health care agent [named] under the [state] Power of Attorney for Health Care Law. When no health care agent is authorized and available, the health care provider must make a reasonable inquiry as to the availability of possible surrogates.... . The surrogate decision makers, as identified by the attending physician, are then authorized to make decisions...for patients who lack decisional capacity...without court order or judicial involvement in the following order of priority:

(1) the patient's guardian of the person; (2) the patient's spouse; (3) any adult son or daughter of the patient; (4) either parent of the patient; (5) any adult brother or sister of the patient; (6) any adult grandchild of the patient; (7) a close friend of the patient; (8) the patient's guardian of the estate.

The health care provider shall have the right to rely on any of the above surrogates if the provider believes after reasonable inquiry that neither a health care agent under the Powers of Attorney for Health Care Law nor a surrogate of higher priority is available. Where there are multiple surrogate decision makers at the same priority level in the hierarchy, it shall be the responsibility of those surrogates to make reasonable efforts to reach a consensus as to their decision on behalf of the patient regarding the forgoing of life-sustaining treatment. If 2 or more surrogates who are in the same category and have equal priority indicate to the attending physician that they disagree about the health care matter at issue, a majority of the available persons in that category shall control, unless the minority initiates guardianship proceedings...No health care provider or other person is required to seek appointment of a guardian.

DISCUSSION QUESTIONS

How helpful do you believe a surrogate decision-making statute like this is likely to be in actual practice? What potential practical problems might you foresee in implementing this statute in real situations? Can you think of a better legal alternative to such a statute?

Exercises

Mr. G is a 75-year-old man admitted to the hospital with right hip fracture after a fall. Before this admission he had lived at home with the wife he married 10 years ago after being widowed many years earlier. He has a grown daughter with medically controlled bipolar disorder with whom he has had little recent contact because she does not get along well with Mr. G's current wife. Mr. G has had several strokes, as well as mild vascular dementia, much difficulty in retaining information, hypertension, and hyperlipidemia. Before hospital admission the wife had been caring for Mr. G despite him being a large man and the wife's own health difficulties. A couple of years ago, Mr. G filled out a do-it-yourself durable power of attorney form naming his wife as his health care agent in the event of his decisional incapacity.

The hospital's multidisciplinary geriatrics team has evaluated Mr. G from a variety of professional perspectives. His wife, who is being advised by her own nurse daughter from a previous marriage, and Mr. G's daughter disagree strongly about the best course of treatment and rehabilitation for Mr. G, indeed even on whether he should be subjected to a rehabilitation regimen.

How should the geriatrics team handle the issue of decision making for Mr. G? What is the legal status regarding medical decision making of, respectively, the wife and daughter? Would resolving the legal question pertaining to surrogate decision-making authority also resolve the handling of the interpersonal dynamics in play in this case?

NOTES

Sections of this chapter were originally published in Marshall B. Kapp, Ethics and Medical Decision-Making, *Encyclopedia of Gerontology* (2nd ed., pp. 526–528) (James E. Birren, ed.). Copyright Elsevier 2007; Marshall B. Kapp, *The Business Case for Medical Informed Consent,* 19 Intl. J. Risk Safety Med. 57–64 (2007); and Marshall B. Kapp, *Informed Consent Implications of Diagnostic Evaluations for Dementia,* 21(1) Am. J. Alzheimer's Dis. Other Dementias 24–27 (Jan./Feb. 2006). Reprinted with permission of Sage Publications, Inc.

CHAPTER 3

Legal Aspects of Death and Dying

Decisions often must be made about whether to commence, continue, withhold, or remove life-sustaining medical treatments (LSMTs) for critically ill patients, many of whom are older persons. In the overwhelming majority of these situations, a satisfactory resolution is reached through a process of discussion and negotiation involving the patient (when he or she is still able to participate), family or significant others, physicians, other members of the health care team, and perhaps some form of institutional ethics committee. Most of the time decisions quite properly are made and implemented within a framework set out in applicable federal and state statutes and regulations but without the need for any formal, official involvement of the court system.

In some cases, however, the informal or extrajudicial (i.e., outside of the courts) decision-making process breaks down, and the parties feel the need to go to court to initiate and obtain a judicial ruling. A distinct *corpus* or body of case law has evolved since the famous *In re Karen Quinlan*, 355 A.2d 647 (1976) case was decided in New Jersey. The numerous trial and appellate courts that have confronted these issues have achieved a substantial, but not a total, degree of consensus on the major points (see Table 3.1). Although litigated LSMT cases are relatively small in number (given the potential denominator, if one considers the number of critically ill patients for whom medical decisions must be made and carried out in various health care settings every day), these well-publicized cases exert a tremendous influence on the delivery of health care and the rights

Table 3.1 Judicial Consensus on Decision Making About Withholding or Withdrawing LSMT

Patient Status	Decision Maker	Criteria
Dead	No decision to be made	No decision/No LSMT
Capable patient	Patient	Patient's wishes
Incapacitated patient with an authorized proxy	Authorized proxy	Substituted judgment or best interests
Incapacitated patient with *de facto* proxy	*De facto* proxy	Substituted judgment or best interests
Incapacitated patient without proxy	Patient, if an instruction directive exists	Instruction directive
	Public or volunteer guardian	Substituted judgment or best interests
	Institutional ethics committee	
	Physician	

of patients and families near the end of life. Thus, it is important that the general boundaries or parameters for LSMT decision making set out by the courts, as well as by legislatures and regulators, are understood by those whose role it is to organize, render, and evaluate professional services within those legal limits.

LEGAL LIABILITY ANXIETIES IN THE INTENSIVE CARE UNIT[1]

Legal principles and procedures regarding medical decision making and the implementation of treatment strategies in the intensive care unit (ICU) are considerably more developed and defined in the United States (and in other Western democracies as well) today than they were only a couple of decades earlier. Nonetheless, a high degree of confusion and free-floating anxiety persists among health care professionals about possible adverse

---

[1]*See* Marshall B. Kapp, Legal Liability Anxieties in the ICU, *Managing Death in the Intensive Care Unit: The Transition from Cure to Comfort* (pp. 231–244) (J. Randall Curtis & Gordon D. Ubenfeld, eds.), New York: Oxford University Press (2001). Reprinted by permission of Oxford University Press.

legal consequences (i.e., criminal prosecution, civil liability, and/or regulatory sanctions) of actions or omissions taking place within this context. This pervasive anxiety sometimes drives provider behavior in directions that serve patients poorly near the end of life.

Much of the legal anxiety influencing suboptimal treatment for dying patients is fueled by misunderstanding and misinterpretation. For example, legal experts interviewed by the U.S. General Accounting Office indicated that when an individual's wishes are clear, difficulties in getting requests to withdraw or withhold artificial nutrition and hydration honored by health care providers typically arise from confusion about the legal ramifications rather than because any serious legal impediment actually exists. Today, most states have statutes, regulations, and/or formal guidelines providing criminal, civil, and disciplinary immunity for physicians engaged in justifiable, aggressive pain management practices using opiates, but physician worries still persist. Additionally, health care professionals occasionally cite fear of unwanted legal entanglements as a pretext or justification for conduct that is really determined more by other forces, such as the ICU rescue culture, professional education and socialization, clinical biases about what "works" best, shortcomings or discomfort in communicating with patients and/or families about end-of-life matters, financial incentives, or physicians' tendency to define medical success in bare terms of survival rather than meaningfulness or quality to the patient.

However weak the factual foundations, the law-related anxieties expressed by health care professionals—whether sincere or pretextual—are palpable, powerful influences on the quality and humanity of medical care actually provided to vulnerable ICU patients and the support available to their families. Adverse effects may take the form of overtreatment (e.g., inappropriate resuscitation attempts or artificial feeding), undertreatment (e.g., insufficient pain control), and impaired interaction with patients and families. The problem exists even for physicians and others who understand intellectually that their own legal exposure is minimal when their conduct is medically and ethically proper. The very fact that physician conduct in this most delicate of areas could conceivably be publicly questioned in a legal setting is sufficient to alter behavior. Physician Jack McCue correctly urges, "[t]he exaggerated fears of liability risks that pressure physicians and nurses to withhold palliative treatment or continue futile therapy in patients near the end of life must be addressed in a forthright fashion." (Jack McCue, *The Naturalness of Dying*, 273[13] J.A.M.A. 1039–1043 [1995])

PUTTING LEGAL RISKS INTO PERSPECTIVE

Legal scholar Alan Meisel observed, "[t]he proportion of deaths from fore-going life-sustaining treatment that is litigated is . . . very small. Somewhere between 0.2% and 0.5% have been litigated at all, and between 37 and 55 in 10 million have been litigated to the point of yielding an appellate decision." This statement is consistent with the American Hospital Association's claim, in its *Cruzan* case *amicus curiae* (friend of the court) brief, that 70% of the 1.3 million Americans who die in health care institutions each year die only after a decision to forgo some form of medical treatment has been made and implemented. In the highly publicized Study to Understand Prognoses and Preferences for Outcomes and Risks of Treatments sponsored by the Robert Wood Johnson Foundation, over 11,000 in-hospital patient deaths were investigated, and none of them entailed any after-the-fact legal claims against providers relating to treatment decisions or actions.

It is important to remember that fewer than half a dozen "right to die" legal cases have originated in the procedural posture of a malpractice suit seeking monetary damages from health care providers for improperly abating LSMT for a dying patient. This is quite understandable in light of the four elements that a plaintiff in any civil negligence case (i.e., the category into which all medical malpractice cases except those alleging intentional harm fall) must establish by a preponderance of the evidence, namely (1) a duty owed, defined by the applicable standard of care; (2) breach or violation of that duty; (3) harm or injury to the plaintiff of the sort that tort law is intended to compensate; and (4) a connection of direct or proximate causation between the defendant's deviation from the acceptable standard of care and the plaintiff's injury. In the case of a patient who was inevitably dying with or without aggressive medical intervention, it would be exceedingly difficult for a plaintiff suing for negligence on behalf of a deceased patient or in his or her own right as a survivor to prove these elements to a jury's satisfaction; in such cases, as plaintiffs' attorneys who work on the basis of contingency fees realize, it is the patient's illness or injury that proximately causes death, not any substandard care on the physician's part. (Conversely, there have been a number of malpractice actions filed where there is persuasive evidence that the withheld or withdrawn medical interventions would realistically have cured and restored the patient to good health.)

From the lawsuits requesting equitable orders, as well as the few dealing with after-the-fact complaints seeking monetary damages, a body of case law has evolved since the landmark Karen Quinlan decision in 1976 regarding medical care at the end of life. The various courts that have been confronted by these issues have achieved a high degree of consensus on the major points (see Table 3.1), although there remains diversity among jurisdictions on a number of secondary questions. Congress and the state legislatures have also gotten involved, mainly by enacting legislation intended to promote and facilitate timely advance health care planning by individuals. Additionally, individual hospitals often choose to adopt internal policies and procedures binding on their medical staffs that go beyond the requirements imposed by the federal and state governments as a matter of law.

DISCUSSION QUESTIONS

1. Why are health care providers so anxious about their potential legal exposure regarding end-of-life medical care? What are the sources or etiology of these anxieties?
2. Do you believe these anxieties are realistic or disproportionate to the actual risks? If the latter, why do health care providers exaggerate their legal risks in this context?
3. What are the positive and negative behavioral consequences of health care providers' legal anxieties regarding end-of-life medical care, in terms of the patient's rights and welfare? *See* Marshall B. Kapp, *Legal Anxieties and End-of-Life Care in Nursing Homes*, 19(2) Issues L. & Med. 111–134 (2003).

FUTILE TREATMENT

Sometimes patients or families demand that the physician provide the patient with forms of LSMT that, in the physician's opinion, are "futile" or nonbeneficial for that patient. Such demands for aggressive medical interventions occur even in the face of dismal survival and quality-of-life prospects. These demands may create a clash at the bedside between patient autonomy (asserted personally or through a proxy) and a physician's own conscience. Such a clash can inspire legal apprehension.

The issue of whether a physician has a legal obligation to effectuate a patient's or family's demand for LSMT that the physician believes to be futile is unclear at the present time. This situation exists despite the venerable legal maxim, *"Lex neminem cogit ad vana seu inutilia peragenda!"* ("The law compels no one to do vain or useless things!") and the American Medical Association's opinion that physicians "are not ethically obligated to deliver care that, in their best professional judgment, will not have a reasonable chance of benefitting their patients. Patients should not be given treatments simply because they demand them."

Using cardiopulmonary resuscitation (CPR) as their focus, Marsh and Staver argue persuasively that a physician has no enforceable duty to provide, or even to discuss, a futile intervention. However, actual case law in what one set of commentators has termed the "right to live" area is still quite sparse. Treatment decisions and conflict resolution about futile demands today must take place in the context of a lack of judicial consensus.

Several cases involve requests by either physicians or family members for judicial clarification before any treatments were withheld or withdrawn. In one case, a probate court continued the appointment of the 87-year-old patient's husband as guardian, knowing that he was demanding ventilator support and artificial feeding for his wife despite her status for more than a year in a permanent vegetative state after CPR. The patient's physician initiated a request for the court to switch guardians on the grounds that the husband was not acting in the patient's best interests. The patient died despite aggressive treatment before an appeal could be pursued.

In another case, brought before any treatment had been withheld or withdrawn, a teenaged patient's parents disagreed about treatment, and a court ordered the physicians to provide LSMT to a patient in a condition "between a stupor and a coma." In another case initiated prospectively, a court used the federal Emergency Medical Treatment and Active Labor Act to order a hospital emergency department to attempt resuscitation and ventilator support for an anencephalic infant in the event her mother brought her to the emergency department in cardiac arrest. In a decision running in the opposite direction, one court replaced a patient's son, who demanded doing "everything" to save his father, as guardian with someone else who was willing to consent to a "no code" order.

Only a couple of legal cases in this area have arisen as after-the-fact malpractice lawsuits brought by unhappy families against involved physicians. In one, a jury totally exonerated a physician and hospital who had entered and acted on a no code order, over an adult daughter's protests, for a permanently vegetative patient. In another, a malpractice suit was remanded, per state procedural law, to a medical review panel but with instructions to the panel that "[a] finding that treatment is 'medically inappropriate' by a consensus of physicians practicing in that specialty translates into a standard of care." The court added in a footnote:

> *Also, if, as in this case, a surrogate decision-maker insists on life-prolonging treatment which the physician believes is inhumane, then the usual procedure is to transfer the patient or go to court to replace the surrogate or override his decision. The argument would be that the guardian or surrogate is guilty of abuse by insisting on care which is inhumane.*

Until some more unambiguous legal guidance and societal consensus about delineating futile versus beneficial treatment come about, physicians should act carefully, both legally and ethically, in defining benefit in its most expansive sense and erring on the side of respecting the patient and family as the best evaluators of whether LSMT will be worthwhile for them. When in doubt, the physician probably should presume that the patient would want an intervention whose benefits are uncertain. Concurrently, though, physicians and other members of the intensive care team should be aggressive in explaining to the patient and/or family their point of view concerning an intervention's futility, using information and reason to move toward a responsible choice; few (albeit some) patients and/or families are likely to persist in insisting on truly burdensome, nonbeneficial medical assaults if they trust the physician and hospital.

DISCUSSION QUESTIONS

1. Why do patients or families sometimes demand medical treatments that are very highly likely not going to be beneficial? Who is the best evaluator of "benefit" in the critical illness context? Should any type of "benefit" count?

2. What role can social workers and nurses usefully play in the process of negotiating with the patient and family regarding the patient's treatment plan?

3. Do you agree with the advice, "When in doubt, the physician probably should presume that the patient would want an intervention whose benefits are uncertain"? *See* Thaddeus M. Pope, *Medical Futility Statutes: No Safe Harbor to Unilaterally Refuse Life-Sustaining Treatment*, 75 Tenn. L. Rev. 1–81 (2007). In the critical care context, do most patients want medical interventions whose benefits are uncertain?

4. Are you offended by the use of the term "medical assaults" in the context of LSMTs, or do you consider this term accurately descriptive?

ARTIFICIAL NUTRITION AND HYDRATION

The process of dying is an emotionally draining and tumultuous one for the patient's family and other loved ones and for the physicians and nurses providing professional care during this period. The strain is exacerbated when decisions need to be made and implemented regarding psychologically and ethically laden questions about the initiation, continuation, withholding, or withdrawal of life-prolonging medical interventions, including various methods of artificial nutrition and hydration (ANH). Unfortunately, statutes in many states, although generally well intended, frequently exert the practical effect of clouding and confusing the legally permissible boundaries of end-of-life care and thus harming rather than helping the patient and those who must live through and carry on after the dying process.

The disruption of humane end-of-life care often wreaked by current state statutes (and their implementing regulations) is particularly dismaying to those of us who believed (in hindsight, rather naively) for a while that legal developments in the 1990s would facilitate, not impede, a decent passage for patients in their final days and those surrounding them. In its 1990 *Cruzan* decision, the U.S. Supreme Court appeared to interpret the 14th Amendment's due process clause in a way that resolved the constitutional status of ANH:

> *I agree that a protected liberty interest in refusing unwanted medical treatment may be inferred from our prior decisions, and that the refusal of artificially delivered food and water is encompassed within that liberty interest.*
>
> *The law does not distinguish artificial feeding from other forms of medical treatment. Whether or not the techniques used to pass food and water into the patient's alimentary tract are termed "medical treatment," it is clear they all involve some degree of intrusion and restraint. Requiring competent adults to endure such procedures against their will burdens patients' liberty, dignity, and freedom to determine the course of their own treatment. Accordingly, the liberty guaranteed by the due process clause must protect, if it protects anything, an individual's deeply held personal decision to reject medical treatment, including the artificial delivery of food and water. Cruzan v. Missouri Dept. of Health, 497 U.S. 261 (1990) (O'Connor, J., concurring).*

The *Cruzan* decision was followed quickly by congressional enactment of the Patient Self-Determination Act (PSDA), which was intended, among other purposes, to require organizational health care providers to develop and disseminate formal policies regarding matters such as the handling of decisions about ANH and to encourage individuals to engage in advance medical planning (including the execution of written advance medical directives) in a timely fashion. Every state now has legislation codifying the constitutional right of decisionally capable individuals to execute an instruction or a proxy advance medical directive, and most states explicitly authorize both kinds.

Despite—indeed, perhaps partially because of—the plethora of law on the subject, confusion about the legal parameters of abating ANH persist, and even patients previously capable of making a decision who thought they had prospectively safeguarded their autonomous treatment wishes by timely execution of advance directives may find their final preferences disregarded and disobeyed in the name of risk management. Why does the current state statutory landscape frequently adversely affect clinical practice and patients' rights regarding the use and limitation of ANH?

There are several possible explanations for the problem. First, some state advance directive statutes have the effect of making it more difficult for a person capable of making decisions to prospectively forgo ANH in subsequent end-of-life circumstances precisely because that is the impact intended by the legislators who enacted those statutes. In other words, some statutes function exactly as their sponsors envisioned. The difficulty with statutes in this category is not a lack of linguistic clarity or faulty interpretation but instead the erroneous set of factual presumptions about the likely effects of ANH and its abatement on dying patients (e.g., the discredited idea that forgoing ANH causes the dying patient pain and discomfort) that animates supporters of this legislation.

A different source of legislatively induced harm in the ANH context stems from poor, imprecise drafting of statutes that are not intended to interpose barriers to the effectuation of patients' choices regarding ANH but that have that effect by failing to say clearly what their sponsors meant. A number of statutes with the practical effect of unintentionally and unwittingly interfering with patient autonomy and humane care because of inartful wording (often committed by attorneys with no grasp of the substantive clinical issues) fall into this category.

At the level of clinical application, the inexact legislative drafting that characterizes many states' ANH statutory schemas may work synergistically with erroneous legal interpretations by physicians, health care administrators, and too often the risk managers and attorneys who counsel them to maximize the general sense of legal uncertainty and anxiety among physicians that frequently complicates the handling of ANH issues. Most health care providers understandably exhibit a powerful aversion (i.e., zero tolerance) to perceived personal legal risks, and their (generally misplaced but nonetheless sincere) supposition that their own legal interests are best protected by maximum aggressiveness in medical treatment may be fed by the poorly considered advice of overly conservative risk managers and in-house attorneys who fail to appreciate the intricacies, underpinnings, and rationales of the relevant statutes or the relationship of statutory and constitutional law. The practical impact of the law is determined by how it is perceived, rightly or wrongly, by those in the trenches, not by the elegant intellectual analyses engaged in by legal scholars and appellate judges.

What can be done, realistically and effectively, to improve the quality of end-of-life care available to dying patients who have previously expressed a wish to forgo ANH in specified circumstances? How can prevalent present deficiencies in the inception, drafting, and interpretation and explanation of state ANH statutes be corrected or at least ameliorated? First, legislators and legislative drafters need to be better educated about the factual underpinnings of the natural process of dying. Specific attention in these educational efforts must be devoted to fostering a much better appreciation of the limited benefits versus the substantial burdens to be expected from the provision of ANH to patients at the end of life. The accurate status of ANH as a "comfort care" measure must be clarified in the minds of legislators before it can be managed properly in particular statutes produced by those legislators. Second, state legislative drafting offices should review the wording of pertinent ANH statutes to confirm that the law provides clear, unambiguous guidance to potential patients and their physicians and other health care providers regarding the permissible boundaries within which decisions about ANH may be prospectively expressed and presently implemented. To the extent that a statute fails to directly convey the specific meaning intended by the legislature, appropriate drafting revisions should be recommended. Standardized advance directive forms distributed in each jurisdiction and individualized documents developed by attorneys or health care organizations also should be reviewed for precision in meaning and amended if greater clarity could be achieved.

We must be careful, though, about placing too much faith in the capacity of more legislation and legal documentation to remedy ills that are mainly the product of the poor drafting and misinterpretation of present statutes and forms. The history of end-of-life care in the United States in the recent past points in the opposite direction, with virtually each new legislative and regulatory development confusing instead of calming the situation. Problematic laws—in their conception, wording, or execution—have in practice almost inevitably begat even more problematic laws, contributing to a vicious cycle of inconsistent and apprehension-inducing verbiage rather than resolving the original shortcomings.

Consequently, significant resources might more productively be devoted to serious interdisciplinary and interprofessional educational efforts encompassing physicians, nurses, health care administrators, and the risk managers and attorneys who counsel them. Continuing education initiatives targeted at fostering a clearer, more uniform interpretation of ANH statutory provisions operative in their own jurisdictions can proactively prepare professionals to grapple with the legal and ethical challenges posed by end-of-life decisions when they arise in tangible contexts. Regulators, prosecuting attorneys, ombudsmen, and patient advocates should be involved in these educational efforts to help avoid misunderstandings and inconsistencies in legal enforcement and especially to allay the anxieties of health care providers about the potential imposition of legal sanctions for deviation from a state's ANH statute.

Perhaps of greatest value in overcoming impediments to decent end-of-life care, respecting the previously expressed self-determination of now-dying patients about ANH, lies in a voluntary (as opposed to imposition by legal fiat) commitment by physicians to implement the spirit of the PSDA in their relationships with individual patients. Specifically, each medical office should develop a formal, written statement explaining its philosophy and ordinary practices regarding end-of-life care, including the use or limitation of ANH. This statement, which would implicitly be based on that office's understanding of the boundaries of applicable state law, should be routinely disseminated to each physician's patient population. Just as an advance directive executed by a patient helps the physician understand the patient's goals and expectations, an explicit office policy can avoid later friction through a reciprocal flow of information to the patient. Each patient, while still capable of making decisions (or the patient's surrogate if the patient is already unable to make medical decisions), would have ample opportunity to discuss the office's policies with the physician in advance of a crisis mode. If the differences between patient expectations and the physician's stated sphere of personal conduct are irreconcilable, adjustments (including the possibility of termination) in the patient–physician relationship could be made in a timely way, protecting the autonomy interests of both patient and physician.

In too many instances statutory law does send the wrong message. Here, as in so many other areas, well-intended laws often end up, in practice, producing antitherapeutic results that harm real people. That result is ethically intolerable. Professionals who write, enforce, interpret, advise about, and ultimately implement the laws owe it to the patients and families who are caught in the dying process to ensure that the statutes and practices pertaining to ANH send forth a message that promotes personal dignity and autonomy at life's most difficult juncture.

DISCUSSION QUESTIONS

1. Have you witnessed patients and/or families encountering difficulties in getting their end-of-life medical choices, including choices to forgo ANH, honored by health care providers? As a general rule, do you believe such choices should be obeyed by health care providers? *See* Neil J. Farber et al., *Physicians' Decisions to Withhold and Withdraw Life-Sustaining Treatment,* 166(5) Arch. Intern. Med. 560–564 (2006). Whatever general rule you advocate regarding compliance with patient or family wishes, what exceptions would you make?

2. Should the law distinguish between decisions regarding the withdrawal of artificially delivered food and hydration, on one hand, and decisions regarding the withdrawal or withholding of other types of LSMT (such as resuscitation, dialysis, antibiotics, or mechanical ventilation), on the other? What, if anything, is legally and ethically special about artificial feeding? *See* Kathleen M. Boozang, *Divining a Patient's Religious Beliefs in Treatment Termination Decision-Making,* 15(2) Temp. Pol. & Civ. Rights L. Rev. 345–360 (2006); Robert D. Truog & Thomas I. Cochrane, *Refusal of Hydration and Nutrition: Irrelevance of the "Artificial" vs. "Natural" Distinction,* 165 Arch. Intern. Med. 2574–2576 (2005).

3. How would you describe the political climate in your state regarding the forgoing of ANH by, or on behalf

of, critically ill older patients? Do you agree with Justice O'Connor's opinion in *Cruzan* that ANH is just one form of medical treatment, to be governed by the same legal principles that cover other forms of medical treatment? *See* Kathy L. Cerminara, *Collateral Damage: The Aftermath of the Political Culture Wars in* Schiavo, 29(2) West. N. Eng. L. Rev. 279–308 (2007).

4. Why do many health care professionals believe that the most aggressive end-of-life medical treatment is necessarily the most protective of the professional's legal interests? What can be done to alter that attitude and the behaviors that accompany it? *See* Lois Shepherd, *In Respect of People Living in a Permanent Vegetative State— And Allowing Them to Die*, 16(2) Health Matrix 631–691 (2006). What other factors (besides apprehension about potential legal liability) naturally push physicians in the direction of aggressive medical treatment of seriously ill older patients? *See* Janet K. Shim et al., *Late-Life Cardiac Interventions and the Treatment Imperative*, 5(3) PLoS Med. 0344–0346 (2008), *available at* www.plosmedicine .org. What can be done to improve the quality of communication between physicians and dying patients and their families about end-of-life options? *See* Susan DesHarnais et al., *Lack of Concordance Between Physician and Patient: Reports on End-of-Life Care Discussions*, 10(3) J. Palliative Med. 728–740 (2007); Dennis McCullough, *My Mother, Your Mother: Embracing "Slow Medicine," the Compassionate Approach to Caring for Your Aging Loved Ones*, New York: HarperCollins Publishers (2008).

5. What do you think of the advice that each medical office should develop and disseminate a formal, written statement explaining its philosophy and ordinary practices regarding end-of-life care, including the use or limitation of ANH? What are the primary pros and cons of this approach? As an exercise, draft a model statement that individual medical offices could adopt.

Exercises

Case 1

Mrs. C, a 75-year-old woman with severe emphysema, was found unresponsive at home. Emergency medical service personnel performed endotracheal intubation and resuscitated her. She was admitted to the hospital and treated for respiratory failure and pneumonia and is now quite lucid and able to communicate. However, the medical team has not been able to wean Mrs. C from the respirator.

After several weeks in this condition, Mrs. C expresses a desire to have the respirator removed, knowing that action would lead to her death. Although she had not executed an advance directive nor discussed her treatment wishes with anyone else previously, she now clearly claims that she would not have wanted to be resuscitated in the first place.

If the medical team respects Mrs. C's expressed desire to have the respirator removed, what should be done to ensure her dying process is as comfortable as possible? Are there any limits on doing whatever is necessary to achieve comfort for this patient? In replying to Mrs. C's request, what is the significance (if any) of the fact that the respirator is already in place? Does that fact make it more or less difficult for the medical team to remove it now, as compared with making a decision about starting a respirator in the first place? What are the potential legal consequences if Mrs. C's expressed wishes are not honored by the medical team?

Case 2

Mr. V is an 86-year-old man with advanced dementia who resides in a sectarian nursing home. As his dementia progressed, he was able to take in less and less food orally. At a certain point he stopped eating altogether, and a nasogastric tube was inserted. He is now bedridden, incontinent, and lies in a nearly fetal position. He appears to be in distress and pulls at his feeding tubes. Wrist restraints are being used to keep him from pulling out the tubes. In addition to the dementia, Mr. V has several comorbidities.

Mr. V's only involved relative is his cousin, who requests that the feeding tube be discontinued. The cousin recounts a conversation many years ago during which Mr. V said, "If I ever become senile like my neighbor, please shoot me." The nursing home refuses the request, citing the religious beliefs of its sponsoring organization. The attending physician agrees with the nursing home that removing the feeding tube would amount to "starving" Mr. V to death.

Are there any viable methods available for providing Mr. V with nutrition and hydration less invasively and with less discomfort? Is there any moral or legal distinction between Mr. V's condition (advanced dementia) and a persistent vegetative state? What is the significance, if any, of the fact that this nursing home is affiliated with a religious sponsor? If the nursing home persists in insisting on continuation of the tube feeding, what alternatives does the cousin have? What impediments would the cousin face in trying to enforce her request on behalf of Mr. V? Regarding the role of the nursing home's religious convictions, *see* Joshua E. Perry, *Biblical BioPolitics: Judicial Process, Religious Rhetoric, Terri Schiavo and Beyond*, 16(2) Health Matrix 553–630 (2006).

If the cousin initiates court action seeking to have the feeding tube removed, what standard should the court use in deciding upon this request: substituted judgment (what Mr. V would have chosen if currently able to make and express his own autonomous choice) or an objective assessment of Mr. V's best interests (weighing the likely benefits of continued tube feeding against the likely burdens)? The substituted judgment standard is theoretically more respectful of the patient's autonomy but often more difficult to apply. *See* David I. Shalowitz et al., *The Accuracy of Surrogate Decision Makers: A Systematic Review*, 166(5)

Arch. Intern. Med. 493–497 (2006). If the court relies on the substituted judgment standard, what burden of proof should the cousin/petitioner have to meet in establishing what Mr. V would have wanted: preponderance of the evidence (i.e., it is more likely than not that Mr. V would want the feeding tube removed), clear and convincing evidence (a more demanding requirement), or proof beyond a reasonable doubt (the most rigorous standard of proof)? What are the arguments pro and con for each standard? Can the evidence relied on be inferential rather than direct? Should a higher standard of proof be required if the surrogate is not a family member?

How would your analysis of this case be different if, instead of being an 86-year-old man with dementia, Mr. V were a 26-year-old man with severe traumatic brain injury suffered as a result of a motorcycle accident?

Case 3

Mrs. M is an 88-year-old woman with moderate dementia who has resided in a nursing home for the past 2 years. She is very confused but in generally good physical health. She has some regular interaction with the other residents. Her only relative is a son, whom she named as her agent under a durable power of attorney (DPOA) instrument she executed when she entered the nursing home.

The nursing home notified the son when Mrs. M developed a bad tooth abscess and it requested the son's consent to have Mrs. M treated by a dentist. To the facility's surprise, the son denied this request. He stated, "Mom has lived a good, long life. At this point, she shouldn't be burdened with a bunch of dentists and doctors poking and prodding her." Despite being informed about the details of treating a tooth abscess, the high likelihood of success, and the risks (including pain and death) of letting the tooth become or remain infected and untreated, the son is insistent that Mrs. M be "left alone."

What should the nursing home do? What is the role of the facility medical director in this situation? The facility director of nursing? If the nursing home follows the son's direction, must staff participate? Would the nursing home and its staff be exposed to any sort of legal risk, perhaps criminal prosecution for adult abuse or neglect, if they comply with the son's direction? If the nursing home defies the son's direction and takes Mrs. M to the dentist for treatment, what are the potential liability consequences? *See* Jeannie Kayser-Jones & Marshall B. Kapp, *Advocacy for the Mentally Impaired Elder: A Case Study Analysis,* 14(4) Am. J. L. & Med. 353–376 (1989).

Case 4

Mrs. L is an 85-year-old severely demented widow who was admitted to a nursing home from a hospital about 2 years ago. She had been hospitalized for treatment of a hip fracture incurred in an automobile accident when she was still driving. She now also suffers from chronic lymphocytic leukemia and hypertension. Before the hospitalization that led to her present nursing home admission, Mrs. L had lived in an apartment with a sister with whom she has maintained close contact.

Mrs. L seemed to do well in the nursing home, even though her dementia became progressively more severe. Like most demented individuals, she paces and talks to herself a lot. She periodically needs blood transfusions to control her leukemia. During these transfusions, Mrs. L cannot understand what is happening and sometimes vigorously resists the procedure despite the best efforts of facility staff, who are dismayed by her consternation, to calm her. Before administering the transfusion, it became necessary to give her a sedative and then physically hold her in bed while the procedure was begun. Otherwise, Mrs. L would remove the transfusion apparatus. The nurse had become quite upset with the whole situation but was too intimidated to raise the issue of possible discontinuation of the transfusions with Mrs. L's physician, who was strongly committed to the transfusion plan.

Two years before the accident that began this chain of events, Mrs. L. had gone to a legal aid office and executed advance medical directives. One document was a DPOA for health care naming the sister as Mrs. L's decision-making agent if necessary. The other document was an instruction directive stating, among other things, "If I become unable to make and express my own treatment wishes, I do not want medical interventions that prolong my life if I have an incurable or irreversible medical problem that is not terminal, but which inflicts upon me severe or progressive physical and/or mental deterioration and loss of ability to function normally."

What should the nurse do in this situation? What is the interpersonal dynamic between the nurse, the physician, and Mrs. L's sister? *See* Jiska Cohen-Mansfield et al., *Medical Decision-Making in the Nursing Home: A Comparison of Physician and Nurse Perspectives,* 32 J. Geront. Nursing 14–21 (2006). How should the nurse balance her role as a patient advocate with her need to maintain a good working relationship with the physician who is intent on continuing the transfusions? Is there a legal obligation to follow Mrs. L's instruction directive? Does the directive even apply to this scenario? If the physician will not relent, what legal alternatives are available to the sister?

ADVANCE HEALTH CARE DIRECTIVES

Every state has one or more advance health care directive statutes. Many states have several statutes: one for an instruction (living will) type of directive and one for a proxy directive or DPOA for health care. The DPOA document names a proxy or agent (the "attorney-in-fact") who is authorized to make future medical decisions on behalf of the individual delegating the authority (the "principal" or "maker") in the event of the latter's subsequent decisional incapacity. There often is a separate statute addressing default surrogate decision-making authority ("family consent" laws) when there is no guardianship order or timely executed advance directive but the patient is personally unable to make decisions at the time. Table 3.2 gives a sample of a family consent statute, and related discussion questions are provided. Additionally, a number of states have enacted separate legislation regarding out-of-hospital "do not resuscitate" (DNR) orders. Table 3.3 gives a sample statute, and related discussion questions are provided.

Table 3.2 Sample Family Consent Statute

IL. ST. CH. 755 § 40/25

(a) When a patient lacks decisional capacity, the health care provider must make a reasonable inquiry as to the availability and authority of a health care agent under the Powers of Attorney for Health Care Law. When no health care agent is authorized and available, the health care provider must make a reasonable inquiry as to the availability of possible surrogates listed in items (1) through (4) of this subsection. The surrogate decision makers, as identified by the attending physician, are then authorized to make decisions as follows: ...(ii) for patients who lack decisional capacity and have a qualifying condition, medical treatment decisions including whether to forgo life-sustaining treatment on behalf of the patient may be made without court order or judicial involvement in the following order of priority:

  (1) the patient's guardian of the person;
  (2) the patient's spouse;
  (3) any adult son or daughter of the patient;
  (4) either parent of the patient;
  (5) any adult brother or sister of the patient;
  (6) any adult grandchild of the patient;
  (7) a close friend of the patient;
  (8) the patient's guardian of the estate.

(continues)

The health care provider shall have the right to rely on any of the above surrogates if the provider believes after reasonable inquiry that neither a health care agent under the Powers of Attorney for Health Care Law nor a surrogate of higher priority is available.

Where there are multiple surrogate decision makers at the same priority level in the hierarchy, it shall be the responsibility of those surrogates to make reasonable efforts to reach a consensus as to their decision on behalf of the patient regarding the forgoing of life-sustaining treatment. If two or more surrogates who are in the same category and have equal priority indicate to the attending physician that they disagree about the health care matter at issue, a majority of the available persons in that category (or the parent with custodial rights) shall control, unless the minority (or the parent without custodial rights) initiates guardianship proceedings....No health care provider or other person is required to seek appointment of a guardian.

(e) The surrogate decision maker shall have the same right as the patient to receive medical information and medical records and to consent to disclosure.

DISCUSSION QUESTIONS

1. Do you agree with the priority order of surrogates contained in this statute? Is this the priority order that most people would want if they became decisionally incapacitated? Is this the priority order of surrogates that you would want making decisions for you?
2. What limits, if any, should be imposed on the surrogate's authority? For example, should the surrogate be allowed, without any formal external oversight, to enter the incapacitated person into a nursing home? A mental institution? A research protocol? A managed care plan?

3. Under what circumstances should health care professionals insist that a surrogate obtain formal legal authority? What are the pros and cons of insisting on explicit clarification of legal authority before following the surrogate's treatment instructions?
4. What should a health care professional do when a surrogate, whether or not formally empowered by a surrogate consent statute, is making choices that seriously deviate from both the patient's substituted judgment and the patient's best interests? *See* Lois Shepherd, *Shattering the Neutral Surrogate Myth in End-of-Life Decisionmaking: Terri Schiavo and Her Family,* 35(3) Cumberland L. Rev. 575–595 (2004–2005).

Table 3.3 Sample Out-of-Hospital Resuscitation Statute

Texas Health and Safety Code § 166.081
(6) "Out-of-hospital DNR order":
 (A) means a legally binding out-of-hospital do-not-resuscitate order, in the [prescribed] form ... prepared and signed by the attending physician of a person, that documents the instructions of a person or the person's legally authorized representative and directs health care professionals acting in an out-of-hospital setting not to initiate or continue the following life-sustaining treatment:
 (i) cardiopulmonary resuscitation;
 (ii) advanced airway management;
 (iii) artificial ventilation;
 (iv) defibrillation;
 (v) transcutaneous cardiac pacing; and
 (vi) other life-sustaining treatment specified by the board [of health] ...; and

(continues)

(B)   does not include authorization to withhold medical interventions or therapies considered necessary to provide comfort care or to alleviate pain or to provide water or nutrition.

(7) "Out-of-hospital setting" means a location in which health care professionals are called for assistance, including long-term care facilities, in-patient hospice facilities, private homes, hospital outpatient or emergency departments, physicians' offices, and vehicles during transport.

DISCUSSION QUESTIONS

1. Some states impose medical prerequisites (e.g., diagnosis of terminal illness, permanent vegetative state, resuscitation would be medically futile) in order for an out-of-institution DNR to be effective. Do you agree with these prerequisites? Which particular ones would you include in legislation? Do such prerequisites violate the 14th Amendment Equal Protection rights of the patient?

2. Do you agree with the requirement that there be a physician's order before emergency personnel may withhold LSMT outside of the hospital, or should a competent patient be able to execute a binding out-of-hospital DNR directive without a physician's order?

3. Many states use some form of specially designed identification (e.g., a bracelet) to be kept on or near the patient as part of the out-of-institution DNR process. Is this requirement necessary and helpful?

4. Under what circumstances should an emergency health care provider be permitted to attempt resuscitation despite the existence of a DNR order?

On the other hand, there is a legislative trend toward simplifying the process by combining these components into one comprehensive statute. About half the states have statutes that combine in one place provisions for instruction directives, proxy directives, surrogate proxy decision-making authority, and DNR orders for various settings. Many current state statutes have provisions that are consistent with the Uniform Health Care Decisions Act created by the National Conference of Commissioners on Uniform State Laws (www.law.upenn.edu/bll/archives/ulc/fnact99/1990s/uhcda93.pdf) and/or the Five Wishes advance directive published by the not-for-profit organization Aging With Dignity (www.agingwithdignity.org). In many states the relevant statute(s) contains recommended, but not obligatory, advance directive forms for use as models by individuals who desire to engage in prospective health care planning.

Regarding instruction directives such as living wills, several models have been proposed for effectuating the competent patient's rights. Some of these suggested devices focus on specific clinical scenarios and medical interventions (e.g., "Do not resuscitate me if I suffer cardiac arrest when I am permanently and severely demented"), whereas others concentrate more on identifying the patient's key values and goals (e.g., "I want to minimize pain and indignity more than I care about living forever"). Ideally, the physician and other health care team members have discussed these issues previously with the patient and have guided the patient to draft the desired instruction directive in a calm, proactive setting while the patient still possesses sufficient decisional capacity.

Regarding proxy directives, the standard POA is a written agreement authorizing an agent or attorney-in-fact to sign documents and conduct transactions on behalf of a principal or maker who has delegated away that authority. The principal can delegate as much (e.g., a general delegation) or as little (e.g., specifically delineating what types of decisions the agent may or may not make) power as desired. The principal may end or revoke the arrangement at any time, as long as the principal remains competent to do so.

The big problem, however, is that the POA in its traditional form is unsuitable as a method for dealing with medical (or financial) decision-making authority for older persons on a voluntary basis. The traditional, ordinary POA ends automatically with the death or decisional incapacity of the person who assigned it. The underlying theory is that because a deceased or incapacitated person no longer has the ability to revoke the POA, the law should exercise that right automatically for the principal. Thus an older person who establishes an ordinary POA to help in managing medical (as well as other) affairs would be cut off from such assistance at exactly the moment when assistance is needed the most.

In an effort to overcome this deficiency, every state has enacted legislation authorizing the execution of a *durable* power of attorney (DPOA). In contrast to the ordinary POA, the effect of a DPOA—when proper indication is given by a decisionally capable delegating principal—may endure beyond the principal's subsequent incapacity. To remove any ambiguity about the applicability of the DPOA concept to the realm of medical decision making (including choices regarding LSMT), almost every state has enacted legislation that explicitly authorizes the use of this legal device in the medical decision-making context. Some statutes use terminology such as "health care representative," "health care agent," or "health care proxy."

In some states, drivers' licenses may exhibit a notation that the licensee has executed an advance directive. Some states have created centralized advance directive registries to which residents may submit their advance directives that can subsequently be located to guide health care professionals regarding that person's future medical treatment. Advance directive forms for any state may be obtained by members of the public for free from the respective state medical society or bar association.

Exercises

Case 1

Mr. B is a 76-year-old widower who suffers from chronic obstructive pulmonary disease, peripheral vascular disease, and mild dementia. During his 3-year nursing home stay, he has remained relatively stable physically but has slowly but noticeably declined in terms of cognitive status. He has a fair amount of regular interaction with his family, the facility staff, and other residents. When he first entered the nursing home, Mr. B executed a health care proxy appointing his daughter as his agent and his son as alternate agent. Simultaneously, Mr. B executed a living will that stated, among other things, that Mr. B would not want dialysis if he became terminally ill or permanently unconscious.

Based on complaints of chest pain and shortage of breath, Mr. B has just been admitted to the hospital. He was found to have undergone a mild heart attack, to be in acute renal failure, and to be acting confused and agitated. His internist and nephrology consultant want to order a few dialysis treatments to improve his kidney function and possibly improve his mental status while the extent of his heart damage is studied. Judging that Mr. B did not have decisional capacity, the health care team turned to Mr. B's children to obtain consent to this treatment plan. The daughter readily consents, but the son argues that Mr. B's living will expressly precludes this plan.

What should the health care team do here? Is this the kind of situation contemplated by Mr. B's living will? What governs when a living will and a DPOA appear to conflict? What assistance might an institutional ethics committee or an ethics consultant provide in this kind of situation? Should the health care team initiate the courts' involvement in resolving this apparent dispute? *See* Alan Meisel, *The Role of Litigation in End of Life Care: A Reappraisal,* 35(6) Hastings Cent. Rep. S47–S51 (2005).

Case 2

Mr. R is an 81-year-old hospitalized man with pneumonia and severe dementia. He also has advanced metastatic prostate cancer. During the diagnostic process, Mr. B was discovered to be suffering from a leaking aortic aneurism and bilateral muscle abscesses. The abscesses were drained. He was started on a course of antibiotics and given a blood transfusion. The remaining issue is whether to perform surgery to repair the aneurism.

Mr. R's dementia makes him rather unconnected mentally to his surroundings and to other people. Although he usually appears comfortable, his discomfort as a result of his most recent medical difficulties was demonstrated by his behavior and agitated reactions to clinical procedures.

In the opinion of the medical team, surgically repairing Mr. R's aneurism will reduce his risk of a fatal rupture but will leave his declining mental status unchanged. His pain will be increased postoperatively, and the risk of death during surgery can run as high as 30%. Mr. R is unable to participate meaningfully in a discussion about his treatment options. He has no interested and available family members or friends.

Who should make the decisions about Mr. R's care? What standards of decision making should the surrogate(s) utilize? Why? Is court involvement necessary in these circumstances? If court involvement is initiated and the judge asks for your professional opinion, how should you respond? *See* Sumeeta Varma & David Wendler, *Medical Decision Making for Patients Without Surrogates,* 167(16) Arch. Intern. Med. 1711–1715 (2007); Douglas B. White et al., *Life Support for Patients Without a Surrogate Decision Maker: Who Decides?* 147(1) Ann. Intern. Med. 34–40 (2007).

DISCUSSION QUESTIONS

1. What effect, if any, have your jurisdiction's advance directive statute(s) had on the quality of end-of-life medical care? *See* Joan M. Teno et al., *Association Between Advance Directives and Quality of End-of-Life Care: A National Study,* 55(2) J. Am. Geriatr. Soc'y 189–194

(2007). Do patients and health care professionals avail themselves of the advance planning opportunities made explicit by these statutes? Why do some patients resist making advance directives? Do these advance directive laws make it more likely that medical care will comply with the patient's or family's wishes? *See* Hana Osman & Marion A. Becker, *Complexity of Decision-Making in a Nursing Home: The Impact of Advance Directives on End-of-Life Care*, 42(1) J. Geront. Social Work 27–40 (2004); Steven B. Hardin & Yasmin A. Yusufaly, *Difficult End-of-Life Treatment Decisions: Do Other Factors Trump Advance Directives?*, 164(14) Arch. Intern. Med. 1531–1533 (2004). Or, do these laws function mainly as risk management "cover" for the professional caregivers? Do you believe the use of advance directives has helped to avoid court involvement in some circumstances? *See* Henry S. Perkins, *Controlling Death: The False Promise of Advance Directives*, 147(1) Ann. Intern. Med. 51–57 (2007).

2. What are the implementation problems regarding medical decision making for dying patients that persist despite, or that are actually caused by, your state's advance directive law(s) and/or by the advance directive documents people in your state write?

3. Which type of advance instruction directive do you believe is most helpful at the bedside when clinical decisions actually need to get made: one that focuses on specific clinical scenarios and medical interventions or one that focuses on the patient's particular values and goals?

4. What are the advantages, from a patient's perspective, of using a proxy directive in the LSMT context? From the health care provider's perspective? What are the shortcomings or limitations of this approach, from the patient's and provider's respective perspectives?

5. Why do all state proxy directives disqualify certain categories of persons (e.g., the principal's attending physician)

from serving as the named agent? What problems might such automatic disqualification cause?

6. Once a health care proxy is in place, how could that proxy's effectiveness in the substitute decision maker's role be optimized?

7. Why are most people (of all ages) very reluctant to make written advance directives, or even to discuss their own future medical treatment wishes with their loved ones? For a survey finding that Americans are more likely to talk with their children about drug use or sex than with a seriously ill parent about their end-of-life medical wishes, *see* www.nationalhealthcaredecisionsday.org/userfiles/File/ NHDD_release_040708–_v4.pdf. Why are persons from some demographic groups much less likely to execute advance directives than others? *See* Dan K. Kiely et al., *Racial and State Differences in the Designation of Advance Directives in Nursing Home Residents,* 49 J. Am. Geriatr. Soc'y 1346–1352 (2001). Should we be encouraging more people to execute written or oral advance directives? If so, what strategies might work best?

8. How should health and human services professionals assess whether an individual has sufficient present cognitive and emotional capacity to execute an advance directive? Do you agree with the provision found in most state statutes in this area presuming all adult patients to be competent to execute advance directives? How much evidence should be required to rebut or overcome such a presumption? *See* Brooke M. Sorger et al., *Decision-Making Capacity in Elderly, Terminally Ill Patients With Cancer,* 25 Behav. Sci. & L. 393–404 (2007).

9. Besides, or instead of, encouraging them to execute advance directives, what should health and human services professionals advise individuals to do to maximize their future autonomy regarding LSMT? *See* Bernard Lo & Robert Steinbrook, *Resuscitating Advance Directives,* 164(14) Arch. Intern. Med. 1501–1506 (2004).

Excerpted from PSDA of 1990, Pub. L. 101–408:

> *§ 4206 Medicare Provider Agreements Assuring the Implementation of a Patient's Right to Participate in and Direct Health Care Decisions Affecting the Patient.*
>
> *(a)(2):*
> *(f) (1) ...the requirement of this subsection is that a provider of services [defined earlier as hospitals, skilled nursing facilities, home health agencies, and hospice programs] or prepaid or eligible organization [i.e., a managed care organization] maintain written policies and procedures with respect to all adult individuals receiving medical care by or through the provider or organization—*
> *(A) to provide written information to each such individual concerning—*
> *(i) an individual's rights under state law (whether statutory or as recognized by the courts of the state) to make decisions concerning such medical care, including the right to accept or refuse medical or surgical treatment and the right to formulate advance directives, and*
> *(ii) the written policies of the provider or organization respecting the implementation of such rights;*
> *(B) to document in the individual's medical record whether or not the individual has executed an advance directive;*
> *(C) not to condition the provision of care or otherwise discriminate against an individual based on whether or not the individual has executed an advance directive;*
> *(D) to ensure compliance with requirements of state law (whether statutory or as recognized by the courts of the state) respecting advance directives at facilities of the provider or organization and*
> *(E) to provide (individually or with others) for education for staff and the community on issues concerning advance directives.*
> *Subparagraph (C) shall not be construed as requiring the provision of care which conflicts with an advance directive.*
> *(2) The written information described in paragraph (1)(A) shall be provided to an adult individual—*

(A) in the case of a hospital, at the time of the individual's admission as an inpatient,
(B) in the case of a skilled nursing facility, at the time of individual's admission as a resident,
(C) in the case of a home health agency, in advance of the individual coming under the care of the agency,
(D) in the case of a hospice program, at the time of initial receipt of hospice care by the individual from the program, and
(E) in the case of an eligible organization..., at the time of enrollment of the individual with the organization.
(3) In this subsection, the term "advance directive" means a written instruction, such as a living will or DPOA for health care, recognized under state law (whether statutory or as recognized by the courts of the state) and relating to the provision of such care when the individual is incapacitated. [...]
(c) Nothing [in this Act] shall be construed to prohibit the application of a state law which allows for an objection on the basis of conscience for any health care provider or any agent of such provider which, as a matter of conscience, cannot implement an advance directive.

§ 4751 (d) Public Education Campaign

(1) In general—The Secretary [of DHHS]... shall develop and implement a national campaign to inform the public of the option to execute advance directives and of a patient's right to participate [in] and direct health care decisions.
(2) Development and distribution of information—The Secretary shall develop or approve nationwide informational materials that would be distributed by providers under the requirements of this section, to inform the public and the medical and legal profession of each person's right to make decisions concerning medical care, including the right to accept or refuse medical or surgical treatment, and the existence of advance directives.
(3) Providing assistance to states—The Secretary shall assist appropriate state agencies, associations, or other private entities in developing the state-specific documents that would be distributed by

providers under the requirements of this section. The Secretary shall further assist appropriate state agencies, associations, or other private entities in ensuring that providers are provided a copy of the documents that are to be distributed under the requirements of the section.

DISCUSSION QUESTIONS

1. What are the goals of the PSDA? What are the factual assumptions regarding human behavior underlying the belief that this legislation is the most effective way to achieve these goals?
2. Are these goals and the underlying assumptions of this legislation realistic? How successful has the PSDA been in accomplishing Congress' goals for it? How would you improve this legislation? What other kinds of strategies would you recommend to pursue the goals embodied in the PSDA?
3. Note that the PSDA does not impose any requirements on individual physicians in their office settings. Why were physicians and individual medical offices not included? Should they be included in the statutory mandates? *See* Sharda D. Ramsaroop et al., *Completing an Advance Directive in the Primary Care Setting: What Do We Need for Success?*, 55(2) J. Am. Geriatr. Soc'y 277–283 (2007); K. Michael Lipkin, *Identifying a Proxy for Health Care as Part of Routine Medical Inquiry*, 21 J. Gen. Intern. Med. 1188–1191 (2006).

ASSISTED DEATH

A 1971 regulation published by the Attorney General required that prescriptions written for substances that fall within the Controlled Substances Act (CSA) be used "for a legitimate medical purpose by an individual practitioner acting in the usual course of his professional practice." In 1994, Oregon voters enacted through the referendum process the Oregon Death With Dignity Act (ODWDA), which explicitly exempts from civil or criminal liability a state-licensed physician who, in compliance with ODWDA's specific safeguards, dispenses or prescribes a lethal dose of drugs upon the request of a terminally ill patient. In 2001, the Attorney General issued an Interpretive Rule to address the implementation and enforcement of the CSA in light of the ODWDA, declaring that using controlled substances to assist suicide is not a legitimate medical practice and that dispensing or prescribing them for this purpose is unlawful under the CSA.

The state of Oregon initiated litigation to challenge the authority of the Attorney General to issue and enforce that Interpretive Rule. After protracted wrangling in the lower federal courts, on January 17, 2006 the U.S. Supreme Court in *Gonzales v. Oregon,* 546 U.S. 243, invalidated the Interpretive Rule. The announcement of this judicial decision was accompanied by loud celebration on the part of a variety of proponents of effective pain management for suffering patients. The problem, however, is that enthusiastically optimistic assessments of what the Supreme Court did in *Gonzales v. Oregon* overwhelmingly have emanated from observers who are responding to the case's particular outcome, but because they have not closely (or actually) read the legal majority and dissenting opinions of the Court in this case, they have not formulated an appreciation of the narrowly confined legal reasoning underlying the majority's decision. A closer reading and appreciation of the majority's opinion in *Gonzales v. Oregon,* I believe, may substantially subdue the enthusiasm of pain control advocates about the real impact of this case on the legal environment surrounding pain control clinical practice.

According to Justice Anthony Kennedy, writing for the six-Justice majority in *Gonzales v. Oregon:*

> [T]he question before us is whether the Controlled Substances Act allows the United States Attorney General to prohibit doctors from prescribing regulated drugs for use in physician-assisted suicide, notwithstanding a state law permitting the procedure. ...The dispute before us is in part a product of ...political and moral debate, but its resolution requires an inquiry familiar to the courts:

interpreting a federal statute to determine whether Executive action is authorized by, or otherwise consistent with, [the CSA]. ... The [Attorney General's] Interpretive Rule's validity under the CSA is the issue before us.

Under constitutional principles (the "delegation doctrine") and the federal Administrative Procedure Act, an executive branch agency, such as the Department of Justice, may promulgate only those administrative rules or regulations that Congress, within a specific statute it has enacted, has empowered that agency to promulgate. Put differently, a cabinet officer, such as the Attorney General, does not have legal authority to initiate a regulation just because he or she believes it is desirable as a public policy matter; rather, every regulation must be justified with a specific statutory basis provided by the democratically elected legislative branch of government. Thus the legal question decided in *Gonzales v. Oregon* was the rather narrow one of statutory interpretation; namely, whether the CSA, as currently written, authorizes the Attorney General to promulgate an administrative rule that defines what is a "legitimate medical purpose by an individual practitioner acting in the usual course of his professional practice." The Supreme Court did *not* find that Congress is *precluded* from authorizing the Attorney General to promulgate such a regulation but did find that Congress had *not chosen* to include such administrative lawmaking authorization in the language of the CSA, as presently written.

The big concern for advocates of effective pain control, including the option for physicians to prescribe opioids when necessary and appropriate, ought to be that Congress still does have the power under the Constitution to statutorily authorize the Attorney General to promulgate precisely the kind of regulation that was promulgated (without proper statutory authority at the time) in 2001 and that the Supreme Court's *Gonzales v. Oregon* decision may inspire Congress to take exactly that action. Or even worse, Congress could directly use an amended CSA to bypass the Department of Justice altogether and directly outlaw the prescription of lethal drugs within the physician-assisted suicide context. There have already been significant political rumblings in the halls of Congress proposing these very legislative actions.

DISCUSSION QUESTIONS

Should Congress amend the CSA so as to directly make it, or empower the Attorney General to make it through regulation, criminal for a physician to prescribe a drug for a patient with the knowledge that the patient will use the drug to hasten his or her own death? Is a physician who writes a prescription with such knowledge engaging in a "legitimate medical purpose by an individual practitioner acting in the usual course of his professional practice"?

The current controversy in the United States over the morality and constitutionality of state statutes that prohibit physicians from assisting patients to commit suicide entails a variety of difficult ethical and legal issues. In policy terms, the debate has tended to focus on whether legislatures can erect sufficiently stringent yet workable safeguards within state statutes authorizing physician-assisted suicide to protect against serious ethical abuses of this patient–physician prerogative. Proponents of decriminalizing physician-assisted suicide take the affirmative position on this question. Skeptics, on the other hand, suggest that opening the door to physician-assisted suicide, however cautiously and conservatively, would inevitably lead (as it apparently has in the current Netherlands experiment with nonprosecution of physicians for participating in physician-assisted suicide) to a movement in principle and practice down a moral slippery slope toward unintended consequences that almost everyone would condemn.

Most of the arguments on both sides of this discussion have been crafted in generic terms. Although a persuasive case against recognition of a constitutional right to physician-assisted suicide generally can be mounted, the anxieties of the slippery slope skeptics appear especially compelling. These are anxieties evidently shared by a substantial portion of the elderly population, because public opinion polls consistently show lower support for legalization of physician-assisted suicide among older citizens than among younger citizens. The primary reasons for these well-founded worries are briefly outlined below.

Decision-Making Capacity

In health care decision making generally, legally and ethically valid choices depend on (besides adequate information and voluntariness) the presence of a cognitively and emotionally capable decision maker. Although defining and evaluating a patient's decision-making capacity is an extremely complex and uncertain endeavor, in essence an individual capable of making decisions has the functional ability to make and express authentic choices, give reasons for those choices indicating deliberation, comprehend and manipulate information material to those choices, and understand the potential personal consequences of the choices.

As even proponents of physician-assisted suicide have acknowledged, capability is an especially indispensable prerequisite in a physician-assisted suicide situation, as the costs of error are so great and irremediable. Notably, there are at least a couple of grounds for suspecting that a suicidal individual's capacity may be particularly problematic in cases of purported requests for physician-assisted suicide by older persons.

First, the prevalence of dementia increases dramatically in older patients. Although the presence of dementia (a diagnostic category) by itself, particularly in its early stages, does not necessarily equate with decisional incapacity (a functional concept), in its more severe stages dementia ordinarily does substantially interfere with an individual's ability to engage in a rational decision-making process with respect to important and complicated matters. Physician-assisted suicide certainly qualifies as such a matter.

Much has been made in contemporary ethical and legal discourse of the possibilities for competent patients to guide their future medical care in the event of subsequent decisional incapacity through the execution of various forms of advance directives. Proposals set forth thus far for physician-assisted suicide would all limit this option to patients with sufficient *present* decision-making capacity to request physician-assisted suicide very shortly before its implementation. It is questionable whether such a restriction, if embodied in a statute, could withstand Equal Protection scrutiny, especially if a right to physician-assisted suicide were not only recognized by the courts but held to be fundamental in kind.

Perhaps more pertinent from a practical perspective is the fact that most people want to stay alive as long as they remain mentally intact; indeed, it is only at the point of severe mental deterioration, including decisional incapacity, when some persons would anticipate such a gruesome quality of life that they might ever contemplate an assisted (or an unassisted) suicide option. As G. Kevin Donovan stated,

> *After all, if assisted suicide is a benefit, why should it be denied to those who waited too late to ask, aren't yet sick enough to merit it, or will never be competent enough.... If the guidelines are meant to protect the most vulnerable members of society, how do we justify at the same time depriving them of this benefit? The conflict is both inherent and inevitable. (G. Kevin Donovan, "Letter— Physician-Assisted Suicide," 274[24] J.A.M.A. 1911 [1995])*

At the same time, allowing physician-assisted suicide for patients incapable of making decisions through previously executed advance directives, with all the ambiguities and uncertainties already attending the rise of advance directives in other contexts, would open the door to precisely the types of abuse that proposals to limit physician-assisted suicide to presently capable patients are intended to prevent. On the other hand, legalizing physician-assisted suicide while restricting its availability to individuals with contemporaneous decisional capacity creates a significant risk that individuals diagnosed with early stage dementias would panic and request physician-assisted suicide preemptively and prematurely out of fear of waiting too long. It is likely, too, that unassisted suicides by early stage dementia patients would become more common in this scenario out of the patients' feeling of necessity to act defensively within an accelerated time frame. The rapid scientific refinement and public availability of genetic testing techniques that may be useful in making more definitive differential diagnoses of early Alzheimer's disease can only complicate this scenario.

A second, and closely related, decisional capacity problem is the prevalence of depression among older, and especially seriously ill, patients. As with dementia, the simple bestowal of a diagnostic label on older patients should not inevitably lead to an assumption of the global inability of these patients to make medical choices. Nonetheless, an impressive body of evidence indicating a clear connection between severe depression in elderly individuals (not infrequently exacerbated by excessive use of alcohol) and difficulties in complex medical decision-making processes, as well as a connection between treatable depression and a desire for death in critically ill patients, should heighten the discomfort about potential abuses of physician-assisted suicide with the older population.

Further, the notion that physicians are able to distinguish ethically and with any socially acceptable degree of confidence and precision between individuals who are capable of making decisions and older individuals who are not is suspect. Even if psychiatric consultation is sought in difficult cases (and most situations of physician-assisted suicide requests ought to be placed in this category), as suggested by Timothy Quill and colleagues, there is no assurance either that the psychiatrist would have any special training and expertise in evaluating the decisional capacity of older persons for physician-assisted suicide purposes or that insurers would routinely pay for such consultations.

Voluntariness

In health care decision making generally, and certainly in the context of physician-assisted suicide, only voluntary patient requests made without duress, undue influence, or coercion have any plausible claim to legal and ethical legitimacy. Several factors may significantly and perhaps inherently impinge on the voluntariness of purported requests for physician-assisted suicide made by elderly patients. First, the United States is currently a fundamentally ageist society in which older individuals are often made to believe they are of little value or have vastly reduced worth. Despite the tremendous (arguably even disproportionate) public financial resources devoted to the health care and income support of the elderly mainly for political reasons, the continual social message to which the elderly are exposed is a theme that glorifies youth and vitality while devaluing the present contributions of the aged. The upshot of this psychological atmosphere is a potential endangerment of older individuals' freedom of choice. As Nancy Osgood noted,

> *Older people, living in a suicide-permissive society characterized by ageism, may come to see themselves as a burden on their families or on society and feel it is incumbent on them to take their own lives.... The right to die then becomes not a right at all but rather*

*an obligation.... In a society that devalues old age and older people,
in which older adults are seen as "expendable" and as an economic
burden on younger members, older people may come to feel it is
their social duty to kill themselves.*

*Put somewhat differently, the problem...involves the voluntari-
ness of the decision. If choosing death becomes a socially acceptable
alternative, then patients needing much care may begin to consider themselves selfish merely for choosing to live. The pressure on
the elderly... would be particularly great if death came to be seen
as "a solution" to...old age.*

*Notably, the impact of an ageist society is evidenced already in
the disproportionately high rate of suicide attempts and comple-
tions among the elderly in the United States. By contrast, the suicide rate of the elderly in societies which hold and communicate
more respect for the aged is a much rarer event.*

A second ground for suspicion about the voluntariness of an older
individual's purported request for physician-assisted suicide arises from
the role of an individual's family in this decision. Although normally
families of older patients are an integral, positive force in supporting and
assisting the effectuation of the patient's autonomous decision making,
this is not always the case. The psychological, physical, and financial
burdens on family members of very sick and frail individuals, especially
those with chronic conditions requiring extensive, ongoing provision of
care in the home, are great and can affect the patient's exercise of autonomy
in many different ways. With respect to the present analysis, even the
most sincere and well-intentioned families in such circumstances may
end up, consciously or not, subtly or more directly pressuring the older
patient to relieve the family's burden by selecting the physician-assisted
suicide option. The stress on the family, regardless of its palpability and
magnitude, can never be a morally or legally acceptable justification for
unduly influencing a vulnerable older person to agree to premature active
death hastening. Nevertheless, when combined with an older person's
own sense of guilt about imposing a burden on the family because of
continuing life and thus continuing the individual's provision of care, any
pressure brought by the family can exert a powerful psychological force
on the dependent patient's choices and actions.

Ageism in the Health Care System

As noted previously, the voluntary nature of an older person's purported request for physician-assisted suicide is threatened both by general ageism in American society and by caregiver burden and other forces acting on the patient's family. Voluntariness, as well as the "informed" component of an older patient's physician-assisted suicide decision, may also be jeopardized by ageist attitudes and practices that directly pervade the present health care delivery system.

From the earliest part of their training, physicians and other health care professionals are taught to devalue the lives of older patients. One important way in which this attitude becomes manifested in practice is demonstrated by the overwhelming evidence that chronological age, *by itself* (that is, not used as a proxy for or indicator of some other, more clinically and ethically defensible consideration such as likely prognosis), frequently is a large risk factor for specific older patients being offered less aggressive medical treatment than normally would be offered to a younger, otherwise identical patient. Thus, as verified in the major national Study to Understand Prognoses and Preferences for Risks of Treatment, old age *per se* is used consciously or subconsciously by many physicians as the basis for (1) slanting the information and options provided to the patient (or surrogate decision maker, in the case of patients incapable of making decisions), thus diminishing the "informed" part of informed consent; and for (2) applying gentle or more firm pressure on the patient to accept less aggressive care than might otherwise be advised, thus jeopardizing the voluntariness of the patient's decision. This specter of age discrimination in medical practice (see Chapter 10) bodes poorly for any reasonable expectation of just, fair administration of a legalized physician-assisted suicide option for older patients.

The elderly as a group based solely on chronological age are also targeted for proposed discrimination on the macro, or social policy, level as well as at the individual bedside. As American society continues to struggle with the challenge of health care cost containment, a number of serious proposals have been put forward which would, through various strategies, categorically ration health care according to the age of the patient. Although vigorous ethical, legal, economic, and social objections to these proposals have been mounted, the enthusiasm with which age-based rationing proposals have been received, if not embraced, by key decision makers ought to shake confidence in our ability, and indeed even our desire, to effectively implement legalized physician-assisted suicide in a non-age discriminatory fashion.

Alternatives to Physician-Assisted Suicide

The emotional and intellectual appeal of physician-assisted suicide appears to derive from fears patients harbor about suffering unremitting physical pain, psychological indignity, loss of control and independence, and abandonment during a time of critical illness that for most individuals is likely to occur near the end of life. Although end-of-life concerns may be relevant to persons of all ages, the elderly correctly believe they are particularly vulnerable to the risks of poor and insensitive care in this context.

The track record of health care professionals in humanely and respectfully caring for patients near the end of their lives surely leaves much to be desired. Trying to avoid dealing with deficiencies in current end-of-life care, however, by allowing and thereby encouraging older persons and others to opt out of the health care delivery system near what elderly persons perceive is the end of their life and to preempt objectionable care by allowing physician-assisted suicide is not the answer.

Instead, a more ethically and legally viable alternative is to confront current deficiencies directly and improve the ethical as well as clinical quality and process of end-of-life medical care. The Ethics Committee of the American Geriatrics Society (and many other professional organizations) has endorsed enhanced pain control through active palliation efforts. Improved professional and public support of nonprofessional caregivers would help assure older patients that they will not be left to die alone and impersonally, thereby reducing a primary incentive for individuals to seek physician-assisted suicide as a preemptive measure.

Unlike actively intervening for the purpose, intention, and expectation of hastening older patients' deaths by complying with questionably valid physician-assisted suicide requests, physicians who work at improving the quality and process of end-of-life care to make it more responsive to and respectful of the authentic values and preferences of older patients are performing a noble and life-affirming service. To accomplish this objective, initiative is demanded at three distinct but interrelated levels: clinical practice, institutional change, and political action. Legalizing physician-assisted suicide, particularly through judicial fiat, would probably destroy

DISCUSSION QUESTIONS

1. Is "physician-assisted suicide" a useful term to use? What are the drawbacks of using this term? What terms might be better for advancing a more productive debate? *See* Kathryn L.Tucker & Fred B. Steele, *Patient Choice at the End of Life: Getting the Language Right*, 28(3) J. Legal Med. 305–325 (2007).

2. After the article reprinted above was written, the U.S. Supreme Court resolved the issue of whether states may enforce statutes making physician-assisted suicide unlawful, holding unanimously that states have such power because individuals have no fundamental constitutional right to hasten their own deaths with the assistance of a physician (or anyone else). *See Vacco v. Quill*, 521 U.S. 793 (1997); *Washington v. Glucksberg*, 521 U.S. 702 (1997). Do you agree with these decisions?

3. The Supreme Court made clear in its 1997 *Quill* and *Glucksberg* decisions that states have the power, even though they do not have any obligation, to decriminalize physician-assisted suicide. Thus far, only Oregon and Washington have taken advantage of that state power. As a public policy matter, should other states follow their lead in this respect? Why or why not? *See* Norman L. Cantor, *On Kamisar, Killing, and the Future of Physician-Assisted Death*, 102(8) Mich. L. Rev. 1793–1842 (2004).

4. Even if physician-assisted suicide in general were decriminalized in individual states, should such decriminalization apply to older persons? Or, are older persons particularly vulnerable and in need of special protections against abuse?

5. How would you respond to a patient's request that you help him or her in some way to commit suicide? What factors would be relevant in shaping your answer to this question? How would you protect yourself legally?

health care professionals' incentive to take these needed initiatives and expose vulnerable, fearful elders to the serious and unnecessary risk of being prematurely deprived of the fullness of their days.

EUTHANASIA

Acting to hasten a patient's death may subject a physician or other health care professional to state prosecution for homicide under the legal theories of murder, attempted murder, or voluntary manslaughter. Worries about criminal prosecution may well exert the effect of discouraging physicians from responding adequately to the needs of dying patients for relief of their intractable pain. The undesirable result too frequently is unnecessary emotional and physical suffering on the part of dying individuals and the families who have to watch them suffer. Health care professionals, state prosecutors and law enforcement officers, and the general public need to understand the fundamental legal and ethical difference between proper pain control, on the one hand, and the illegal practice of euthanasia, on the other.

Euthanasia is the doing of an affirmative act, such as the giving of a lethal injection, by one person to another for the exact purpose of speeding up the other person's death and with the accurate anticipation and actual result of doing exactly what was intended. Euthanasia at present is outlawed in every state and most of the rest of the world, even if done with the permission (voluntary euthanasia) or even at the request of the euthanized individual. However, providing sufficient pain medication for a dying patient is a very different kind of act than euthanasia. For at least two reasons, it should be treated quite distinctly under the law. First, the purpose of prescribing adequate pain medication for a suffering patient who is approaching the end of life is to provide palliation for the person's suffering. As one might expect, the experience of physical pain is the main reason that patients ask their physicians to provide relief through prescription drugs. The patient's death is a foreseeable and anticipated event, but *directly causing* that death is not the physician's goal in prescribing pain medications. In this situation, the patient's death is not resisted, but it is a by-product rather than the *intended* outcome of compassionate palliative care. Therefore the philosophical principle of *double effect* (engaging in an act for a morally good purpose even though acknowledging the act also might contribute to a morally bad result) would excuse, if not applaud, the prescription of adequate pain medications for suffering dying patients. *See* Bernard Lo & Gordon Rubenfeld, *Palliative Sedation in Dying Patients,* 294(14) J. Am. Med. Ass'n 1810–1816 (2005).

Second, and more importantly, it may not even be necessary for proponents of prescribing sufficient pain medications for patients nearing death to rely on the double effect principle for moral justification and legal protection. This is because the physician's palliating conduct may not really be contributing to a hastening of the patient's death anyway. There is growing evidence that even when it takes the form of sedating the patient so deeply as to render the patient unconscious or stuporous until death has taken place, the administration of pain medication may not have any measurable effect on shortening the patient's life.

As expressed by legal scholar Norman Cantor, "Since deep sedation is administered to patients who are gravely deteriorated and unavoidably dying, it may be almost impossible to know whether the underlying disease process or the effects of sedation caused the death." Regarding the administration of pain relievers short of inducing terminal sedation, Cantor notes, "In the context of a debilitated, fatally afflicted patient, it is difficult to establish whether the analgesics actually hasten death. That evidentiary difficulty helps explain why very few criminal prosecutions [for homicide] have involved physician administration of analgesics."

The medical literature overwhelmingly concurs that "[o]pioids, which are recognized worldwide as the most appropriate drugs to treat severe pain, can be taken in large doses without having a lethal effect" and that "fears over the perceived life-shortening side effects of higher doses of opioids (known as 'opiophobia'), the risk for abuse of opioids and possible legal consequences" are "probably often unrealistic." Ben A. Rich, *A Prescription for the Pain: The Emerging Standard of Care for Pain Management,* 26 Wm. Mitchell L. Rev. 1 (2000). Internationally, there is a "growing notion that the effect of opioids on survival might be much smaller than frequently thought" and that "opioids are safe [that is, not death enhancing] in the terminally ill when their doses are titrated against the symptom response."

DISCUSSION QUESTIONS

1. Why does every jurisdiction in the United States make active conduct intentionally hastening another human being's death a criminal offense? Are there any exceptional circumstances in which you believe such conduct should be legal?

2. Do you agree that, for legal purposes, providing pain medication for a dying patient should be considered qualitatively different than an act of euthanasia? Should we legally accept the ethical principle of *double effect*? Do you believe we need to rely on that principle in this context, or do you agree with those who suggest that pain medication—even if it amounts to terminal sedation—does not really hasten death and therefore has no legal significance?

3. Besides the evidentiary problems in proving the actual cause of death, why else do you believe we have seen so few criminal prosecutions involving physician prescribing or administration of analgesics to dying patients? If such prosecutions are rare, why are physicians' anxieties about negative repercussions for controlling patients' pain through drug prescription so great?

PAIN CONTROL FOR DYING PATIENTS

In spite of the foregoing discussion, there is substantial evidence that inadequate assessment, recognition, and treatment of patients' pain is a significant deficiency in the United States health care system generally. At particular risk for inadequate treatment are older persons generally, nursing home residents, and especially older postoperative or institutionalized persons with severe cognitive impairments, including dementia. The technical ability to effectively assess and treat pain in older patients now exists, through pharmacological (including opioids such as morphine, sulfate, and codeine) and nonpharmacological interventions. Nonetheless, powerful barriers impede effective pain management in too many instances.

One problem is insufficient up-to-date education about the present state-of-the-art in pain assessment and control for older patients, sometimes exacerbated by health care professionals' erroneous beliefs about the likely effects of prolonged use of analgesics. Another problem is that current third-party payment practices may act as a disincentive to proper pain care for older individuals.

Importantly, there is also the barrier to good pain management created by providers', and most significantly physicians', anxiety about negative legal repercussions. Physicians worry about criminal prosecutions brought by the Drug Enforcement Agency or its state counterpart for violation of the federal or state CSA, criminal prosecutions brought by local prosecutors for assisting in patient suicides, regulatory sanctions including license revocation or suspension, and medical malpractice lawsuits alleging negligence.

To address the impediment to adequate pain management of older individuals posed by physicians' legal anxieties, most states have enacted Intractable Pain Statutes that explicitly allow physicians to prescribe controlled substances to alleviate severe or intractable pain. These statutes confer criminal, civil, and disciplinary immunity on physicians who are engaged in justifiable pain management practices utilizing opioids. A number of professional organizations, including the American Geriatrics Society, American Academy of Pain Management, American Pain Society, the American Medical Directors Association, and the Joint Commission on the Accreditation of Healthcare Organizations, have developed and disseminated evidence-based clinical guidelines or practice parameters on pain management for dying patients. State medical boards have altered their policies and practices regarding the prescribing of controlled substances to encourage physicians to treat severe or intractable pain in dying patients more effectively; many of these alterations are based on the *Model Guidelines for the Use of Controlled Substances for the Treatment of Pain* promulgated in 2004 by the Federation of State Medical Boards, www.fsmb.org/pdf/2004_grpol_Controlled_Substances.pdf.

Of course, maintaining ethical practice while also effectively managing legal risks depends on both acting properly and being able to prove you did so afterward. When a physician properly prescribes opioids and other analgesic medications to treat the effects of specific pain symptoms, that physician should fully and honestly document in the patient's medical record the factual basis for the physician's clinical judgment and conduct. Assuming good professional practice that is correctly documented (see Table 3.4), a humane physician should not realistically fear adverse legal consequences for supporting the comfort of patients, even (or perhaps especially) at the end of their lives.

Influence of Economics and Other Factors on LSMT Decisions

Ethical and legal challenges concerning the making and implementation of difficult medical decisions have, in large part, arisen within, and been shaped by, the particular economic environment engulfing the participants in those decisions. Ethics and economics both concern the process and outcome of arriving at choices, and thus their intersection at critical points of analysis and action is inevitable.

As attention in the health care arena during the past few decades has increasingly focused on the management and containment of financial costs, substantial anxiety has been expressed about the likely negative ramifications of the ethics–economics interface. One particular area

---

Table 3.4 Elements of Correct Documentation of Opioid Prescription for Severe or Intractable Pain

Medical history
Physical examination
Evaluations and consultations
Treatment objectives
Discussion of risks and benefits
Informed consent
Medications
Other treatments
Instructions and agreements
Periodic reviews

Reprinted with permission from the Federation of State Medical Boards, Model Guidelines for the Use of Controlled Substances for the Treatment of Pain (2004), *available at* www.fsmb.org/pdf/2004_grpol _Controlled_Substances.pdf

DISCUSSION QUESTIONS

Despite the efforts enumerated previously to improve the quality of pain management in end-of-life situations by alleviating some of the physicians' apprehensions concerning possible adverse legal consequences, the Federation of State Medical Boards still acknowledges the following:

Notwithstanding progress to date in establishing state pain policies recognizing the legitimate use of opioid analgesics, there is a significant body of evidence suggesting that both acute and chronic pain continue to be undertreated. Many terminally ill patients unnecessarily experience moderate to severe pain in the last weeks of life. The undertreatment of pain is recognized as a serious public health problem that results in a decrease in patients' functional status and quality of life...

Why do such problems in pain management for older persons, especially in end-of-life scenarios, persist? What additional or alternative policy or practice strategies might be tried to bring about some improvement in this area? What should be done to educate prosecutors and staff of state medical licensing boards about the proper medical prescribing and administration of opioids and other analgesic medications for suffering dying patients? Contrast the prescribing of opioids in this kind of situation with the prescribing of opioids under other circumstances. *See* Jennifer F. Wilson, *Strategies to Stop Abuse of Prescribed Opioid Drugs*, 146 Ann. Intern. Med. 897–900 (2007).

around which ethical speculation about the potential impact of the prevailing cost containment climate has concentrated is the sphere pertaining to medical decisions made about, and care provided to, individuals who are approaching the end of their lives. Such speculation, fueled to a high degree by an often expressed worry about the amount of health care resources supposedly consumed—wastefully and voraciously—by patients in their final days is not well-informed at this point by credible empirical evidence. The present state of mind prevalent among many regarding the interface of ethics and economics in the end-of-life context might best be summarized as, "We really don't know very much, but we're worried anyway!"

Many individuals fear the pointless initiation and, worse, the continuation of excessive technological intervention in end-of-life scenarios and a concomitant loss of personal dignity and control over the management of their own dying process. This fear has inspired the development, promulgation, and (albeit with only limited success) implementation of advance medical planning mechanisms designed to abate medical intervention when—according to the patient's or surrogate's judgment— the burdens of treatment have or are likely to become disproportionate to the reasonably foreseen benefits. Apprehension about overtreatment has also led, in more extreme cases, patients to consider or pursue proactive measures (i.e., suicide done alone or with a physician's assistance) to hasten their own deaths prematurely. There are even anecdotal stories about persons executing advance directive documents with stop-loss provisions of the nature, "When I only have X dollars remaining in my bank account, stop all medical treatment keeping me alive, because I don't want excessive health care expenses to erode the estate I wish to leave to my family."

Although anxiety about excessive end-of-life treatment is widespread today, it stands in stark contrast to the fears held by many that they might be undertreated as a result of perverse behavioral incentives placed on health care providers by third-party payers' financial pressures to contain costs and, in the case of for-profit insurers and managed care organizations, to maximize profits to shareholders. For example, a newspaper editorial criticizing the practice of assisted suicide and voluntary euthanasia in the Netherlands suggested that the U.S. government, in its role of both payer for and provider of significant amounts of health care, has a pernicious financial conflict of interest regarding patients (and, by implication, families) who want aggressive end-of-life medical intervention and hence a vested interest in pushing patients to accept more limited care. In a similar vein is the published accusation by a prominent plastic surgeon attributing the advance directive movement mainly to a massive plot by the American insurance industry. There is an irony to this accusation. If it were true, it would logically behoove third-party payers to pay physicians to encourage their patients to execute advance medical directives. As it is, physicians complain that lack of payment for time spent counseling patients about these matters acts as a serious barrier impeding such conversations.

Family members also may have conflicts of interest that motivate them toward limiting the extent of medical intervention in end-of-life situations. One set of authors, for instance, documented a relationship between financial hardship in studied families due to medical expenses, on one hand, and the rejection of aggressive treatment options, on the other. (It should be noted, though, that the families' choices for less aggressive intervention generally were consistent with the patients' own values.)

There is little if any quantitative data now available establishing whether cost considerations really lead to inappropriate end-of-life under-treatment, but fears of such a connection may discourage some individuals from executing advance directive instruments or agreeing to treatment limitation techniques like do not resuscitate orders. We know that reluctance to prospectively agree with treatment abatement is common among some specific population groups who historically have had valid reasons to distrust the evenhandedness of the American health care system (although those grounds for apprehension were just as present during the time that fee-for-service medicine was dominant and no one was paying attention to how much was being spent on health care).

Additionally, anxiety about health care providers' current financial incentives for end-of-life undertreatment no doubt has encouraged some individuals to execute the will-to-live form, in which particular kinds of medical interventions may be prospectively requested rather than rejected, made available by the National Right to Life Committee (see Table 3.5). Further, this anxiety may drive some persons and their families or other advocates to demand more arguably futile medical interventions rather than being willing to rely on their clinicians' judgment about the appropriateness (i.e., the burden-to-benefit proportionality) of particular treatments. According to one set of authors, "[A]ssertions of the right to live may have less to do with societal conceptions of death or the legal doctrine of patient autonomy and more to do with money." Other authors warned, "[S]hould people suspect that they are being pressured to sign advance directives and that such directives might be used inappropriately to limit care, then the result might be both higher costs and more use of advanced technologies that patients or families would forego in an environment of greater trust."

Table 3.5   Excerpt From Model Will-to-Live Form

General Presumption for Life

I direct my health care provider(s) and health care attorney in fact(s) to make health care decisions consistent with my general desire for the use of medical treatment that would preserve my life, as well as for the use of medical treatment that can cure, improve, reduce, or prevent deterioration in, any physical or mental condition.

Food and water are not medical treatment, but basic necessities. I direct my health care provider(s) and health care attorney in fact to provide me with food and fluids, orally, intravenously, by tube, or by other means to the full extent necessary both to preserve my life and to assure me the optimal health possible.

I direct that medication to alleviate my pain be provided, as long as the medication is not used in order to cause my death.

I direct that the following be provided:

- The administration of medication
- CPR
- The performance of all other medical procedures, techniques, and technologies, including surgery

all to the full extent necessary to correct, reverse, or alleviate life-threatening or health-impairing conditions or complications arising from those conditions.

I also direct that I be provided basic nursing care and procedures to provide comfort care.

I request and direct that medical treatment and care be provided to me to preserve my life without discrimination based on my age or physical or mental disability or the "quality" of my life. I reject any action or omission that is intended to cause or hasten my death.

Reprinted with permission from the National Right to Life Committee "Will to Live" Project

Cost consciousness may encourage certain actors to overdo the encouragement of advance health care planning, contributing to an atmosphere of coercion instead of choice and an excessive quickness to "respect autonomy" by latching onto patients' earlier statements to limit end-of-life interventions without adequate reflection and investigation of a statement's intended applicability to the situation at hand. The ethical danger is that an undue eagerness to exhibit "respect for autonomy" may become a respectable cloak or cover for providers to inappropriately or prematurely limit either potentially curative or palliative care—a defensible form of asking "Why bother?"—just to save money.

Economic considerations always have influenced, and properly will continue to influence, end-of-life decision-making processes and practices, as participants strive to behave ethically in a real world of finite resources. We must be vigilant, though, to prevent financial factors from attaining disproportionate weight in the ethical calculus and thereby driving out other important influences on the quality and compassion of end-of-life care. The conduct and interpretation of more descriptive research to provide a better understanding of how economic incentives actually do influence, for better or worse, the ways in which the health care system treats people at the end of their lives would be a useful first step in formulating an effective prescriptive plan for ensuring that ethical principles guide care at this most vulnerable juncture of the human experience.

DISCUSSION QUESTIONS

1. Do you agree that end-of-life medical decisions must inevitably be influenced by economic concerns? Can't we eliminate, or at the least reduce, the influence of money on treatment decisions?

2. What other factors besides economic incentives and dis-incentives influence the behavior, both positively and negatively, of the various actors (namely, health care professionals and institutions, patients, families, and advocates) who become involved in health care scenarios at the end of life? What about such factors as a techno-logical imperative that infuses the entire enterprise of modern medicine with a powerful bias in favor of max-imizing the aggressive use of advanced technological

interventions whenever possible? Or, an educational and socialization process that instills new health care professionals with an ethos that death is the ultimate failure, to be avoided as long as possible by any means available? Or, multimedia coverage that actively feeds two kinds of public expectations: medical miracles on the imminent verge of discovery, on one hand, and fears about medical sadists running amok inflicting unwanted and inappropriate overtreatment at the end of life, on the other? Or, perhaps, anxieties about adverse legal repercussions, both for overtreatment (e.g., prescribing too many opioids for pain relief) and undertreatment? How about ageist prejudices and stereotypes as factors influencing the actors' end-of-life behavior?

3. Do we spend too much money on end-of-life medical care, especially for older persons? If so, why do we spend too much? How much should we spend? How might we spend what we currently spend in better ways? Doesn't a patient have a legal right to all the end-of-life care available?

4. Should older persons who are worried about health care costs eroding the financial legacy they intend to leave to their family be permitted to execute stop-loss advance medical directives? Should such provisions be legally enforceable? What happens if the health care providers for that patient find such directives morally offensive?

5. Are the anxieties of some patients that they will be undertreated because of their providers' perverse financial incentives valid? Do you believe these fears discourage people from executing advance directives or agreeing to DNR orders? What can be done to alleviate these anxieties?

6. Would you encourage a patient/client to sign a will-to-live form (see Table 3.5)? Why or why not?

Exercise

Mrs. A is a 90-year-old widow with severe dementia due to Alzheimer's disease and serious ischemic cardiomyopathy. She lives in a nursing home and is bedridden. She occasionally responds to commands but otherwise does not communicate in any consistent way. Staff cannot tell if she actually recognizes anyone. She never executed an advance directive or discussed medical treatment wishes with anyone else.

Mrs. A developed increasing shortness of breath and was transferred to an academic medical center, where she was treated for pneumonia and congestive heart failure. Despite very aggressive treatment for her medical problems, her condition is bleak. She has a heart rate of 110, an ejection fraction of 18%, and bilateral pleural effusions. She has an oxygen saturation of 70% to 80% while receiving oxygen by face mask. Nothing being done appears to improve the medical situation.

In accordance with hospital policy, Mrs. A's physician initiates a conversation with the family about Mrs. A's resuscitation status. The patient's son and grandson become very upset and insist that the hospital "do everything" to keep Mrs. A alive, a sentiment echoed long distance by her granddaughter, who is a first-year medical resident in radiology. The granddaughter wants Mrs. A's physician to obtain cardiology and pulmonary consultations, transfer the patient to the ICU, perform a second thoracentesis to completely drain effusions, and perform chemical pleurodesis. Mrs. A's physician resists on the grounds that these various interventions would be intrusive, painful, unlikely to improve the patient's overall medical prognosis, and may even be counterproductive medically. The physician believes Mrs. A's family is just behaving unreasonably.

How should discussions proceed with the family? Who else ought to be involved in these discussions? Is the family behaving unreasonably? Is Mrs. A's physician legally obligated to follow the family's demand for maximum medical treatment? What are the alternatives?

Definitions of Death

For most of our history, cessation of cardiorespiratory functioning has served society adequately as a definition of death for all purposes. The usefulness of this definition has been seriously impaired in more recent times, however, as advances in biomedical technology have made it possible to sustain cardiorespiratory functioning artificially in certain individuals almost indefinitely. Thus states have had to search for a definition of death that is comprehensive (legal, ethical, and clinical) and that responds to the following questions: (1) When is a person dead, so that there is no question about withholding or withdrawing LSMT? (2) When is a person dead, so that organs may be removed and transplanted into another, still living, human being? *See* Janet M. Torpy, *Patient Page—Brain Death,* 299(18) J. Am. Med. Ass'n 2232 (2008).

In 1981, the President's Commission for the Study of Ethical Problems in Medicine and Biomedical and Behavioral Research recommended a Uniform Determination of Death Act, which stated the following:

> *An individual who has sustained either (1) irreversible cessation of circulatory and respiratory functions, or (2) irreversible cessation of all functions of the entire brain, including the brain stem, is dead.*

Either by statute or judicial decision, virtually all states have now adopted the Uniform Determination of Death Act, although ethical and clinical controversies persist.

The Uniform Determination of Death Act states that "[a] determination of death must be made in accordance with accepted medical standards."

All state statutes on this subject concur. The clinical state of the art in this realm continues to evolve, along with the rest of medicine. The so-called Harvard Criteria, first published in 1968 and regularly updated since then in light of advances in medical knowledge and technology, propose that a permanently nonfunctioning brain (i.e., patient death) could be accurately diagnosed on the basis of four factors:

1. Unreceptivity and unresponsivity
2. No spontaneous movements or spontaneous breathing
3. No reflexes and the absence of elicitable reflexes
4. As a confirmatory measure only, flat electroencephalograms, taken twice within at least a 24-hour intervening period

Because the law leaves to clinical discretion the selection of which specific tests to perform to confirm a patient's death, individual hospitals

DISCUSSION QUESTIONS

1. Current law requires irreversible cessation of the entire brain, including the stem, before an individual is dead. This "whole brain" definition means that someone in a persistent vegetative state is alive as long as the brain stem still functions. Some commentators have suggested that the states should change their laws to consider dead those individuals who have suffered irreversible cessation of all upper, or cognitive, brain function even if the brain stem continues to function. Do you agree with the current whole brain definition of death or would you favor adopting an upper brain definition? What are the arguments for and against each of these approaches?

2. Some people hold religious objections to the concept of brain death, believing that a person is alive as long as the heart and lungs are working, even if artificially. Should other states join New Jersey, N.J. Stat. § 26:6A-5, in taking such religious beliefs into account in drafting their statutes defining death?

frequently develop their own policies to guide—loosely or tightly—physicians declaring death within the institution. Thus, for example, a particular hospital might choose as a matter of policy to require a specific kind of blood flow as a confirmatory test, even though neither this nor any other specific procedure is required by the state or federal government as a matter of law.

Once a patient satisfies the clinical criteria, and therefore meets the legal definition, the physician is obligated to make a declaration of death. Once the criteria are met, there also is an obligation to respect the family's request to discontinue any further LSMT and to release the body, or else liability for emotional distress to family members may be imposed on the health care institution.

Exercise

Mr. F decided to jump from an airplane to celebrate his 70th birthday. His head hit the ground hard when his parachute opened only partially. He was taken by ambulance to Holy Smokes Hospital, where he was admitted. The next day, having performed the medical procedures required by Holy Smokes' policy (which was based on the Harvard Criteria), the neurologist found that Mr. F's whole brain had irreversibly stopped functioning. Mr. F's family was told that Mr. F was "brain dead" and was only being kept alive now by the respirator; the family was asked to consent to removal of the respirator. They refused, saying they were "hoping for a miracle."

What went wrong in this scenario? Who is at fault? How should a hospital and its health care professionals appropriately deal with such a situation? For another example of a problematic misunderstanding about the meaning of a declaration of death, see Arthur I. Applbaum et al., *A Family's Request for Complementary Medicine After Patient Brain Death*, 299(18) J. Am. Med. Ass'n 2188–2193 (2008).

Certification of Death and Autopsies

When any person dies, a death certificate must be filed with the local department of vital records. Certain deaths must be referred to a coroner or medical examiner, depending on the particular jurisdiction's death investigation system. Once a referral has been made, the coroner or medical examiner must determine what steps, possibly including autopsy or postmortem examination, are needed to properly investigate the circumstances of the deceased's death. When a coroner or medical examiner conducts an autopsy, some states treat the results as an easily accessible public record.

DISCUSSION QUESTIONS

1. What is the public health rationale for requiring that death certificates for every person be filed in a central location?
2. Should the results of an autopsy conducted by a coroner or medical examiner be accessible to the public?

There are cases in which referral to a coroner or medical examiner is not legally mandated, but the attending physician may recommend that a hospital autopsy be performed. In situations in which referral to a coroner or medical examiner is not required by statute, an autopsy may be performed only if there is valid informed consent either from the individual while alive or a legally authorized surrogate after the person's death.

DISCUSSION QUESTIONS

1. Why might an attending physician recommend that an autopsy be performed even though it is not legally required?
2. What are the potential legal uses of voluntary autopsy results regarding, for example, disputes about civil liability or probate or estate matters? What are the potential positive and negative risk management implications of autopsy findings for health care providers who had earlier been involved in the deceased's care?

NOTES

Sections of this chapter were originally published in Marshall B. Kapp, Legal Liability Anxieties in the ICU, *Managing Death in the Intensive Care Unit: The Transition from Cure to Comfort* (pp. 231–244) (J. Randall Curtis & Gordon D. Rubenfeld eds.), New York: Oxford University Press (2001). Reprinted by permission of Oxford University Press; Marshall B. Kapp, *Regulating the Foregoing of Artificial Nutrition and Hydration: First, Do Some Harm*, 50(3) J. Am. Geriatr. Soc'y 586–588 (Mar. 2002); Marshall B. Kapp, *The U.S. Supreme Court Decision on Assisted Suicide and the Prescription of Pain Medication: Limit the Celebration*, 2(2) J. Opioid Mgt 73–74 (March/April 2006); Marshall B. Kapp, *Old Folks on the Slippery Slope: Elderly Patients and Physician-Assisted Suicide*, 35(1) Duquesne L. Rev. 443–453 (1996); and Marshall B. Kapp, *Economic Influences on End-of-Life Care: Empirical Evidence and Ethical Speculation*, 25 Death Studies 251–263 (2001).

CHAPTER 4

Legal Interventions for Incapacitated Older Persons

As discussed in Chapter 2 (generally) and Chapter 3 (in the specific context of end-of-life medical treatment), ordinarily the person most directly affected by any particular decision about health care, finances, social services, residential issues, or other personal matters is the person who gets to make that decision. That ordinary practice is most consistent with the ethical principle of self-determination. There are times, however, when the affected individual is not capable of making and expressing difficult personal choices competently and voluntarily. In *State of Tennessee v. Northern,* 563 S.W.2d 197, 210 (Tenn. 1978), for example, the court stated, "If ... this patient could and would give evidence of a comprehension of the facts of her condition and could and would express her unequivocal desire in the face of such comprehended facts, then her decision, however unreasonable to others, would be accepted and honored by the Courts and her doctors. The difficulty is that she cannot or will not comprehend the facts."

BACKGROUND

Ethical Underpinnings

The ethical principles of beneficence (doing good for others) and nonmaleficence (avoidance of doing harm) translate into the legal concept of *parens patriae* (literally, "father of the country") (see Table 4.1). The *parens patriae* power is society's (i.e., the state's) inherent authority to act

---

Table 4.1   Relevant Ethical Principles

Autonomy (self-determination) = informed consent doctrine
Nonmaleficence (preventing harm) = state's *parens patriae* authority
Beneficence (doing good) = state's *parens patriae* authority

---

to protect individuals who are not able to protect themselves. It is under the states' *parens patriae* authority that the legal system has created a variety of mechanisms for intervening (or for empowering private parties to intervene) in the lives of nonautonomous persons without their consent.

Legal mechanisms created under the state *parens patriae* power include involuntary commitment to a public mental institution (or to a private institution that is licensed by the state to accept involuntarily committed mental patients), guardianship, adult protective services (APS), representative payeeships, and ordinary power of attorney and durable power of attorney (DPOA) (see Table 4.2). Some of these mechanisms have already been referred to in Chapter 3.

Because many of the existing legal interventions in this sphere are products of state, and even local, legislation, regulation, and common law decisions, there is substantial variation in legal specifics across geographical locations. This pluralistic spreading of authority acts as a barrier to

DISCUSSION QUESTIONS

Why should the state exercise *parens patriae* power to intervene on behalf of older individuals who lack decisional capacity? Why shouldn't such persons be allowed (or forced) to sink or swim on their own? What business does the state have "butting into" private affairs?

Table 4.2   Potential Legal Interventions

Involuntary civil commitment
Guardianship
   Voluntary
   Involuntary
APS
Representative payeeships
Powers of attorney*
   Ordinary
   Durable
      Immediate
      Springing

*National Conference of Commissioners on Uniform State Laws, Uniform Power of Attorney Act (2007), available at www.law.upenn.edu/bll/archives/ulc/dpoaa/2008_final.htm.

DISCUSSION QUESTIONS

Should states and localities be allowed, and even encouraged, to innovate in this arena? Would older persons be better off with a more uniform national approach to the question of what should be done about some individuals' decisional incapacity?

uniformity but allows for experimentation and innovation as the different jurisdictions attempt to fashion their own policy solutions to the challenges of decision making on behalf of nonautonomous persons.

Legal interventions that impinge on the personal freedoms or liberties of individuals are limited by both legal doctrine (based on the prohibition in the federal Constitution's 14th Amendment against a state depriving any person of life, liberty, or property without due process of law) and the ethical doctrine of least restrictive or least intrusive alternative. Under the least restrictive/intrusive alternative concept, government intrusion into personal autonomy should not be any more extensive than is necessary to accomplish the legitimate public goal of protecting the vulnerable person against avoidable harm. Because of the least intrusive/restrictive alternative doctrine, a number of relatively nonintrusive legal and financial mechanisms have been developed to help vulnerable people who are presently decisionally impaired or who might become impaired in the future to maintain self-determination as long as feasible rather than to lose control before that loss is necessary. These mechanisms, intended to protect the vulnerable against exploitation but without unduly limiting their autonomy, include (among others) DPOA, daily money management services, joint bank accounts, and living (*inter vivos*) trusts.

Decisional Incapacity

Incapacity to make and express valid decisions is a problem that involves older persons in disproportionate terms. The extent of mental disorders in old age, representing decrements in both intellectual and emotional functioning, is considerable (see Table 4.3). For some older persons, mental dysfunction may be a carryover condition from earlier life. For most older people, though, mental health problems develop later in life as a result of organic brain disorders (primarily degenerative disorders or multi-infarct dementia), paranoid disorders, drug reactions, excessive use of alcohol, or as the by-product of various physical illnesses. These problems may take the form of cognitive impairment (dementia) in memory, attention, or

---

Table 4.3   Sources of Mental Impairment for Older Persons

Mental illness from younger life
Developmental disabilities
Organic brain disorders
  Degenerative disorders
  Multi-infarct dementia
Paranoid disorders
Drug reactions
Alcohol
Physical illness

information processing; emotional lability (psychosis), often manifested as aggression; or pseudodementia (depression).

The formal trigger for moving from respect for an individual's autonomous decisions to reliance on some form—voluntary or involuntary—of surrogate decision making for that individual is a determination that the person is no longer capable of engaging in a rational decision-making process. Such a determination may take place in the context of a formal, official adjudication of incompetence by a court of law with appropriate jurisdiction. More frequently, working assessments of incapacity are made outside of the court setting by medical, legal, or other clinicians; even though these assessments by themselves carry no actual formal legal authority, involved health care and human service professionals ordinarily act on the basis of these *de facto* or factual judgments without waiting for a formal legal adjudication.

Consistent with its primary emphasis on maximizing personal autonomy, the law treats the evaluation of decisional capacity ideally as a decision-specific matter. Under this approach, the inquiry ought to focus on whether the individual under scrutiny currently possesses enough capacity to make the particular decision on the agenda at that point in time. This is instead of the type of more global or all-encompassing assessment that was embodied in earlier American law and that still characterizes statutes in some other places. Although the law on the books in the United States has improved substantially in the past two decades in this regard, in practice most guardianships (discussed below) still are ordered by the court on a plenary or total basis; courts' legislatively granted authority to order guardianship on a partial or limited basis is only rarely used by the judges.

Current legal and bioethical opinion also recognizes that incapacity is not always a permanent condition. For some individuals, including some demented persons, capacity and incapacity may be transitory in duration, subject to waxing and waning depending on factors such as the time the person is asked to make a decision, the surrounding location and environment, medications taken, support or aggravation systems available, and the effects of temporary, treatable physical ailments. Thus the issue of decisional capacity really needs to be revisited periodically for many persons. This fact makes it inefficient for the judiciary and most service delivery systems but enhances societal respect for individual autonomy.

DISCUSSION QUESTIONS

1. Discuss the social attitudes that make us unwilling to tolerate (and therefore make us more eager to intervene legally regarding) an impractical decision in an 80-year-old that we would much more readily condone in a person half that age. Why are older women more likely than older men to be found in need of protective legal intervention?

2. Why is looking at an individual's decisional capacity on a decision-specific basis most consistent with the ethical goal of maximizing personal autonomy? Why do many health, human service, and legal professionals continue in actual practice to evaluate decisional capacity on a global, all-or-nothing basis?

3. Given that a particular individual's decisional capacity may get better or worse over a period of time, what strategies can health and human service professionals implement to try to ensure the maximum capable involvement of the client in decisions affecting that client?

4. How does the type of decision to be made affect the standards of cognitive and emotional capacity we would impose on the older individual before honoring that person's autonomy? To what extent should the consequences of a decision, for both the decision maker and others, be taken into account in setting the necessary standards of capacity? For example,

   a. What is the proper test of an older person's capacity to choose to own working firearms and keep them in the home? Who should be doing the capacity assessment for this purpose? *See* Edith Greene et al., *Granny, (Don't) Get Your Gun: Competency Issues in Gun Ownership by Older Adults*, 25 Behav. Sci. & L. 405–423 (2007).

b. What is the proper test of an older person's capacity to vote in an election? When should a formal capacity assessment be conducted, how often, and who ought to do the evaluation? What can and should be done to enhance elders' capacity to vote? *See Symposium, Facilitating Voting as People Age: Implications of Cognitive Impairment,* 38 McGeorge L. Rev. 843–1137 (2007).

Planned, Voluntary Legal Interventions

The U.S. legal system provides individuals who currently have sufficient capacity to make all or most of their own personal and financial choices with the opportunity to plan ahead for future situations in which decisions may need to be made but sufficient personal capacity to make them autonomously has been permanently or temporarily lost. Taking advantage of these planning opportunities allows an individual who is presently capable of making decisions to maintain some control, exercised prospectively, while obviating the need for later court involvement to resolve intrafamily or family/professional disagreements about how the person or property of the person should be treated after severe dementia or another type of mental deterioration has occurred.

Among the several voluntary legal mechanisms available for advance financial planning are the DPOA for financial matters (authorizing a named agent to act as a surrogate for the principal under delineated circumstances), creation of *inter vivos* (living) trusts, joint ownership of property (e.g., banking and securities accounts), and money management services. The major legal devices used for advance planning of medical or other personal matters are the DPOA for health care (in some jurisdictions referred to as the health care proxy) and instruction directives, usually called living wills or declarations.

The development of legal planning mechanisms designed to avoid involvement of the courts reflects a fundamental social value that difficult personal decisions pertaining to people with dementia and other severe cognitive and emotional impairments should be handled privately whenever possible within the person's informal circle of family, friends, and health care and human services team. It follows logically from the fact that the actual workings of these planning mechanisms ordinarily are not subject to any external oversight that now-capable persons planning for a future with dementia or other mental disability must be able to confidently trust the relatives, friends, and professionals to whom they are delegating the authority to advocate, represent, and make decisions.

In turn, persons in whom such trust has been placed are legally and ethically required to act in a fiduciary or trust capacity. Traditionally, a fiduciary or trust agent was supposed to be dedicated to serving the best interests of the person who delegated away decision-making authority (the principal). The best interests model is functionally akin to a parent–child relationship. The modern trend in proxy decision making, though, has been toward enforcement of a substituted judgment standard. Under this approach, the fiduciary is obligated to make those decisions that the principal would make personally, according to the principal's own preferences and values to the extent those preferences and values can be accurately ascertained, *if* the patient were able at this time to make and express his or her own competent decisions.

DISCUSSION QUESTIONS

1. Do you agree that it is best to avoid court involvement in resolving intrafamily or professional/family disagreements about how the person or property of the incapacitated individual should be treated? Why should minimizing judicial involvement in such matters be a goal?

2. How can health and human service professionals encourage clients to engage in advance planning through the legal mechanisms described? Should they encourage such planning? Why or why not?

3. What are the particular challenges health and human services professionals confront in dealing with the

decision-making agents named by clients in their DPOAs rather than with the client directly and exclusively? How would you as a professional caregiver build a legally and ethically satisfactory relationship with your clients' surrogates? *See* Nancy N. Dubler, guest ed., *Symposium: The Doctor-Proxy Relationship,* 27(1) J. L., Med. & Ethics (1999); Alexia M. Torke et al., *The Physician-Surrogate Relationship,* 167 Arch. Intern. Med. 1117–1121 (2007).

4. As a standard to guide the conduct of surrogate decision makers for decisionally incapacitated individuals, which is preferable: best interests or substituted judgment? Why? Which test is easier to apply in practice? *See* Brian J. Zikmund-Fisher et al., *A Matter of Perspective: Choosing for Others Differs from Choosing for Yourself in Making Treatment Decisions,* 21 J. Gen. Intern. Med. 618–622 (2006); Karen B. Hirschman et al., *Why Doesn't a Family Member of a Person With Advanced Dementia Use a Substituted Judgment When Making a Decision for that Person?,* 14 Am. J. Geriatr. Psychiatry 659–667 (2006).

5. How do you feel about the absence of routine external monitoring (by the court or some other legal or organizational body) of the conduct of a person named to be a client's agent in the client's DPOA? If we require routine external monitoring, won't that defeat the main purpose of the DPOA, namely, handling personal matters privately and informally? On the other hand, if we do not require external oversight, what is the likelihood the agent will abuse this position of trust for the agent's own benefit? *See* Jane A. Black, *The Not-So-Golden Years: Power of Attorney, Elder Abuse, and Why Our Laws Are Failing a Vulnerable Population,* 82 St. John's L. Rev. 289–314 (2008); Nina A. Kohn, *Elder Empowerment as a Strategy for Curbing the Hidden Abuses of Durable Powers of Attorney,* 59 Rutgers L. Rev. 1–53 (2006).

Unplanned, Involuntary Interventions

The inability or unwillingness to place sufficient trust in available others, as well as ignorance of possible alternatives and, frequently, simple inertia, account for the many individuals with significant decision-making deficits who do not engage in the sort of advance planning exercises just discussed. In such cases, society relies on its inherent *parens patriae* authority to establish several mechanisms for imposing surrogate decision makers on the incapacitated person without that person's agreement or even over his or her active objection. These specific *parens patriae* intervention mechanisms are discussed below.

SPECIFIC INTERVENTION MECHANISMS

Involuntary Civil Commitment/Hospitalization

Every state has legislation that permits the involuntary (civil) commitment to a mental health facility licensed by the state of persons who have been adjudged dangerous to themselves or others because they are mentally ill. Older persons sometimes are the subject of involuntary commitment proceedings. In most jurisdictions, anyone may file a petition initiating a commitment proceeding. In this proceeding, the state bears the burden of proving by at least clear and convincing evidence (a few states require proof beyond a reasonable doubt, as in criminal prosecutions) both the mental illness and the dangerousness of the person to be committed. *See Addington v. Texas,* 441 U.S. 418 (1979). In most cases, both the petitioning state and the allegedly mentally ill, dangerous person are represented by legal counsel. The role of the health care or human services professional may be to initiate the proceeding and/or, once the case goes to court, to provide evidence through sworn affidavit or live testimony on the issues of mental illness and dangerousness. These professionals also may be instrumental beforehand in helping the patient, family, and other caregivers to explore less intrusive alternatives that may keep the matter out of the court system altogether.

Additionally, a person may gain admission to a public mental institution through a process of voluntary hospitalization. In theory, this represents the free, competent, informed choice of the patient, but the "voluntary" label may be misleading. In practice, it is likely that many individuals (especially older persons) presenting themselves for admission to public mental health institutions, usually under threat of involuntary commitment if they do not cooperate, have substantially impaired capacity to understand their choices and select among them knowingly and voluntarily. It is also suspect whether the material risks of, and the viable alternatives to, voluntary commitment have been adequately explained to most mental institution applicants. Thus the similarities between voluntary and involuntary admission ordinarily are much more important than the distinctions. *See Zinermon v. Burch,* 494 U.S. 113 (1990).

DISCUSSION QUESTIONS

1. Should voluntary admissions to public mental institutions be abolished, with all admissions instead processed as involuntary, with formal procedural protections required accordingly? What purposes are served by maintaining the option of a voluntary admission status?

2. If truly voluntary admissions to a public mental institution are implausible, are voluntary admissions to a nursing home any more believable? Who has the authority to consent to a person's admission to a nursing home? *See* Marshall B. Kapp, *The "Voluntary" Status of Nursing Facility Admissions: Legal, Practical, and Public Policy Implications,* 24(1) N. Eng. J. Civ. & Crim. Confinement 1–35 (1998); Marshall B. Kapp, *"A Place Like That": Advance Directives and Nursing Home Admissions,* 4(3) Psychol., Pub. Pol'y & L. 805–828 (1998).

Under the Due Process clause of the U.S. Constitution's 14th Amendment, intrusions by the government into fundamental individual freedoms must be based on the principle of using the least intrusive or least restrictive alternative available consistent with the purpose of the intrusion. Thus there has been a trend in recent years toward outpatient involuntary commitment. Under this approach an individual who is

DISCUSSION QUESTIONS

1. From the perspectives of public policy and therapeutic care, respectively, what are the likely advantages and problems associated with outpatient commitment? *See* Bruce G. Link et al., *Stigma and Coercion in the Context of Outpatient Treatment for People With Mental Illnesses,* Soc. Sci. Med. (2008); John Petrila & Annette Christy, *Florida's Outpatient Commitment Law: A Lesson in Failed Reform?* 59(1) Psychiatric Serv. 21–23 (2008); Bruce J. Winick, *Outpatient Commitment: A Therapeutic Jurisprudence Analysis,* 9(1–2) Psychol., Pub. Pol'y, & L. 107–144 (2003).

2. What particular benefits and/or difficulties might be encountered with outpatient commitment for older mentally ill individuals? What are the characteristics of older persons who might be viable candidates for outpatient commitment?

found to satisfy the criteria for commitment may be ordered by the court to comply with an outpatient treatment plan as a condition of not being placed involuntarily inside a public mental health institution.

Guardianship

Under the *parens patriae* authority, statutes in every state allow designated courts, pursuant to petitions filed by "interested" parties (who usually do not have to be family members), to adjudicate a person to be mentally incompetent and appoint a guardian or conservator (terminology varies among jurisdictions) for the incompetent ward. The appointed guardian may be another individual (most frequently a relative or close friend of the ward), but—when no individual is willing and able to accept court appointment—the court may appoint a financial or health care institution, a for-profit guardianship service, or a nonprofit volunteer guardianship program. Most jurisdictions have statutes establishing public guardianship programs, under which government agencies provide the guardianship services, either directly or by contracting with a private sector entity for the services, as a last resort for "unbefriended" individuals who have no one else to fulfill the guardian role as surrogate decision maker and advocate. *See* Pamela B. Teaster et al., *Wards of the State: A National Study of Public Guardianship,* 37 Stetson L. Rev. 193–240 (2007). The sufficiency and sources of funding for public guardianship programs varies markedly from place to place.

DISCUSSION QUESTIONS

1. What would you foresee as the possible advantages and disadvantages of having a family member or friend of the ward appointed as the guardian? A financial institution such as a bank? A health care institution such as a hospital? A for-profit guardianship business? *See* Alison Barnes, *The Virtues of Corporate and Professional Guardians,* 31(3) Stetson L. Rev. 942–1026 (2002). A nonprofit volunteer guardianship organization? *See* Ellen M. Klem, *Volunteer Guardianship Monitoring Programs,* Washington, DC: ABA Commission on Law and Aging (2007). A public (governmental) guardian? *See* Pamela B. Teaster, *When the State Takes Over a Life: The Public Guardian as Public Administrator,* 63(4) Pub. Admin. Rev. 396–404 (July/Aug. 2003); Pamela B. Teaster, *The Wards of Public Guardians: Voices of the Unbefriended,* 51(4) Fam. Relations 344–350 (2002); Winsor C. Schmidt, Jr., *The Wingspan of Wingspread: What is Known and Not Known About the State of the Guardianship and Public Guardianship System Thirteen Years after the Wingspread National Guardianship Symposium,* 31(3) Stetson L. Rev. 1027–1046 (2002).
2. Who makes the ideal guardian? What qualities are most important? Why?

The guardian traditionally has had a fiduciary or trust responsibility to act in the ward's best interests. As indicated previously, however, there is a growing preference that instead of just relying on their personal judgment about what would be in the principal's or ward's best interests, fiduciaries should make decisions based on the principle of substituted judgment when it is realistically feasible to know what the principal or ward would have wanted done. For example, the Uniform Guardianship and Protective Proceedings Act (UGPPA) § 314 (a) provides the following:

> ...A guardian ... to the extent possible, shall encourage the ward to participate in decisions, act on the ward's own behalf, and develop or regain the capacity to manage the ward's personal affairs. A guardian, in making decisions, shall consider the expressed desires and personal values of the ward to the extent known to the guardian.

The principle of decision-specific capacity has inspired every state to enact legislation creating the mechanism of partial or limited guardianship, with decision-making authority granted by the court only to the extent that the ward really needs a surrogate. Limited guardianship legislation reflects a "person-centered" approach. The UGPPA § 311 (b) provides as follows:

> The court, whenever feasible, shall grant to a guardian only those powers necessitated by the ward's limitations and demonstrated needs and make appointment and other orders that will encourage the development of the ward's maximum self-reliance and independence.

UGPPA § 314 (a) provides, "A guardian shall exercise authority only as necessitated by the ward's limitations...." Nonetheless, most guardianship orders still get issued by the courts in global, all-encompassing terms. Similarly, temporary guardianships that must be reviewed periodically, rather than permanent proxy appointments, currently are in favor among state statutes.

Unlike the situation a few decades ago, state guardianship statutes now uniformly contain fairly tight substantive criteria, that is, narrow definitions of incompetence. These definitions generally contain a "disabling condition" clause, describing the mental, emotional, or physical condition necessary for incompetence; a "cognitive functioning" clause, specifying that incompetence requires a finding of inability to make and communicate informed decisions; and an "essential needs" or "functional behavior" clause, referring to the individual's inability to care for himself or herself or to manage his or her own affairs.

State statutes also contain procedural requirements, such as the right of the proposed ward to be notified of and to be present and participating at the hearing and to have legal representation, as well as a strict burden and form of proof, relating to the appointment and monitoring of a guardian. In practice, however, courts continue to defer heavily in guardianship matters to medical affidavits and to the oral and written reports of other health care and social service professionals. The National Probate Court Standards, a set of recommended practices for judges, tell the courts to avail themselves of professional evaluations of the alleged incompetent person's (respondent's) abilities that address the following, among other, factors:

- The respondent's diagnosis;
- The respondent's limitations and prognoses, current condition, and level of functioning;
- The degree of personal care the respondent can manage alone or with some assistance, and the decisions requiring the supervision of a guardian;
- The respondent's current ability to provide for personal needs; and
- Whether current medications affect the respondent's demeanor or ability to participate in the legal proceedings.

Additional guidance for judges regarding the clinical evaluation process appear in American Bar Association Commission on Law and Aging & American Psychological Association, Judicial Determination of Capacity of Older Adults in Guardianship Proceedings (2006), *available at* www .abanet.org/aging/publications/docs/judgesbooksum.doc.

DISCUSSION QUESTIONS

1. Despite changes in state legislation over the past two decades, why do courts routinely continue to create guardianships/conservatorships on a plenary or total rather than a limited basis? What are the impediments to a more narrow, focused approach to the appointment of surrogate decision makers? *See* Lawrence A. Frolik, *Promoting Judicial Acceptance and Use of Limited Guardianship*, XXXI Stetson L. Rev. 735–755 (2002).

2. In considering guardianship/conservatorship petitions, why are courts so deferential to medical affidavits and the opinions of other health care and social service professionals? The UGPPA § 306 provides the following:

   At or before a [guardianship] hearing, the court may order a professional evaluation of the respondent [the alleged incapacitated person] and shall order the evaluation if the respondent so demands. If the court orders the evaluation, the respondent must be examined by a physician, psychologist, or other individual appointed by the court who is qualified to evaluate the respondent's alleged impairment. The examiner shall promptly file a written report with the court. Unless otherwise directed by the court, the report must contain: (1) a description of the nature, type, and extent of the respondent's specific cognitive and functional limitations; (2) an evaluation of the respondent's mental and physical condition and, if appropriate, educational potential, adaptive behavior, and social skills; (3) a prognosis for improvement and a recommendation as to the appropriate treatment or habilitation plan.

   How valuable do you believe such professional evaluations would be in the context of guardianship proceedings? Would the reports be given too much or too little weight by the courts? Should courts order such evaluations liberally or sparingly? Who should pay for court-ordered evaluations?

Guardianship is a legal approach to surrogate decision making for impaired individuals that still inspires controversy over many basic policy questions. The following are some observations from one participant at the 2001 Wingspan Conference sponsored by several national organizations (including the American Bar Association), during which invited experts struggled with these policy questions:

> *My most striking observation concerns the extent of vigorous disagreement among conference participants regarding the fundamental nature, goals, and methods of the contemporary guardianship system in this country, at what should be a rather mature stage in the development of that system. Specifically, the assembly as a whole appeared uncertain about the basic purpose of the legal structure encompassing guardianship. Some argued that the basic purpose was to protect the autonomy rights of heroically independent individuals struggling valiantly against the unwelcome, paternalistic intrusions of either self-interested or well-meaning, but frequently misguided, family members, health-care providers, financial institutions, or other third parties. Others argued that the basic purpose was to protect and promote the well-being of seriously disabled persons who cannot fend for themselves in a perilous world, and to do so at the smallest economic and psychological cost possible. The former model emphasizes and embraces the adversarial, due process aspects of the legal system, in which allegations of opponents are hotly contested until the ultimate available level of review has been exhausted, and a presumption of impermissible conflicts of interest encourages a multiplying of layers of protection. One example of this protection is separate legal counsel for the guardian, the guardian ad litem, the alleged incapacitated person, family members, and other petitioners. The latter model, by contrast, proposes that the guardianship system serves a therapeutic role, both in terms of facilitating the benevolent provision of helpful services to the incapacitated individual and doing so with a minimum of unnecessary hassle and expense. In this model, courts are therapeutic agencies rather than neutral referees of disputed facts and technical points of law. Attorneys for the parties are more like the caregiving team for the ward than combatants in search*

of decisive legal victory. Diversion of individuals to alternative arrangements short of formal guardianship proceedings, including advocating on the basis of trust and goodwill among the parties, is part of the therapeutic theme. Although the term was not specifically mentioned during the 2001 Wingspan Conference, this consequentialist approach to guardianship is consistent with viewing this area of law through the analytical lens of therapeutic

DISCUSSION QUESTIONS

1. Which model of guardianship is preferable: the adversarial, due process approach or the collaborative, therapeutic paradigm? Is diversion of individuals to alternative dispute resolution arrangements short of formal guardianship proceedings a good (therapeutic) end or a denial of due process rights? *See* Mary F. Radford, *Is the Use of Mediation Appropriate in Adult Guardianship Cases?* XXXI Stetson L. Rev. 616–686 (2002); Susan N. Gary, *Mediation and the Elderly: Using Mediation to Resolve Probate Disputes Over Guardianship and Inheritance,* 32 Wake Forest L. Rev. 397–444 (1997).

2. What is the proper role of the attorney in the guardianship process: a zealous advocate using "scorched-earth" tactics to win a zero-sum contest or a therapeutic agent working as a member of the social services team? Which role is most consistent with most attorneys' training and predisposition? *See* Joan L. O'Sullivan, *Role of the Attorney for the Alleged Incapacitated Person,* XXXI Stetson L. Rev. 687–734 (2002). Should the attorney himself or herself ever act as the guardian? What are the potential advantages and disadvantages of the attorney taking on the guardian role? *See* Edward D. Spurgeon & Mary Jane Ciccarello, *Lawyers Acting as Guardians: Policy and Ethical Considerations,* XXXI Stetson L. Rev. 791–866 (2002).

jurisprudence.... Excerpt from Marshall B. Kapp, *Reforming Guardianship Reform: Reflections on Disagreements, Deficits and Responsibilities,* 31 Stetson L. Rev. 1047–1055 (2002).

The diversion of decisionally impaired individuals to alternative arrangements short of formal guardianship proceedings raises a number of questions. The substantive, procedural, and administrative aspects of formal legal guardianship and formal diversion alternatives to guardianship certainly are important. However, for most people in the *de facto* "gray zone" or netherworld of decisional capacity and their families, there are (as will be explained) more directly relevant considerations.

According to contemporary American legal theory, citizens live in an arm's-length world of strangers. In this world, the adult individual makes all of his or her own decisions unless and until decision-making authority is transferred by formal legal means (namely, judicial appointment of a guardian or the execution of a valid DPOA instrument) to another specific person or entity. Decisional authority regarding personal issues in this legalistic model is atomistic, individualistic, singular, and sequential; only one person at a time can hold power. All adults are legally presumed to be capable of making their own decisions. In theory, that presumption can be rebutted or overcome only when a court finds sufficient evidence of incapacity.

Moreover, the legitimacy of this current model for protecting both the rights and the well-being of alleged or actual incapacitated persons rests heavily on society's faith that the courts and the medical profession, utilizing appropriate consultation with mental health experts, are able to accurately and reliably determine when an alleged incapacitated person is so cognitively and/or emotionally impaired that the sequential transfer of legal decisional authority should be triggered. The judicial process and medical professionals working in concert are depended on as being able to definitively distinguish between capacity and incapacity in particular persons, even on a decision-specific and time-specific basis.

In real life, autonomy in making personal choices often is not exercised in the atomistic and sequential manner embodied in legal theory. In practice, many older persons regularly delegate their decision-making authority to chosen agents without any formal legal trappings ("Doctor, ask my daughter"). Even more frequent is a voluntary, informal, nonexplicit sharing of authority between the individual and one or more partners in decision making ("Doctor, talk to my daughter and me together"). Although a variety of legal mechanisms, such as joint ownership of property, are in place to enable the sharing of financial decision-making authority among multiple parties, there do not exist comparable mechanisms recognizing and facilitating the sharing of authority regarding nonfinancial, personal decisions about such matters as medical care and residential arrangements. When a person is *de facto* incapable of explicitly delegating decisional authority to, or sharing decisional authority with, another party, the authority to make decisions for that person very often gets transferred to others anyway as a matter of custom and expediency without a formal legal stamp of approval. This occurs, for instance, when third parties such as health care providers look to family members to make crucial medical decisions for a relative who cannot speak for herself, even in the absence of a guardianship order or a prior or contemporaneously explicit delegation of authority by the patient/client.

Real life also diverges from legal theory in another essential respect. In contrast to the law's hopeful belief that judges and medical professionals have the ability to draw neat, clean, either/or distinctions between decisional capacity and incapacity, accurately determining capacity in particular cases often turns out to be a much more complex and difficult task.

Most individuals in the gray zone of decisional capacity, and even many who are quite clearly factually incapacitated, never have the capacity issue formally raised. Therefore, for them, the legal process of guardianship (or the process of placement in a formal guardianship alternative/diversion program) never gets invoked. The courts, who interpret and administer the guardianship statutes enacted by state legislatures, do not generate their own caseload. They are limited to involvement in controversies that are brought to the courts by parties who cannot resolve their problems less formally. Rather than initiating formal guardianship proceedings whenever there are concerns about someone's decisional capacity, the various parties generally "bumble through" outside of the legal system as best they can. This occurs based on working, clinical judgments about capacity and the cooperation (or complicity, depending on what one believes about the propriety of "bumbling through") of willing and available family members, friends, and health care and social service providers. "Although incompetence denotes a legal status that in principle should be determined by a court, resorting to judicial review in every case of suspected impairment of capacity would probably bring both the medical and legal systems to a halt." Paul S. Appelbaum, *Assessment of Patients' Competence to Consent to Treatment,* 357 N. Eng. J. Med. 1834 (2007).

There are a variety of reasons that initiating a formal guardianship process is the exception rather than the usual circumstance, besides concerns about the financial, time, and emotional costs of involving the courts. For one thing, families and professionals tend to understand pragmatically that obtaining a court's legal blessing for a decision-making arrangement that would have occurred informally anyway would rarely change the decisions made or provide additional protections to the incapacitated person. There is also the powerful force of inertia; because the current process of "bumbling through" ordinarily works well and without negative legal or other kinds of consequences, there is not much benefit seen for anyone in changing everyday practice in a way that certainly would create financial and other kinds of costs.

When the formal guardianship process does get called into action, it usually is more for the benefit of a third party, such as a service provider, financial institution, or feuding family member, than to provide any primary or incidental benefit to the ward. A legally authoritative ruling on the alleged incapacitated person's legal status by a court is commonly seen and obtained as a way to protect the legal and financial interests of the third party from potential liability. It is really a matter of guardianship as a form of defensive medicine, with the court used to shield or immunize the third parties.

Hence, often there is a big gap between legal theory and practical approaches to decision making for persons with questionable capacity. Given this gap, we must ask what messages advocates and policymakers should be sending to, and what behaviors we should be trying to encourage in, health care, social service, and financial professionals and agencies who implement the clinical, daily reality that actually affects the lives of people with questionable capacity, their families, and others who care about them. In other words, what kind of psychological climate should we be promoting, through professional education and otherwise, for those who make the important decisions about whether to convert any specific life situation into a legal case?

DISCUSSION QUESTIONS

1. Should we be encouraging or discouraging professional caregivers as a general, presumed practice to initiate (or encourage the family to initiate) a formal, legalistic approach to situations involving individuals whose decisional capacity is ambiguous? Conversely, should we be encouraging or discouraging a more pragmatic "bumbling through" approach when decisional capacity is unclear? What should be the default rule for professionals in this circumstance?

2. Should we be encouraging the risk of more false positives (the risk of guardianship actions being initiated unnecessarily while the person is still able to make his or her own decisions) or more false negatives (the possibility that incapacitated individuals who really do need legal protection will not receive it because no one asks the court to get involved)? In evaluating these conflicting approaches to the problem, what is the "success" we are trying to achieve?

3. Regarding professionals and the public, should we be pushing the legal process as the best way to protect a vulnerable citizen's rights? Or, should we be criticizing the guardianship process as a wasteful, superfluous, and negative experience for its victims?

4. How can we deal productively with the risk management worries of professional caregivers, financial institutions, and others that often explain the filing of otherwise unnecessary or premature guardianship petitions? Is it desirable to encourage caregivers and financial institutions running to, or running away from, attorneys and risk managers to resolve issues about who has the legal right to make particular decisions involving an older person?

5. What should we be teaching present and future health care and human service professionals about the best

process for measuring decisional capacity? In ambiguous situations, should we be encouraging or discouraging the conduct of more formal, elaborate, highly documented capacity evaluations than are normally done for most patients/clients? Should we encourage or discourage professional caregivers to administer formal mental status assessment instruments to help determine and document a person's capacity to make his or her own important life decisions?

6. Is it best to scare professional caregivers and financial institutions into an adversarial, legalistic model of interacting with individuals who have questionable decisional capacity and their families, a model in which the rights and obligations of each party are explicitly delineated in advance by the court? Alternatively, would it be preferable to calm third parties into an informal, therapeutically driven model of pragmatically sorting out rights and duties collaboratively along the way? Would the latter approach risk depriving people with questionable decisional capacity of their due process liberty rights?

The way that we answer these questions has pragmatic consequences. On one hand, if we choose to encourage greater use of the formal legal guardianship system, the courts should be quicker to err on the side of disallowing or voiding decisions and transactions involving people with questionable legal capacity. In that case, statutes and common law should be amended or interpreted to put caregivers, financial institutions, and even family members at risk of being found liable for taking some action (for example, agreeing to and performing surgery) regarding a person of ambiguous decisional capacity when there was uncertain legal authority to take such action. Probably the most powerful way to move behavior in this direction would be convincing those involved that judicial appointment of a guardian would be accompanied by real, meaningful, ongoing court monitoring that actually protects the vulnerable ward, that is, that makes a difference in how and what decisions are made for the ward. Put differently, a believable argument that the probable benefits would outweigh the sure disadvantages of initiating guardianship would be a big motivation for embracing the legalistic due process approach.

On the other hand, we could encourage more "bumbling through," rather than reliance on the formal legal system, in situations with questionably capable elders in several ways. First, we could make it harder for third parties and questionably capable individuals to successfully void decisions and transactions involving people whose decisional capacity was unsettled when the decision or transaction was made. Second, policymakers could encourage third parties to deal with questionably capable persons without a formal guardianship adjudication by reducing the risk management apprehensions of those third parties. Today, legal worries incline those third parties more toward formal, adversarial approaches to capacity determination; court involvement is now seen as a source of legal protection for third parties who are providing services or doing business with individuals of questionable decisional capacity. Finally, creative informal approaches to handling the challenge of cloudy decisional capacity in many older individuals could be encouraged by the development and dissemination of good resources and programs, such as money management services, that protect the rights and well-being of mentally compromised individuals without exposing them to the undesirable aspects of undergoing legal guardianship.

In evaluating the wisdom of initiating guardianship proceedings for an older person, one confronts a paradox. On one hand, there just is no way to achieve—in either theory or practice—the supposed protections of a legalistic approach to decision making for incapacitated persons without taking on the monetary, time, and emotional costs engendered by that approach. On the other hand, though, we want to produce the flexibility and chance for innovation and creativity in coming up with responses to the challenge of impaired decisional capacity that is allowed by the unspoken but prevalent practice of "bumbling through" outside of the courthouse; this is unachievable, however, unless we are willing to take the serious risk of relying heavily on trust and goodwill rather than external monitoring and enforcement.

DISCUSSION QUESTIONS

How should we refine both the guardianship system and professional practice so that we achieve the best balance of formality and pragmatism that improves the lives of vulnerable individuals who need protection against harm not only from themselves and others who mean to exploit them, but also from their well-intentioned but sometimes excessively zealous would-be protectors?

Once a guardianship or conservatorship has been established, "[c]ourt monitoring of guardians is essential to ensure the welfare of incapacitated persons, identify abuses, and sanction guardians who demonstrate malfeasance. Despite a dramatic strengthening of guardianship statutory standards in recent years, judicial monitoring practices vary substantially by jurisdiction." Naomi Karp & Erica Wood, *Guarding the Guardians: Promising Practices for Court Monitoring,* AARP Public Policy Report #2007-21 (2007). *See also* Sally B. Hurme & Erica Wood, *Guardian Accountability Then and Now: Tracing Tenets for an Active Court Role,* XXXI Stetson L. Rev. 867–940 (2002). Consider the following observation from the 2001 Wingspan Conference:

The adversarial-versus-therapeutic-model debate also was highlighted by discussions regarding the proper role of continuing judicial monitoring of guardianships after their creation. Participants who supported retaining the zealous advocacy requirement for attorneys also tended to support an aggressive policing-and-enforcement role for the courts regarding oversight of guardians and their fiduciary duties to their words. This position was based on an image of widespread, incompetent, or even unscrupulous conduct by untrustworthy guardians who, left solely to their own devices, would take advantage, or at least seriously endanger the well-being, of the wards whom the courts had placed at the guardians' mercy.

By contrast, most proponents of responsible advocacy favored a more collaborative, counseling role for ongoing post-appointment judicial involvement, concentrating on the courts trying to help guardians perform their functions better, rather than catching and punishing fiduciary miscreants. A pejorative characterization of this disagreement might be as a battle between extreme cynicism, on one hand, and hopeless naïveté, on the other.

One contentious piece of the monitoring debate was the degree, if any, to which the courts, which were universally acknowledged to operate with grossly inadequate financial and human resources, should be allowed to delegate some of their specific post-guardianship appointment duties to public or private social-service agencies or other suitable entities. Participants all agreed that ultimate legal and moral responsibility for assuring proper conduct of the guardian rests with the court having jurisdiction over that guardianship. There also was fairly widespread acceptance of the idea that most probate court systems today are considerably more skilled and prepared to oversee the financial aspects, as opposed to the personal aspects, of guardianship, employing professionals with accounting expertise, rather than social work expertise. Advocates of a therapeutic, collaborative role for the courts wanted to grant courts considerable discretion in contracting out some of their monitoring tasks to agencies who might be better equipped than the judiciary to evaluate and attend to a ward's ongoing health- and human-service needs and choices. Proponents of a policing-and-punitive-enforcement paradigm, however, would severely limit or completely deny the courts such leeway, on the grounds that oversight of behavior and punishment for transgressions are tasks for which the judiciary is uniquely well-suited. For these participants, the remedy for current monitoring deficiencies is a massive infusion of additional resources into the infrastructures of the overworked court bureaucracies.

The UGPPA § 317, Monitoring of Guardianship, provides:
(a) Within 30 days after appointment, a guardian shall report to the court in writing on the condition of the ward and account for money and other assets in the guardian's possession or subject to the guardian's control. A guardian shall report at least annually

thereafter and whenever ordered by the court. A report must state or contain: (1) the current medical, physical, and social condition of the ward; (2) the living arrangements for all addresses of the ward during the reporting period; (3) the medical, educational, vocational, and other services provided to the ward and the guardian's opinion as to the adequacy of the ward's care; (4) a summary of the guardian's visits with the ward and activities on the ward's behalf and the extent to which the ward has participated in decision-making; (5) if the ward is institutionalized, whether the guardian considers the current plan for care, treatment, or habilitation to be in the ward's best interest; (6) plans for future care; and (7) a recommendation as to the need for continued guardianship and any recommended changes in the scope of the guardianship. (b) The court may appoint a [visitor] to review a report, interview the ward or guardian, and make any other investigation the court directs. (c) The court shall establish a system for monitoring guardianships, including the filing and review of annual reports. Excerpt from Marshall B. Kapp, *Reforming Guardianship Reform: Reflections on Disagreements, Deficits and Responsibilities*, 31 Stetson L. Rev. 1047–1055 (2002).

DISCUSSION QUESTIONS

How closely should the courts monitor the activities of guardians? Why? What standards should be used as the basis for judging the acceptability of guardians' performance? Do courts have the resources and expertise to perform the oversight function? If a lot of money became available to pour into the guardianship system tomorrow, how could that money be spent? Should the courts be permitted to hire out some of their guardianship monitoring duties to private or public social service agencies or other organizational entities?

Exercise

Mrs. A is 79 years old. When she was admitted to the nursing home, her oldest daughter was already her plenary legal guardian, having been appointed several months earlier when Mrs. A suffered a stroke that left her with garbled speech and mild aphasia. Mrs. A did not object to the appointment of her daughter as her guardian.

The social worker in the nursing home is bothered by the daughter's conduct as Mrs. A's guardian. Even in the best of situations, the social worker ordinarily dreads asking guardians to spend more money on behalf of their wards. In the case of Mrs. A, the social worker always has to plead with the daughter to spend any money at all to meet Mrs. A's basic needs. Mrs. A was left a very comfortable estate by her late husband and the social worker observes the daughter driving a new, expensive automobile, always dressed in the latest fashions, and sporting a home address in the toniest part of town.

The social worker has concluded that the daughter does not really have Mrs. A's best interests at heart. What action, if any, should the social worker take to protect Mrs. A? What remedies are potentially available? What are the arguments against the social worker trying to disturb the current relationship between Mrs. A and her daughter?

Additional Resource

National Guardianship Association, www.guardianship.org

Adult Protective Services

Every state, in reaction to a federal financial incentive created by the Older Americans Act and Title XX of the Social Security Act, has legislatively created its own APS system. The APS system, operating through local social service agencies, makes available to willing older persons a variety of health care and social service (including legal counseling and advocacy) interventions designed to protect those persons from the dangers of abuse and neglect (including self-neglect). In addition, state laws generally allow local APS agencies to impose their beneficial services on unwilling recipients. With a few exceptions, under most relevant statutes nonvoluntary interventions of this type may be instituted for a very short period of time on an emergency basis, but the interventions must then either be discontinued or continued only under authority of a court order that is based on a finding that the proposed services recipient lacks an adequate level of capacity to consent or refuse concerning the specific decisions confronting that person.

The complex philosophy involved in this arena is exemplified in the legislative intent section of the Florida Adult Protective Services Act, Fla. Stat. § 415.101(2):

> *The Legislature recognizes that there are many persons in this state who, because of age or disability, are in need of protective services. Such services should allow such an individual the same rights as other citizens and, at the same time, protect the individual from abuse, neglect, and exploitation. It is the intent of the Legislature to provide for the detection and correction of abuse, neglect, and exploitation through social services and criminal investigations and to establish a program of protective services for all disabled adults or elderly persons in need of them.... In taking this action, the Legislature intends to place the fewest possible restrictions on personal liberty and the exercise of constitutional rights, consistent with due process and protection from abuse, neglect, and exploitation. Further, the legislature intends to encourage the constructive involvement of families in the care and protection of disabled adults or elderly persons.*

This legislative philosophy can be seen at work in Fla. Stat. §415.1051 (1) (d), which says:

> *If at the hearing the court finds by clear and convincing evidence that the vulnerable adult is in need of protective services and lacks the capacity to consent, the court may issue an order authorizing*

the provision of protective services. If an order for protective services is issued, it must include a statement of the services to be provided and designate an individual or agency to be responsible for performing or obtaining the essential services on behalf of the vulnerable adult or otherwise consenting to protective services on behalf of the vulnerable adult.

Representative Payee Programs

Federal law establishes several different representative payee programs to manage the proceeds of regular government benefit payments (e.g., Social Security retirement and disability checks) that are sent to beneficiaries incapable of making decisions. A representative payeeship may be set up by the government agency distributing the benefit on the basis of someone's allegation that the beneficiary lacks capacity to manage the payment

DISCUSSION QUESTIONS

When APS interventions are forced on nonconsenting older individuals, is it an infringement of rights or protection for the vulnerable? Do you agree with the statement of a group of clinicians: "Until recently, many health care professionals did not pay attention to self-neglect by vulnerable elders believing these behaviors were simply a lifestyle choice. Unlike children, adults are presumed to be autonomous.... . It is wrong to impose medical or social remedies on eccentric elders who have capacity, but health care professionals should not allow cognitively impaired elders to live in extreme squalor without either electricity or running water."? Carmel B. Dyer et al., *Vulnerable Elders: When It Is No Longer Safe to Live Alone*, 298 J. Am. Med. Ass'n 1448–1450 (2007). Does the same argument also apply to disturbing, but somewhat less extreme, living circumstances?

and request for appointment to the payee position. The beneficiary's permission is not required to establish a representative payeeship, although an appeals procedure exists for challenging the agency's finding of incapacity. The representative payee is supposed to act as a fiduciary in spending the government-paid dollars strictly for the beneficiary's benefit, but meaningful external monitoring of the payee's performance is relatively rare. Thus the representative payee alternative embodies a compromise between the formality, time, expense, and emotional turmoil entailed in the guardianship/conservatorship process, on one hand, and a totally nihilistic abandonment of incapacitated persons who cannot handle their own affairs, on the other.

Usually, the representative payee is an individual friend or relative of the program beneficiary. Certain private not-for-profit organizations also may serve as representative payee, under authority of the Omnibus Budget Reconciliation Act of 1990, Public Law No. 101-508.

DISCUSSION QUESTIONS

1. How much external oversight of representative payees' conduct as managers of beneficiaries' government benefit checks is desirable? What form should that oversight take? At what point does external oversight become so extensive it threatens the goal of operating a protective model that is less intrusive than guardianship?

2. What are the advantages and disadvantages of having the representative payee function carried out by a private organization versus an individual family member or friend of the program beneficiary? What qualities should a good individual or organizational representative payee possess?

EVALUATING INTERVENTION STRATEGIES

How well has the United States done in terms of developing and implementing desirable legal interventions for persons with dementia? This is an inquiry whose answers depend on a combination of existing and future empirical research and social policy examination. How effectively and efficiently the various legal intervention strategies that are available to deal with issues presented by individuals with severe dementia in the United States work must be evaluated in terms of their correlation, in actual operation, with the ethical and social values and presumptions that underlie those strategies.

Put succinctly, the central measurement standard ought to be the extent to which particular legal interventions, as well as the constellation of available legal alternatives considered *in toto,* effectively maximize the personal autonomy of vulnerable persons with dementia and other severe mental disabilities while at the same time protecting those persons from serious, avoidable harm resulting from their inability to fend for themselves. Does our current mixture of trust-based (hence extrajudicial) alternatives and more formal (hence more closely externally monitored) mechanisms best promote these goals? Do we achieve a sufficiently decent job of fitting specific interventions to specific individuals?

At the same time, efficiency in achieving delineated social goals must be carefully assessed. How well does the present American legal approach to dealing with the problems of persons with dementia perform in terms of minimizing not only financial transaction costs (i.e., the costs of running this segment of the legal system), but also time expenditures and emotional turmoil for family members, health care and human service professionals, and the individual with dementia?

The U.S. legal landscape must also be evaluated in terms of how well it deals with the growing social challenge of "the unbefriended." This term applies to the increasing number of persons in this country who are growing older and seriously impaired in terms of decision making but who have no suitable family members or friends available to act as either informal or formal surrogate decision makers for them. Neither the unbefriended nor the health care and social service professionals and the financial institutions that seek to engage in transactions with

DISCUSSION QUESTIONS

1. Do you agree that the key social goal should be efficiently maximizing individual autonomy while protecting vulnerable persons from serious, avoidable harm? Are all three aspects of this goal (efficiency, autonomy, and protection) realistically achievable simultaneously? What might be some alternative and/or additional goals for the legal system regarding older persons who face life choices?

2. How well does the legal system do in achieving its goals regarding older persons with diminished decisional capacity? How could the system, and the results it produces, be improved? At what costs, and to whom?

3. What should we do, both within and outside of the legal system, about the growing "unbefriended" population? *See* Naomi Karp & Erica Wood, *Incapacitated and Alone: Health Care Decision-Making for the Unbefriended Elderly,* Washington, DC: American Bar Association Commission on Law and Aging (2003).

4. Are you aware of how the legal systems of any other countries deal with the challenges posed by decisionally impaired older persons?

the unbefriended are well served by the presently available array of either planned or unplanned legal alternatives. As American society struggles with this challenge, potential lessons from other countries should be assiduously sought out and scrutinized.

CHAPTER 5

Regulation and Financing of Geriatric Services and Settings

HOME CARE

Regulating Quality and Safety

The activities of home health agencies are highly regulated, primarily for the purposes of ensuring that the quality of services the agencies provide meets defined minimum levels and protects the rights and interests of service consumers and agency employees. This regulation takes a panoply of forms (see Table 5.1).

Traditionally, we have attempted to ensure that the quality of services provided in home- and community-based long-term care (HCBLTC) settings meets minimally acceptable standards mainly by imposing strict structure and process regulatory requirements on providers. This strategy is predicated on the theory that the demand that providers possess prescribed qualifications and credentials and deliver services within defined behavioral parameters would necessarily bring about desired outcomes or results. Some structure and process regulations, such as those contained in the federal Conditions of Participation, pertain only to publicly funded providers; others, like state licensure laws, apply to all providers of specified services regardless of funding source. In addition, tort law allows a service recipient to bring a civil malpractice action against a provider seeking money damages for causing the recipient injury (a legal outcome measure) by negligently or intentionally deviating from acceptable professional

---

Table 5.1   Forms of Home Health Care Regulation

State licensure of
- Home health agencies
- Individual professionals whom agencies employ or with whom they contract

Federal Medicare and Medicaid Conditions of Participation, 42 C.F.R. Part 484 and 42 C.F.R. § 440.70(d)

Quality Improvement Organization assessment of compliance with professionally recognized standards of care

Tort litigation seeking financial recovery for alleged injury directly caused by professional malpractice

Antifraud and Abuse laws aimed at controlling the amount and propriety of financial payments

Antitrust laws

Fair Labor Standards Act and other regulation of the agency as an employer

Antidiscrimination laws pertaining to home health agencies as employers and providers of services:
- Americans With Disabilities Act
- Age Discrimination in Employment Act
- Civil Rights Act

---

standards of care under the circumstances (a process measure). This remedy takes as one of its chief justifications the assumption that decent quality care can be ensured through the threatened punishment and hence deterrence of poor quality care (although the validity of this premise is highly debatable).

When services are provided by Medicare-certified home health agencies, federal regulations (42 C.F.R § 440.10) explicitly spell out each service recipient's right to the following, among other things: to have his or her property treated with respect, to voice grievances regarding treatment that is (or fails to be) furnished or regarding the agency's lack of respect for property, to be informed about and participate in planning individualized care, to confidentiality of clinical records maintained by the agency, and to be advised of the availability of the toll-free home health agency (HHA) hotline in the state. Many states have enacted even more extensive recipients' rights mandates of their own, enforceable against home health agencies licensed by the state (*see* Florida Statutes § 400.495).

DISCUSSION QUESTIONS

1. Do you share the assumptions that underlie the current system of structure and process regulation of home health agencies as the best way to ensure the quality and safety of home health services?
2. What signals, positive and negative, does it send to consumers, families, home care workers, and the public that the rights of home health recipients need to be specified in federal and state law?

Terminating the Home Care Agency–Client Relationship

HHAs generally derive the bulk of their income from payments received, either directly from clients or through third-party payers, for rendering professional services to clients. Consequently, most HHAs devote substantial marketing efforts to enrolling and retaining as many suitable clients as possible. Sometimes, however, the client or the HHA may initiate a termination or reduction of their professional relationship and the alteration is mutually agreed on by both parties, such as when home health care was originally undertaken for a specific purpose (such as helping the client recover at home from surgery) and that purpose has now been satisfied. At virtually any time, a client may exercise the right unilaterally to terminate a relationship with an HHA. However, a more tenuous situation, from a legal and ethical perspective, may arise if it is the HHA that attempts unilaterally to terminate or reduce its existing relation with an established client.

There are several potential motivations that might underlie an HHA's wish unilaterally to discontinue or reduce its provision of services to a particular client. The HHA may believe that the client's condition has changed in a way that has made the client now ineligible to receive further home health coverage under the Medicare program or other pertinent public or private third-party insurance arrangement. A Medicare-eligible beneficiary's treating physician may refuse to certify an acceptable plan of care for the patient, as required for HHA payment by 42 C.F.R. § 484.18(a)–(b), or the HHA anticipates that the treating physician will not certify an acceptable plan of care for the client. Additionally, an HHA may terminate or reduce its relationship with a client because providing certain services to the client is no longer economically efficient or profitable for the HHA, continuing to care for a client poses untenable physical and/or legal risks to the HHA and/or its staff, or the client and informal caregivers are unduly noncompliant or actively undermine the care plan.

In earlier times, the legal relationship present between an HHA and a client (or the client's surrogate, in the case of mentally incapacitated clients) was characterized as voluntarily and freely entered into. The right of an HHA to terminate or reduce a relationship that has been entered into voluntarily and freely was limited only by two kinds of legal considerations: (1) any pertinent promises negotiated by the parties and contained within the express or implied provisions of the HHA–client contract and (2) common law tort principles prohibiting health care providers from abandoning their patients/clients by unilaterally and abruptly leaving them "high and dry" in need of continuing services without sufficient anticipatory notice of the change in the relationship. By contrast, the prerogatives of Medicare-certified HHAs in the United States today regarding their relationships with clients are constrained not only by contract and tort principles but also by federal statutes and regulations establishing "Conditions of Participation," including provisions concerning clients' rights, that HHAs must fulfill to receive payments for services rendered through the Medicare program, 42 U.S.C. § 1395bb[a].

A 2004 important federal judicial decision interpreted and significantly expanded the legal responsibilities of HHAs to give formal notice to their Medicare clients before terminating or reducing home health care services to those clients, regardless of an HHA's reason(s) for terminating or altering the relationship. The background, holding, and practice implications of the *Lutwin v. Thompson* (361 F.3d 146 [2d Cir. 2004]) case are important to discuss here. This case commenced in 1998 when a group of public interest law firms initiated a civil lawsuit on behalf of a class of elderly and disabled Medicare beneficiaries who at one time received or who at the time of the lawsuit filing were receiving home health care services provided by an HHA but who were facing the involuntary reduction or termination or the threat of involuntary reduction or termination of those services. The declaratory and injunctive relief (i.e., relief that would order the defendant to do or refrain from doing specified acts other than paying the plaintiffs money damages) requested by the plaintiff class was "meaningful notice and appeal rights when their home health benefits are reduced or terminated."

On July 3, 2000, U.S. Department of Health and Human Services (DHHS) published a final rule implementing the Home Health Prospective Payment System, effective October 1, 2000, 42 C.F.R. parts 409–411, 413, 424, and 484. In conjunction with these changes to the Medicare payment system, the Secretary promulgated a written "Transmittal" to all Medicare-certified HHAs instructing them to provide mandatory notice to Medicare beneficiaries when making adverse coverage decisions in the form of a Home Health Advance Beneficiary Notice (HHABN). The HHABN must be "written in plain language" and purports to serve the dual purpose of providing written notification of an HHA's adverse coverage determination and apprising the beneficiary of the appeals process. "Specifically, the notice provides a reason why the HHA does not believe the services ordered by a physician are covered under Medicare, the cost of the services, and the conditions precedent to initiating the appeals process." As noted in the *Lutwin v. Thompson* opinion, "HCFA Transmittal A-01-05 and the new HHABN process it established have directly addressed many of plaintiff's concerns regarding notice by requiring notice of reductions or terminations of service and notice of a beneficiary's appeal rights whenever an HHA makes an adverse coverage determination."

Nonetheless, controversy remained over what notice obligations, if any, are owed by HHAs to Medicare beneficiaries when an HHA seeks unilaterally to terminate or reduce its services for a reason(s) *other* than the HHA's determination that the client is no longer eligible to be covered for home health care by Medicare. In Transmittal A-01-05, the DHHS Secretary took the position that an HHA's notice obligations extend only to terminations or reductions of service predicated on adverse Medicare coverage decisions, but the plaintiffs urged the court to require DHHS to impose on HHAs a more expansive set of notice duties.

In rejecting the validity of the Secretary's 2001 Transmittal, a two to one majority of the panel of the U.S. Court of Appeals for the Second Circuit hearing the *Lutwin* litigation held "that the Medicare statute requires that HHAs give written notice before they terminate or reduce home health services for any reason...." This finding was based on the Court's interpretation of the Medicare statute's mandate that, to participate in the Medicare program:

> *(1) The agency protects and promotes the rights of each individual under its care, including each of the following rights:*
> *(A) The right to be fully informed in advance about the care and treatment to be provided by the agency, to be fully informed in advance of any changes in the care or treatment to be provided by the agency that may affect the individual's well-being...*
> *(E) The right to be fully informed orally and in writing ...of (iv) any changes in the charges or items and services [furnished by the HHA to the beneficiary].*

The judicial majority construed these statutory provisions clearly and unambiguously to require that when an HHA is no longer willing—for *any* reason whatsoever—to continue providing previously provided services to a current client, there is a change in the "items and services furnished by ... the agency" that requires advance written notice.

Besides relying on the language of the Medicare statute, the plaintiffs in this case also asserted that the Fifth and Fourteenth Amendments of the U.S. Constitution, which prohibit units of government from depriving any citizen of life, liberty, or property without due process of law, compels advance notice of unilateral termination or reduction of home care services to Medicare beneficiaries. Because it found that the Medicare statute requires HHAs to provide written notice before they terminate or reduce home health services for any reason(s), and there is a long-standing tradition of courts trying to avoid deciding constitutional issues needlessly, the *Lutwin* court wisely declined to consider (thereby leaving open for future exploration) the question of whether written notice might also be required by the Due Process clause.

The *Lutwin* plaintiffs, in addition to their claim for notice rights, asserted that the constitutional Due Process clause requires the Secretary to implement a predeprivation review procedure for the appeal of an HHA's adverse coverage determination for an HHA client. The Court of Appeals unanimously rejected this procedural due process argument, agreeing with the District Court "that the fiscal and administrative burden to the government associated with such an alteration in the Medicare process outweighs the risk of erroneous deprivation of the plaintiffs' property interest in home health benefits under the present regime."

For HHAs faced with the pragmatic challenge of figuring out how actually to implement the *Lutwin* decision satisfactorily, there are several rather disconcerting aspects of the court's ruling. Additionally, the court's aggressive overreaching in this case ought to bother those who are interested in the policy aspects of home health care regulation.

First, a group of home health physicians filed an *amici* (friend of the court) brief supporting the plaintiffs in this case, asserting that when the HHA reports that the treating physician concurred in the decision to reduce or terminate home health services, there is an unacceptably high risk that the HHA has misled, misinformed, or, worse, never even consulted the treating physician before taking it upon itself to reduce or terminate necessary patient services. The defendant's policy, if upheld, would allow HHAs to make their own independent determination of the medical need for services and permit HHAs unbridled autonomy to unilaterally stop treatment without physician concurrence and without notice to the beneficiary.

To the extent that these allegations are truthful (as opposed merely to being self-serving rhetoric by a few disgruntled physicians), they should be quite ethically troubling to HHAs. When an HHA seeks to justify the reduction or elimination of services on the basis of a medical rationale (i.e., a rationale that home health care is no longer needed for a particular client), the treating physician should be closely involved in that determination and the HHA is obligated to relate to the treating physician honestly and to create, retain, and transmit accurate documentation regarding medical facets of the client's condition.

Second, the majority opinion in *Lutwin* creates a disturbing definitional confusion. In a footnote to its opinion, the majority states, "In holding that [the Medicare statute requires that] HHAs must provide written notice to Medicare beneficiaries before reducing or terminating services, we recognize that *de minimis* alterations in the items and services furnished by the HHA—for example, changes in care personnel or times of arrival or departure of such personnel—would not require written notice." This essentially throwaway comment (in legal terms, *dicta*) leaves wide open the issue of precisely which alterations in items and services furnished by the HHA would be considered so minor that prior notice is not legally compelled. One could realistically envision the very same public interest law firms spearheading the *Lutwin* litigation taking advantage of the court's uncertainty on this point to argue in some future litigation that changes in care personnel or times of arrival or departure are so significant to the client's well-being that prior notice by the HHA to the client about those items is imperative. Indeed, the dissenting opinion in *Lutwin*, in criticizing the majority's reading of the Medicare statute as requiring an HHA to give notice before terminating or reducing services for any reason, perceptively anticipated just such an argument in warning that "written notice of a host of other matters that are of importance to HHA patients, such as changes in care personnel or times of arrival or departure of such personnel, may be included."

Third, the *Lutwin* majority seriously overreached its appropriate judicial role in at least a couple of key respects. To begin, by rejecting the validity of the Secretary's Transmittal A-01-05, the majority explicitly defied the strong presumption of deference that courts ordinarily are supposed to show toward administrative agencies' interpretations of their own governing statutes and regulations. Worse yet, the *Lutwin* majority rebuffed well-grounded tenets of judicial restraint by *sua sponte* (on its own) adopting an even more expansive construction of the Medicare law than the plaintiffs themselves and their *amici* (friends) had urged the court to adopt. The plaintiffs only had asserted that they were entitled to prior written notice when an HHA tries to terminate or reduce services either because of a belief that the client was not eligible for Medicare home health coverage or for lack of physician recertification of a client's care plan. The court went beyond the plaintiffs' own limited request for relief, to hold much more broadly that the Medicare statute "requires written notice prior to any reduction or termination [for any reason] in the items and services furnished by the HHA." The dissenting opinion accurately accuses the majority of converting the Medicare statute into "a general 'patients' bill of rights' covering contractual relationships between HHAs and all their patients to be informed by the Secretary."

Hence, HHAs must be prepared to develop and reliably put into place efficient systems for notifying clients (or their legally authorized representatives) in a timely fashion about an HHA's intent to terminate or reduce the provision of services to a client. Such systems must include effective staff education activities and provisions for timely and comprehensive documentation. The respective responsibilities of particular individuals within the HHA regarding client notice must be delineated clearly and should be written into every involved staff member's job description.

Many elderly and disabled individuals regularly receive valuable services from HHAs. The unilateral termination or reduction of such services by an HHA may exert a significant impact on the life of a client who has come to depend on those services. On one hand, notifying a client of the HHA's intent in this regard in a timely fashion is a matter of common sense and ethical decency, and law enshrining the HHA's notification responsibilities toward clients makes clear policy sense. At another level,

DISCUSSION QUESTIONS

1. Do you believe the physicians' *amici* brief in the *Lutwin* case that HHAs frequently make decisions to reduce or terminate home health services unilaterally, without proper involvement of the client's treating physician?

2. In providing home health care services, are matters such as changes in care personnel or times of arrival or departure of such personnel of such importance to patients that the HHA should have to provide the patient with advance written notice? How far in advance must the notice be provided?

3. What do you think of the majority's opinion in the *Lutwin* case? Did the Court go too far, perhaps for political reasons, in interpreting the Medicare statute here? Does this decision impose inflexible, unreasonable burdens on HHAs? Is this decision ultimately more likely to help or hurt clients?

though, individual clients' conditions and HHA needs and capabilities change constantly, and inflexible legal requirements for formal, written, prior notification of every client concerning the details of every proposed alteration in service delivery may impose an undue administrative burden on numerous HHAs, interfering with rather than enhancing the quality of client care and the HHA–client relationship and entailing negative financial, psychological, and clinical implications for clients and HHAs. The challenge is to devise and implement administrative systems regarding notice that treat clients fairly and therapeutically while allowing enough flexibility for HHAs to carry out their activities productively and profitably.

Exercises

Case 1

Mr. and Mrs. X are well known to all of the HHAs in the community. Mr. X is 84 years old, blind, and has a permanent colostomy. He also has rheumatoid arthritis and needs assistance with such activities of daily living (ADLs) as shaving, bathing, changing and cleaning his colostomy, dressing, ambulating, and food preparation. Mrs. X is able to see and ambulate with only a moderate degree of assistance but otherwise is in very bad shape physically.

Mr. and Mrs. X are well known because they have been clients of almost every home care provider in the community. Mr. and Mrs. X are independently wealthy and able to pay for needed services out of pocket. Over the past year they have sought out HHAs because they do not seem able to retain the private aides they had hired independently earlier. The problem is that nothing is ever done quite to the clients' satisfaction. Each HHA has run through its roster of aides, none of whom have lasted longer than a week. When they get upset with an aide's perceived shortcomings, Mr. X often becomes physically agitated and strikes out at the aide whereas Mrs. X does verbal berating. Not infrequently, aides have asked to be removed from the X home before being fired by the clients. A few of the HHA staff have suggested that Mr. and Mrs. X move into some type of extended facility together. Mr. and Mrs. X have rejected that suggestion, insisting they would be fine in their own home if only they could find "good help."

XYZ Home Care has recently agreed to take on Mr. and Mrs. X as clients. In 2 weeks Mr. and Mrs. X have dismissed three of XYZ's best aides. The aides' grapevine has been working overtime and now XYZ is having difficulty in convincing an aide to agree to this assignment. XYZ is the last chance in this community for Mr. and Mrs. X. How should XYZ Home Care handle this case? What rights and responsibilities are held by the individual employees of XYZ?

Case 2

Mr. J sometimes seems confused and sometimes quite lucid. On some days you can have a normal conversation with him, whereas on others he doesn't remember he ever met you. XYZ Agency has provided homemaker and bathing assistance for several years to Mr. J, who lives alone in a garden apartment. Questions are starting to be raised about Mr. J's capacity to continue living alone in his own apartment. Once, he left the stove on and a small fire resulted. Mr. J's daughter is concerned and would like her father in a safer environment. She has consulted Mr. J's physician. For his part, though, Mr. J is not willing to give up control over his life willingly. He believes he can manage his own affairs just fine and likes his current living circumstances. Based on a short consultation, the physician is willing to say that Mr. J is decisionally incapacitated, but the XYZ Agency case manager does not believe Mr. J is at the stage of incapacity yet. What are the case manager's legal and ethical obligations and options at this point?

Case 3

Mrs. Y, age 88, lives alone in a decaying trailer a few miles from a small town. She has six old, indoor cats that defecate and urinate in the trailer, which is dirty inside and outside. Vermin sometimes visit the trailer. Mrs. Y has a constellation of physical problems for which she ought to have regular help. She accepts meals-on-wheels, and the delivery person has observed that roaches often are drawn to the food that Mrs. Y leaves lying around. Mrs. Y refuses all other homemaker or personal care services. She has always been a loner and keeps in touch with none of her relatives. She has avoided the health care system for many years. According to screening tests administered by a caseworker from the local adult protective services (APS) agency, Mrs. Y is not considered to be decisionally incapacitated. She wants to stay in her trailer with her cats. If she is moved from her home, there will be nobody to care for the cats. What legal and ethical alternatives are available to the APS agency?

Case 4

Mr. W is a 65-year-old man with a complicated medical history that includes a stroke resulting in left hemiparesis, left eye blindness, frequent falls, and alcohol abuse. He is wheelchair dependent and needs assistance with several ADLs. He lives alone in a wheelchair-accessible apartment and has no known family. He has a 10th grade education, served in the army, and worked on the assembly line of a factory for a few years before quitting. He has since subsisted primarily on food stamps and a variety of local charity programs but now qualifies for his state's Medicaid HCBLTC program.

Mr. W's health problems are chronic, and the goal set for him was to maintain community residence and his present level of function while providing social and emotional support. This approach included medical management in the local clinic, recreation in a local community center, and home care for ADL assistance. Mr. W has been assessed as sufficiently capable of making his own health care decisions, despite some mild cognitive impairment.

Mr. W has been counseled both by his physician and the staff of his home care agency regarding the dangers of continued alcohol abuse, but he refuses to cooperate with his treatment plan related to alcohol abuse. Geriatric home care aides reported finding empty liquor bottles under his sink at home and he has been falling down a lot. He has been abusive to the psychologist and the social worker who are part of his managed care team. He continues to drink excessively and lately has exhibited inappropriate behavior toward the aides assigned to provide him with personal care such as bathing and dressing. He sexually harassed an aide in his home and frightened her with his advances. He refuses to have male aides in his home.

What should the home care agency do about Mr. W? What are its legal obligations and options, and what are the potential legal risks related to those obligations and options? What is the role of the state agency administering the HCBLTC program in which Mr. W is enrolled? Where do people like Mr. W usually end up spending their final years?

Consumer-Directed Long-Term Care

Consumer direction in the long-term care context has been defined as follows:

> *[A] philosophy and orientation to the delivery of home- and community-based services whereby informed consumers make choices about the services they receive. They can assess their own needs, determine how and by whom these needs should be met, and monitor the quality of services received. Consumer direction may*

exist in differing degrees and may span many types of services.
It ranges from the individual independently making all decisions
and managing services directly, to an individual using a repre-
sentative to manage needed services. The unifying force in the
range of consumer-directed and consumer choice models is that
individuals have the primary authority to make choices that work
best for them, regardless of the nature or extent of their disabil-
ity or the source of payment for services. National Institute on
Consumer-Directed Long-Term Care Services, Principles of
Consumer-Directed Home- and Community-Based Services.
Washington, DC: Author (1996).

In the traditional, historical, American model of HCBLTC for
individuals with serious and ongoing impairments in the ability to perform
ADLs, most of the important operational facets (the who, what, where,
when, and how) of service financing and delivery have depended mainly
on who is paying the bill. When the individual service recipient personally
pays for desired services, that person is respected as a consumer and gets to
negotiate the content of the service delivery agenda, at least to the extent
that there exists a competitive marketplace of service providers vying for
business in the individual's locale. By contrast, when third-party payers
(ordinarily governmental entities) are involved, the HCBLTC services
received by the person with ADL impairments are primarily driven by
the policies and instructions of the agencies delivering or coordinating
services, within well-delineated programmatic constraints established by
service funders. Consumers have limited choice and control about their
own long-term care once enrollment in the public financing program has
commenced.

The traditional agency- or funder-driven HCBLTC paradigm emphasizes professionally ascertained client needs and the paramount goal of
client safety. In addition, it seeks to accomplish its primary objectives of
quality control and consumer protection through the application of direct
command and control regulation (i.e., regulatory "thou shalts" and "thou
shalt nots") of service providers' conduct. This regulation is done, for
example, via professional and organizational licensing by the states and
federal or state structural conditions yoked to providers' participation in
specific public funding programs such as Medicaid. Additional legal tools

relied on in this regard are the threat of civil and criminal liability for violation of quality standards and the endangerment of client safety. The policy assumption underlying the traditional model is that the behavior of service providers needs to be pushed constantly in the direction of client protection. Creating anxiety among providers about potential personally adverse legal consequences for jeopardizing client safety is likely the most effective way to achieve that behavioral objective. Put differently, the envisioned ideal role of the law is to prevent, detect, and punish provider malfeasance. An appropriate descriptive image is one of the law as a shield, placing a protective barrier between the older consumer and those who would engage in mistreatment.

As already noted, the idea of consumer-driven long-term care is nothing novel as applied to individuals who have the financial means—through personal pensions, invested savings, or private long-term care insurance policies—to pay for services themselves. The power of the purse is the power to negotiate, at least insofar as choices of service providers are available within a particular community. Similarly, a rich tradition of consumer-driven long-term care has developed over the past several decades in the context of publicly funded long-term care services for younger seriously disabled persons who desire to define and control the parameters of their service plans. However, since the mid-1990s there has been a broad conceptual and practical shift, even for the substantial proportion of the older American population that depends on public dollars to finance their HCBLTC. This shift, which represents a logical expansion of the informed choice doctrine beyond its original application to clinical medicine and the more recent consumer-driven health care contexts, has been toward consumer-driven long-term care delivery models within which the older consumer is empowered to control the structural and operational components of the service plan. This shift in the gerontological sphere has been fueled by a variety of social, economic, political, and legal factors.

Publicly financed, consumer-driven HCBLTC models vary significantly across the states in structure and operation. These models are funded through a combination of federally approved state Medicaid waivers authorized by 42 U.S.C. § 1396n(c), dedicated state appropriations, and (at least for the time being) private foundation demonstration grants. The precise methods of transmitting compensation to long-term care providers (e.g., via vendor payments made directly by the governmental or private insurer versus entrusting clients with vouchers or cash to spend themselves, with professional counseling) vary from program to program. Contemporary experimentation with consumer-driven models of long-term care is by no means limited to the United States, and several countries have demonstrated more than a decade's worth of substantial positive experience with these models.

Under the consumer-driven long-term care paradigm, quality control and direct protection of consumers against provider malfeasance remain legitimate, but now secondary, functions of the law. The main function of the law under consumer-driven long-term care is affirmative. Specifically, the law is expected to enable, empower, and facilitate the informed, capable, and voluntary exercise of consumer autonomy or self-determination within a competitive, affordable marketplace of good quality services and goods. Here, the law should be envisioned as a sword with which consumer rights—most notably the right to informed choice—can be carved out. The parameters of the government's proper role within the emerging consumer-driven HCBLTC paradigm include both autonomy-enhancing initiatives and the regulatory limits that arguably ought to be imposed as a matter of client protection, even under a consumer-driven model of HCBLTC.

Several states have been operating consumer-directed HCBLTC programs since the 1980s. These state programs include a significant number of older persons "without any evidence of significant problems for older consumers." The available empirical evidence supports the workability of this model. Nevertheless, private arrangements between consumers and independent contractors for HCBLTC services entail a panoply of risks for the consumer (as well as for in-home long-term care workers). In some circumstances, attempted consumer direction will fail. Even, and perhaps especially, under a robust consumer-driven long-term care model, a certain amount of governmental regulation is essential to protect consumers. For instance, access to the courts must remain available to consumers to enforce the terms of private contracts entered into by those consumers with private long-term care insurers and sellers of long-term care goods and services. Consumers will only be willing to continue to negotiate and join in contracts to the extent they feel confident that the bargained-for terms will be enforced legally if they are not complied with voluntarily. Additionally, civil tort remedies, in the form of monetary damages, must remain available to particular consumers who are seriously injured because of private provider deviation from acceptable standards of care (i.e., negligence) or intentional misconduct such as client physical or financial abuse.

The consumer-driven model begins with an informed consumer. This, in turn, requires that adequate, appropriate, comprehensible information about the benefits, risks, and costs of various alternative services and service providers are readily available to consumers who expect to direct the details of their own HCBLTC. Ideally, consumers should be educated, trained, and supported by objective professional sources to exercise their choices in the manner that best accomplishes a particular consumer's personal goals and preferences. Legal initiatives can positively influence the informational environment in several ways.

Government mandates the collection and public dissemination of a slew of comparative data concerning the quality of services rendered by particular long-term care providers. Further research is needed to clarify how consumers actually use this information to select providers and monitor their performance. The Federal Trade Commission (relying on statutory authority [15 U.S.C. § 45] stemming from Congress' constitutional power to regulate interstate and foreign commerce) and its state counterparts (relying on the states' inherent police power to protect and promote the general health, safety, and welfare of the community) should promulgate rules criminalizing false and misleading advertising or other misrepresentations by service and product sellers. False, misleading commercial speech, designed to sell a service or product rather than to inform political debate, is not as fully protected against governmental prohibition under the free speech clause of the U.S. Constitution's First Amendment, as is political speech. Further, consumers who are defrauded by deceptive practices must be able to seek monetary damages for their injuries in individual civil tort claims brought in state courts. Additionally, government has a valuable role to play in setting standards for the sales practices of private long-term care insurance companies, including regulation regarding product advertising.

Actual consumer preferences lie at the heart of the consumer-driven long-term care paradigm. Those consumer preferences trump policymakers' and long-term care practitioners' externally generated and imposed ideas about what consumers *should* desire. Under the traditional agency or funder-driven long-term care model, consumers were forced to make a trade-off. They forfeited choice regarding most of the details of their own long-term care in exchange for the protection against the risk of harm purportedly provided by an extensive web of command-and-control regulation and tort and criminal liability potential surrounding service delivery. It must be noted that the assumption about the prophylactic consequence of legal regulation underlying the traditional long-term care model has not yet been subjected to rigorous empirical analysis; it persists as an article of faith among adherents of the regulatory approach.

The consumer-driven long-term care paradigm, by contrast, deemphasizes the safety preservation function of legal intervention and, instead, more strongly emphasizes its autonomy enhancement potential. An important policy-relevant assumption, therefore, is that this trade-off of assumed safety for tangible control over long-term care details is acceptable, if not affirmatively desirable, to the majority of potential long-term care consumers and/or their families or other surrogates.

There is a corollary to this assumption about a tolerance, if not a positive preference, for increased autonomy even at the cost of some increased exposure to risk of harm (put differently, a preference for quality of life over quality of care): namely, the supposition that the great majority of consumers and/or their surrogates are capable of intelligently making such trade-offs of some degree of increased exposure to risk of harm to obtain and maintain desired forms of long-term care from desired providers under desired conditions. One (but only one) way that such capability might be measured would be by comparing the consistency of consumer choices with the intent of program planners. Consumer self-determination could be exercised either independently, in collaboration with family, friends, or significant others, or by informally (i.e., without the involvement of formal legal sanction) delegating decision-making authority to another individual(s) selected and trusted by the consumer.

It makes little sense to devise a long-term care model predicated on assumed consumer preferences unless we also assume most consumers are able to act autonomously, by making important decisions voluntarily, competently, and as an outcome of rational manipulation of sufficient information, and that persons lacking this capacity represent an exceptional category within the much larger relevant population. Moreover, long-term care by definition involves the use of a frequently changing array of services over an extended period of time; hence, proponents of consumer-driven long-term care must assume most consumers' adequate capacity to function as autonomous decision makers exists not just at the outset of long-term care but on a continuing, ongoing basis as well.

Nevertheless, even the most vigorous proponents of consumer-driven long-term care acknowledge that there will be some (albeit a relatively small) percentage of older disabled HCBLTC candidates who lack, temporarily or permanently, sufficient cognitive and/or emotional capacity to act as autonomous consumers despite any amount of informational and social support. States could fulfill their *parens patriae* obligation to protect these individuals by enacting legislation requiring (except in those situations where the candidate has previously been adjudicated incompetent by a court as part of a guardianship or conservatorship proceeding) HCBLTC candidates to be evaluated to determine if they currently possess sufficient decisional capacity to participate in a consumer-driven service model.

Regarding those who are determined to lack adequate present decisional capacity, advocates of consumer-driven long-term care suppose that there exist suitable mechanisms for surrogate decision making about long-term care (including HCBLTC options). This assumption contains two general components. First, it is assumed that legal advance planning mechanisms, primarily proxy directives (i.e., durable powers of attorney) supplemented by instruction directives (i.e., living will–like instruments), concerning long-term care decision making either exist, or can be created, to assist almost all decisionally incapacitated long-term care candidates to have their previously indicated long-term care preferences followed. Further, it is assumed that these legal devices will be created in a timely fashion (i.e., while the consumer is still decisionally capable) by most individuals who will become decisionally incapacitated at some point in the future. Moreover, there is faith that reliance on these advance planning documents in real circumstances requiring specific decisions will achieve the results, in terms of the shape of the long-term care service plan, the consumer had intended to achieve.

To assist in the fulfillment of this set of assumptions, the states should amend their respective advance directive statutes to expressly authorize the execution of both proxy and instruction directions specifically referring to planning for HCBLTC (and, for that matter, for future nursing home care). Moreover, federal or state statutes could be enacted, analogous to the Patient Self-Determination Act of 1990 (see Chapter 3), that compel hospital discharge planners, physicians, and designated others to inquire of a patient or the patient's surrogate, at designated points in time (such as when the hospital discharge planning process commences), whether the patient had previously executed an advance long-term care directive. When, as usually would be the case, no advance long-term care directive had been previously executed, the law could require the discharge planner, physician, or other professional to offer to assist the patient to execute such a document. To aid in the enforcement of these long-term care directives, state long-term care directive statutes could contain provisions mandating that discharge planners, area agencies on aging, and other participants who would be involved in the individual's HCBLTC respect and implement the instructions contained in a directive (subject to resource constraints and exceptions based on potential ethically unacceptable risks of harm to the vulnerable individual). Even under such exceptional circumstances, the involved professionals should be prohibited from interfering with a transfer of the consumer to other providers who are willing and able to honor the consumer's long-term care advance directive.

There also is the belief on the part of consumer-driven long-term care advocates that willing and able individuals can easily be identified and convinced to step in to make choices on behalf of decisionally incapacitated long-term care clients. Additionally, it is assumed that an acceptable mechanism for holding these surrogates accountable for acting consistently with the consumer's wishes or, alternatively, in the consumer's best interests can be created. A suitable process of accountability in this context would depend on several factors. These factors include, among others, the prospective achievement of sufficient consensus among interested stakeholders regarding appropriate minimum and optimal qualifications for long-term care decision-making surrogates, agreement on the extent and limits of surrogates' decision-making powers, development of efficient and effective ways of monitoring surrogates' performance as fiduciaries for decisionally incapacitated long-term care clients, and implementation of aggressive but not overly intrusive strategies for intervening when the surrogacy system goes seriously awry.

The various states' APS statutes could be amended to specifically address these factors in ways that facilitate the efficacy of surrogate decision making for matters pertaining to HCBLTC. These modifications to the present APS system could be made as an exercise of each state's inherent *parens patriae* authority to protect from harm those persons who are *de facto* unable to protect themselves and hence vulnerable to ethically and socially unacceptable risks.

Consumer choice, to be engaged in as a matter of private negotiation and agreement, is only meaningful as more than a slogan when consumers actually enjoy the opportunity to pick from and negotiate specific details with an array of potential local providers of long-term care services and goods. To promote the welfare, and thus encourage the participation, of independent long-term care service providers whose availability and willingness to sell their services is integral to the maintenance of a vibrant marketplace, government should attend to a variety of human resource matters. These matters include application to independent providers of the wage and hour provisions of the Fair Labor Standards Act, workers' compensation and unemployment insurance provisions, the Social Security retirement system, and disability programs. To the extent the legal environment and other factors can promote the job satisfaction, safety, and general well-being of independently employed workers, those factors will contribute to the ultimate success of the consumer-driven long-term care model.

Another central aspect of the legal environment concerns providers' exposure to litigation and liability risks. Proponents of consumer-driven long-term care assume (without significant dispute from most advocates of the more traditional, professionally dominated service delivery model) that the prevailing legal environment (both actual and perceived) can exert a powerful effect on the behavior of people trying to avoid or minimize their own exposure to negative legal consequences. Such defensive risk management behavior, whether or not it actually successfully reduces the actor's legal risk, may act either beneficially or antitherapeutically on the lives of the intended beneficiaries (in this case, HCBLTC consumers) of the anxiety-producing legal environment.

In the long-term care context, it is assumed that the actual or perceived climate relating to providers' legal risk exposure may affect the availability, quality, and price of HCBLTC services in any specific locality. More specifically, proponents of consumer-driven HCBLTC assume that a legal environment that concentrates more (and is perceived as concentrating more) on enhancing consumer autonomy and less on constantly policing for provider malfeasance is likely to result in more providers of services and goods vying for economically empowered consumers' business in a competitive marketplace. This would happen by reducing providers' apprehension about potential regulators' aura of distrust and propensity to punish. That development, in turn, is likely to enhance the accessibility, affordability, and quality of long-term care all consumers are able to purchase. That is because these are all attributes every provider wants to excel at to improve its own competitive position in the business world of empowered, informed purchasers.

The starting factual precept of consumer-driven long-term care is that at least a significant proportion of disabled adults, including older persons—even many of those with quite substantial ADL impairments—strongly want to manage all or many of the details of their own long-term care rather than leave the most significant service delivery details to a professional agency or funding entity. This presumption is consistent with the contemporary American cultural commitment to the ethical and legal value of autonomy. This belief in the desire for individual autonomy is a fundamental article of faith nearly universally held among members of the long-term care policy community, rising virtually to the level of a mantra.

Nonetheless, we know there is some amount of heterogeneity on this matter among various components of the relevant population. Individuals, deciding personally or through a surrogate, who want to receive HCBLTC services within a traditional regulatory model should be allowed and enabled to do so. It would ironically defeat the goals of the autonomy principle to force consumers to drive their own HCBLTC plans unwillingly. A scaled down version of the *status quo ante* needs to remain in place for those individuals, or alternatively a default mechanism should exist in the same way that in the health care financing arena traditional Medicare Parts A and B remain in place to be chosen by beneficiaries who do not wish to join with those individuals who are participating in the more autonomy-oriented Medicare Advantage-Part C option.

The paradigm shift to a consumer-driven model for the funding and delivery of home and community based long-term care for older, disabled individuals does not merely entail the removal of a preexisting regulatory regime in which the most important facets of the care plan were determined mainly by professionals and bureaucracies instead of the consumer. Rather, this shift calls for a new and different approach to regulation. The specific form and contents of regulation in the era of consumer-driven HCBLTC depend in significant measure on a rethinking of the role of government in the weighing and balancing of sometimes competing social values implicating both the enhancement of autonomy and protection of the vulnerable.

In 2008, the Centers for Medicare and Medicaid Services (CMS) published a Proposed Rule providing guidance to the states that want to administer self-directed personal assistance services through their State Medicaid Plans. *See* 73 Fed. Reg. 3546-65 (Jan. 18, 2008).

DISCUSSION QUESTIONS

1. Do you agree with (1) the policy assumption underlying the traditional model of long-term care service financing and delivery that "the envisioned ideal role of the law is to prevent, detect, and punish provider malfeasance" or (2) the policy assumption underlying the consumer-driven long-term care model that the function of the law is to enable, empower, and facilitate the informed, capable, and voluntary exercise of consumer autonomy or self-determination within a competitive, affordable marketplace of good quality services and goods? Do older potential consumers of HCBLTC really want to be treated as autonomous shoppers for services or do they want to be spared from having to make their own choices and direct their own service plan?
2. Why did the idea of consumer-driven HCBLTC take hold in the context of the younger disabled community so much earlier than in the world of aging services? What are the relevant differences, if any, for these two populations?
3. What are some of the social, economic, political, and legal factors that have fueled the movement toward consumer-driven HCBLTC in the gerontological sphere? *See* Paula Acosta & Leslie Hendrickson, *Discussion*

Brief—Advancing Medicaid HCBS Policy: From Capped Consumer to Consumer-Directed, Rutgers Center for State Health Policy (Mar. 2008), *available at* www.cshp .rutgers.edu/cle; Suzanne R. Kunkel & Valerie Wellin, eds., *Consumer Voice and Choice in Long-Term Care,* New York: Springer (2006).

4. Why do you suppose several European countries are far ahead of the United States in their implementation of consumer-driven models of HCBLTC?

5. How do consumers actually use the publicly available data concerning the quality of services rendered by particular long-term care providers? How might consumers be assisted to make better use of these data? *See* Kevin J. Mahoney et al., *Cash and Counseling: A Promising Option for Consumer Direction of Home- and Community-Based Services and Supports,* 7(4) Care Mgt J.: J. Long-Term Home Health Care 199–204 (2006).

6. Do you agree with the premise of consumer-driven long-term care that consumer preferences ought to trump policymakers' and long-term care practitioners' ideas about what consumers should desire? Don't policymakers and practitioners know best what is in the best interests of consumers? Are long-term care consumers (and their families) really willing to trade off some degree of protection against the risk of harm to enhance their control over the details of their HCBLTC?

7. Are older individuals who need help with their ADLs capable of making autonomous choices regarding the details of their HCBLTC? How large a problem is consumers' decisional incapacity likely to be in implementing the consumer-drive HCBLTC model of service delivery and financing? *See* Jane Tilly, *Consumer-Directed Home and Community Services for Adults With Dementia,* Alzheimer's Association Public Policy Issue Brief (2007), *available at* www.alz.org/documents/ advocacy_public_policy_issue_brief_71107.pdf;

Ce Shen et al., *Does Mental Illness Affect Consumer Direction of Community-Based Care? Lessons From the Arkansas Cash and Counseling Program,* 48(1) Gerontologist 93–104 (2008). Should formal evaluations of decisional capacity be legally mandated for each potential HCBLTC candidate? Even without a legal mandate, should programs be carrying out formal capacity evaluations?

8. Do you believe that there now exist suitable mechanisms for surrogate decision making about long-term care (including HCBLTC options) for those consumers who are determined to lack adequate present decisional capacity? Are advance planning instruments likely to work well in this context? What other surrogate decision-making mechanisms would you suggest?

9. Should independent home care workers be entitled to the same legal benefits and protections as HHA employees? If so, who will pay for these additional benefits and protections? If benefits and protections are needed to ensure an adequate workforce, won't the free market make sure that they happen? Besides the actions noted above regarding legal protections and benefits for independent home care workers, what might government do to promote adequate person-power to make a meaningful consumer-driven long-term care model work, that is, to promote the willingness and availability of sufficient numbers of independent HCBLTC workers for consumers to hire?

10. Do you believe that the real and perceived legal environment makes a real impact on the availability and price of independent service provider options for HCBLTC consumers? How would you describe the liability risk climate for HCBLTC in your own state; in other words, how anxious are service providers in your state about the legal risks entailed if they are involved in providing HCBLTC to older patients/clients?

In the HCBLTC model, the client must pay attention to his or her status as employer to the independent caregiver, who is an employee for most legal purposes. The employer/employee relationship implicates rights and responsibilities for the parties pertaining to

- Minimum pay and maximum hours under the regulations of the Fair Labor Standards Act, 29 C.F.R. part 552
- Federal and (if applicable) state and local income tax withholding
- Social Security Federal Insurance Contributions Act payroll deductions
- For a growing percentage of the independent provider workforce who are immigrants, the Immigration Reform and Control Act, 8 U.S.C. § 1101.

ASSISTED LIVING

Assisted living is the fastest growing type of senior housing in the United States. *See* Keren Brown Wilson, *Historical Evolution of Assisted Living in the United States, 1979 to the Present,* 47 (Special Issue III) Gerontologist 8–22 (2007); Robyn I. Stone & Susan C. Reinhard, *The Place of Assisted*

DISCUSSION QUESTIONS

1. What are some of the barriers that people who need long-term care might encounter in trying to devise and direct their own home- and community-based care plan? How prevalent are these barriers? How can clients be helped to overcome these barriers? Or, are they insurmountable?
2. Why are both the formal long-term care industry and the pool of available independent caregivers so dependent on immigrants? What are the likely effects of changes in American immigration laws on the availability of long-term care workers?

Living in Long-Term Care and Related Service Systems, 47 (Special Issue III) Gerontologist 23–32 (2007).

Definitions and Regulation

Definitions across the states are inconsistent; there are more than a dozen designations for facilities that could be considered, or that are marketed as, assisted living. In general, though, assisted living may be defined as a residential setting that provides or coordinates personal care services, 24-hour supervision, scheduled and unscheduled assistance, social activities, meals, housekeeping, and some health-related services (such as assistance with medications). Assisted living facilities usually are not designed for (although an increasing number of them do in fact admit and retain as residents) persons requiring around-the-clock nursing care or continuous medical monitoring. The objective of assisted living is to maintain or enhance the capabilities of frail older persons and persons with disabilities so that they can remain as independent as possible in a home-like environment.

The states have the primary responsibility for licensing and overseeing care furnished to assisted living residents. Because neither Medicare nor Medicaid dollars (except for the dollars available under specific state Medicaid waiver programs) pay for assisted living services, few federal standards or guidelines are applicable to assisted living facilities. Individual states address their regulatory role regarding assisted living through a variety of approaches. In terms of specific content, state laws differ significantly in their (1) standards concerning admission and discharge criteria, staffing ratios, and training requirements; (2) inspection procedures that detail frequency, notification requirements, and inspector training; and (3) the range of enforcement mechanisms available to be used. The National Center on Assisted Living compiles an annual list of state regulations that includes contact information for licensing agencies (*see* www.ncal.org/about/state_review.cfm). The major national trade association is the Assisted Living Federation of America (www.alfa.org).

In addition to state regulation via licensure laws, the long-term care ombudsman agency in each state and the APS agency in most states investigate complaints or allegations of problems involving residents of assisted living facilities. Also, state consumer protection agencies are involved in regulating the accuracy of materials produced by assisted living facilities to market their services to the public.

DISCUSSION QUESTIONS

1. Should the states regulate assisted living facilities via command and control licensure requirements, or should rights and responsibilities in this context be left as a matter of contract between the facility and the consumer (with the courts available to interpret and enforce the contractual provisions when there is a disagreement between the parties)?

2. If states are going to directly regulate assisted living facilities, should the regulations focus on the assisted living facility primarily as an institution, as a model of housing, or as a service provider? What particular aspects of assisted living should be targeted in regulations? In this context, are regulations likely to be protective or counterproductive?

3. How can potential consumers be assisted to evaluate the marketing claims of assisted living providers? How can potential consumers best be assisted to understand and negotiate the provisions in the admission contract the assisted living provider asks the potential consumer to sign? What specific subjects ought to be covered in an assisted living facility admission contract? (See Table 5.2.)

Accreditation

Since mid-2000, the Commission on Accreditation of Rehabilitation Facilities (CARF) operates a voluntary accreditation program for assisted living facilities (www.carf.org). Accreditation is the granting of approval or credentials (i.e., a stamp of approval) to an agency or facility based on that agency or facility demonstrating (usually by passing a specific survey or inspection) that standards prescribed by the accrediting body have been met. Accreditation is voluntarily sought by the agency or facility rather than being required by the government, and the accrediting body

Table 5.2 Subjects Included in Assisted Living Admission Contract

- Occupancy date
- Type and size of unit to be rented
- Furnishings
  - Provided by facility
  - Resident is permitted to bring
- Unit structural alterations permitted
- Resident health requirements
  - For admission
  - Permitting the facility to terminate the contract
- Unit maintenance
- Services to be provided
  - Included in the monthly fee
  - Available for purchase at an additional fee
- Monthly occupancy fee*
  - Now
  - Conditions under which the facility may increase the fee
- Residents' rights
- Disputes/liability
  - Any limitations on the facility's liability†
  - Methods of settling disputes (e.g., requirement of mediation or arbitration instead of, or as a precondition to, litigation in the courts)‡

* Note that the consumer obtains no equity or ownership interest in the property in exchange for the monthly fee.
† Most state courts are reluctant to enforce contract provisions that purport to be total waivers of liability by the consumer and/or to exculpate the facility in advance from any liability, and some states have enacted statutes prohibiting the enforcement of such contractual clauses.
‡ Most state courts will enforce contractual clauses, if entered into knowingly and without coercion by all parties, that involve the use of alternative dispute resolution mechanisms.

is a private rather than governmental entity. Among other things, CARF surveyors check for conformance with standards pertaining to:

- Assisted living's core values and mission
- Input from residents, families, and other stakeholders
- Disclosure of information
- Outcomes management
- Individual-centered planning, design, and delivery of services
- Residents' rights
- Quality and appropriateness of services

DISCUSSION QUESTIONS

1. Is voluntary accreditation of assisted living facilities likely to be an effective quality assurance tool? Should CARF or some other private, nonprofit entity be granted deemed status, such that the entity's accreditation would substitute for government inspection of the facility?
2. What kinds of expertise should be represented in a survey team that is accrediting assisted living facilities?

Autonomy and Negotiated Risk

Development of the assisted living concept entails commitment on the part of service providers to a model of individual autonomy or self-determination. Under this model, particular consumers are presumed to be adults who are capable of forming, expressing, and acting on their own values and preferences regarding important choices arising in their everyday life. There are a variety of impediments, however, to translating the autonomy model of assisted living into actual practice. Among the most powerful of these barriers is the widespread anxiety about exposure to potential litigation and legal liability that health and human services professionals and organizations associate with providing services generally and more specifically with permitting and even facilitating consumers to make and implement autonomous "bad" choices that place themselves at risk of avoidable injury.

These law-related anxieties often push provider behavior in a paternalistic direction, influenced by the assumption that restricting client control over living arrangement and service provision details thereby increases the level of risk management for the provider. If the assisted living movement is to fulfill its potential on behalf of older persons who would like such a residential option, it is necessary to harness much of the law-inspired apprehension that now stands as a barrier to the basic shift away from imposed protection and toward meaningful consumer participation in planning and decision making. One promising avenue for doing that is pursuing the process of negotiated or managed legal risk.

The negotiated or managed risk concept builds heavily on the legal and ethical doctrine of informed consent (see Chapter 2), by using the client's autonomous right to make personal decisions about his or her own care plan to clarify and reallocate the risks, responsibilities, and potential liabilities connected to the choices selected. Under the informed consent doctrine, a decisionally capable adult has the liberty right not to have his or her bodily integrity invaded without the individual's voluntary and informed consent. In other words, the person has the prerogative to refuse undesired interventions. Although the informed consent principle usually has been analyzed in terms of specific medical treatments, it applies full force to the various kinds of ongoing health-related, dietary, and residential interventions and restrictions that might make up a long-term assisted living arrangement.

However, rights are accompanied by responsibilities. When a consumer and/or family legitimately exercise the autonomy right, embedded in informed consent, to negotiate a care plan that includes certain risks of consumer injury that the provider would otherwise be attempting to remove, the legal doctrine of assumption of risk comes into play. As a general matter, assumption of risk is available as a defense to a negligence action if the defendant is able to prove that the plaintiff voluntarily and knowingly assumed the risk of certain conduct that might otherwise be deemed negligent. The assumption of risk defense is closely related to the contributory or comparative negligence doctrines, under which a defendant—even if guilty of negligence—is excused from liability altogether or has liability proportionately reduced because of the plaintiff's own negligent contribution to his or her injury.

Both the assumption of risk and contributory/comparative negligence doctrines are premised on a decisionally capable plaintiff or authorized substitute decision maker knowingly and voluntarily deciding to take on a risk of harm. Informed, voluntary choice supposes that the decision maker understand the possibility of an adverse outcome and nonetheless decides (or even demands) to accept the care plan in question.

The courts slowly but noticeably seem to be more willing to place responsibility on the consumer's shoulders by holding the consumer—

rather than the professional or agency—answerable for the results of the risky decisions that the consumer knowingly and voluntarily makes. This development fits logically with the concept of negotiated risk as it is continuously refined and tested in multiple situations arising in the context of assisted living. In some states, the concept of negotiated risk is embodied in statute. For example, Illinois states the following:

> *Assisted living, which promotes resident choice, autonomy, and decision-making, should be based on a contract model designed to result in a negotiated agreement.*

This model assumes that residents are able to direct services provided for them and will designate a representative to direct these services if they themselves are unable to do so. This model supports the principle that there is an acceptable balance between consumer protection and resident willingness to accept risk and that most consumers are competent to make their own judgments about the services they are obtaining.

For the contrary viewpoint, namely, that assisted living residents are all incapable of knowingly and voluntarily negotiating the terms of their own lives within the facility, *see* Eric Carlson, *Protecting Rights or Waiving Them? Why "Negotiated Risk" Should be Removed from Assisted Living Law*, 10(2) J. Health Care L. & Pol'y 287–237 (2007).

Exercises

Apply the concept of negotiated risk in the following hypothetical, but realistic, situations.

Case 1

Jimmy is an assisted living resident who wanders from the facility. He walks several miles and forgets to return home. He will possibly sustain injury if he continues to leave the facility unattended, as he forgets to return home and is unsteady on his feet. The assisted living facility suggests that Jimmy wear an identification (ID) bracelet with his name, address, and phone number; Jimmy only leave the premises when escorted by a family member or facility volunteer; and/or Jimmy alert staff when he is leaving the facility. Jimmy agrees to wear an ID bracelet but insists on being free to leave the assisted living premises unattended and does not want to have to inform staff each time he departs the premises. His family understands and supports his desire to go and return as he pleases.

If Jimmy wanders by himself away from the assisted living facility, falls, and injures himself, should the facility be held legally responsible for his injuries? Why or why not?

Case 2

Shirley is an insulin-dependent diabetic with orders from her physician to adhere to an American Diabetes Association diet. However, she likes sweets and frequently sneaks regular desserts from her tablemates at meals. She says she does not like diabetic desserts. Shirley's physician has informed her, and she has signed an agreement indicating her understanding, that eating regular desserts could elevate her blood sugar to a level that could place her at an extreme health risk.

If Shirley continues to eat nondiabetic desserts and her blood sugar becomes dangerously elevated, who (if anyone) should be held legally responsible for any injuries? Why?

Case 3

Fernando has a physician's prescription to take two pills for his heart condition at bedtime, with assistance from the assisted living facility staff. Medications ordinarily are delivered between 8 p.m. and 8:30 p.m. Fernando frequently tells the staff person to just leave the pills and he will take them right before he goes to bed (at about 10:30 at night). A number of times, however, staff have found the pills on the floor the next morning. If Fernando does not take his medication as ordered, his physician says Fernando could suffer adverse medical consequences, including exacerbation of his heart condition. Both Fernando and his family prefer to accept the consequences if he forgets to take the medication at bedtime rather than to have staff oversee the taking of the medication earlier in the evening.

If Fernando forgets to take his pills and suffers adverse medical consequences as a result, who (if anyone) should be held legally responsible for adverse outcomes? Why?

CONTINUING CARE RETIRE-MENT COMMUNITIES OR LIFE CARE COMMUNITIES

One attempt to address the long-term care needs of an aging population has been the development of continuing care retirement communities (CCRCs). The conventional CCRC is a physical plant (whose parts may run the gamut from high-rise apartments to garden apartments to cottages to nursing facilities) that provides shelter and certain supportive, personal, and health services for as long as one remains in the CCRC in return for a sizable entry fee plus monthly fees. The comprehensiveness of the bundle of services included in the prepaid package varies among CCRCs; the most comprehensive plans, which include long-term nursing care for no additional fees, are often termed life care communities.

State regulation of CCRCs generally deals with three areas: consumer protection, the CCRC's financial stability, and quality of care provided by particular licensed units (e.g., nursing facility care). CCRCs may seek voluntary accreditation from CARF/Continuing Care Accreditation Commission.

DISCUSSION QUESTIONS

1. Why does the CCRC concept appeal to many older persons?
2. Besides the issue of affordability, what are some of the other potential concerns about which older people should be counseled before committing to enter a CCRC?
3. In helping a consumer to review a CCRC admission contract before signing it, on which specific issues should one focus? What items would be included on your review checklist, regarding (among other things) the services to be provided and financial responsibility for receiving those services?
4. What is the state's interest in regulating a CCRC's financial stability? When a consumer enters into a CCRC, what exactly is that consumer actually "buying"?

HOSPICE

For a growing number and variety of terminally ill patients, care is being provided through hospices. Hospice care focuses on providing palliative and supportive services to the patient and family rather than aggressive medical intervention at the end of life. Hospice emphasis is placed on symptom control and preparation and support before and after death, with full-scope health services being provided by an organized interdisciplinary team on a full-time basis regardless of the patient's physical location.

The hospice movement entails several legal implications. First, individual health care professionals who provide hospice care are licensed directly by the state regardless of the specific setting in which they are working. In addition, hospice organizations themselves encounter many of the same types of legal issues that concern both institutional and agency health care providers. For instance, the states each require that hospices be licensed.

Hospices that wish (and almost all do) to participate in the Medicare program must meet federal requirements set out at 42 C.F.R. Part 418. On June 5, 2008, DHHS published extensive new Medicare Conditions of Participation for hospices, representing the first major regulatory overhaul in this arena since 1983. *See* 73 Fed. Reg. 32088-01 (June 5, 2008). CMS has published the *Medicare Hospice Manual,* CMS Pub. No. 21, *available at* www.cms.hhs.gov/manuals/pbm/itemdetail.asp. Survey protocols and interpretive guidelines are available at www.cms.hhs.gov/guidanceforlawsandregulations/07_hospice.asp.

In addition to the formal legal requirements that a hospice must satisfy, it may apply for voluntary accreditation by the Joint Commission on Accreditation of Healthcare Organizations (JCAHO) under its hospice accreditation program. The American Board of Hospice and Palliative Medicine operates a certification program in hospice and palliative medicine for physicians (*see* www.abhpm.org). The National Hospice and Palliative Care Organization (www.nho.org) has promulgated voluntary standards for hospice programs, and the Hospice Association of America has developed and disseminated a Code of Ethics and a Hospice Patient's Bill of Rights for its members (*see* www.nahc.org/haa/billofrights.html).

DISCUSSION QUESTIONS

1. After reading the Hospice Patient's Bill of Rights developed by the Hospice Association of America, are there any items you would remove from or add to this document?

2. Should any private organization be given deemed status for Medicare purposes regarding hospice? Why or why not? Absent deemed status, what is the incentive for any hospice to comply with voluntary standards?

ADULT DAY CARE

Adult day care refers to a variety of services and levels of care that are provided to older and disabled persons in a congregate setting for less than 24 hours per day. Licensure of adult daycare providers is a matter of state option, e.g., Ohio Rev. Code § 3722.16. State laws vary regarding the specific services that a program may provide and the manner in which those services may be provided. Adult daycare programs may seek voluntary accreditation from CARF.

One especially controversial area is the administration of medication. Ohio Rev. Code § 3722.011 provides the following:

> *All medication taken by residents of an adult care facility shall be self-administered, except that medication may be administered to a resident by a HHA, hospice care program, nursing home staff, mental health agency, or board of alcohol, drug addiction, and mental health services ... . Members of the staff of an adult care facility shall not administer medication to residents. No person shall be admitted to or retained by an adult care facility unless the person is capable of taking the person's own medication and biologicals, as determined in writing by the person's personal physician, except that a person may be admitted to or retained by such a facility if the person's medication is administered by a HHA, hospice care program, nursing home staff, mental health agency, or board of alcohol, drug addiction, and mental health services ... . Members of the staff of an adult care facility may do any of the following: (A) Remind a resident when to take medication and watch to ensure that the resident follows the directions on the container; (B) Assist a resident in the self-administration of medication by taking the medication from the locked area where it is stored,...and handing it to the resident. If the resident is physically unable to open the container, a staff member may open the container for the resident. (C) Assist a physically impaired but mentally alert resident, such as a resident with arthritis, cerebral palsy, or Parkinson's disease, in removing oral or topical medication from containers and in consuming or applying the medication, upon request by or with the*

consent of the resident. If a resident is physically unable to place a dose of medicine to the resident's mouth without spilling it, a staff member may place the dose in a container and place the container to the mouth of the resident.

NURSING HOMES

Background on the Legal Environment

As part of the Omnibus Budget Reconciliation Act (OBRA) of 1987, Public Law No. 100-203, Congress enacted the Nursing Home Quality Reform Act (codified at 42 U.S.C. §§ 1395i-3(a)–(h) and 1396r(a)–(h)). This Act contains many of the recommendations made in a 1986 Institute of Medicine report, *Improving the Quality of Care in Nursing Homes,* that Congress had directed the DHHS to commission. OBRA 87 amended the Social Security Act, Titles XVIII (Medicare) and XIX (Medicaid), to require substantial upgrading in nursing-home quality and enforcement.

Under the Nursing Home Quality Reform Act, each nursing facility is required to "care for its residents in such a manner and in such an

DISCUSSION QUESTIONS

1. Are the sorts of legal limitations on medication administration illustrated by the Ohio statute quoted above necessary and sensible, or do they just make the job of the adult daycare program more difficult without really protecting the client? Do such legal restrictions unduly exclude from adult day care some older persons who might benefit from that service?
2. On what aspects of adult day care should regulators and private accrediting bodies place the most emphasis?
3. What are the incentives and disincentives for adult day-care programs to seek CARF accreditation?

environment as will promote maintenance or enhancement of the quality of life of each resident" and to "provide services and activities to attain or maintain, for each resident, the highest practicable physical, mental and psychological well-being." For each admitted resident, a facility must collect information according to a defined minimum data set, using a resident assessment instrument, about an individual's physical, mental, and emotional condition. Using this information, facilities must develop and implement an individualized plan of care for each resident.

To implement this legislation, DHHS published a series of regulations that has been codified at 42 C.F.R. Part 483. Nursing homes must comply with very specific mandates set forth in these Requirements for Participation. These federal requirements for which nursing homes are surveyed concern (1) resident rights; (2) admission, transfer, and discharge rights; (3) resident behavior and facility practices; (4) quality of life; (5) resident assessment; (6) quality of care; (7) nursing services; (8) dietary services; (9) physician services; (10) rehabilitation services; (11) dental services; (12) pharmacy services; (13) infection control; (14) physical environment; (15) administration; (16) laboratory; and (17) other. There are more than 185 individual survey items within those 17 categories.

The federal government contracts with the states to assess, through its survey agencies (usually the state health department), whether nursing homes meet those standards through annual surveys and complaint investigations. The annual standard survey, which must be conducted on average every 12 months and no less than once every 15 months at each facility, entails teams of state surveyors arriving without prior notice and spending several days in a facility. Their purpose is to determine whether care and services meet the assessed needs of residents and whether a facility is in compliance with other regulatory requirements. Through its State Operations Manual (containing interpretive guidelines and survey protocols), CMS establishes specific protocols, or investigative procedures, for state surveyors to use in conducting the surveys. In contrast, complaint investigations, also conducted by state surveyors but following the individual state's procedures (within certain federal guidelines and time frames), usually target a single alleged problem in response to a complaint filed against a facility by a resident, a resident's family or friends, or nursing-home employees. Quality-of-care problems identified during either standard surveys or complaint investigations are classified into 1 of 12 categories according to their scope (i.e., the number of residents potentially or actually affected) and their severity (i.e., extent of possible harm).

Addressing documented deficiencies is a shared federal–state responsibility. CMS is responsible for enforcement actions involving nursing homes with Medicare certification. The scope and severity of a deficiency determines the applicable enforcement action and whether it is optional or mandatory. Enforcement sanctions can involve, among other options, compelling corrective action plans, levying civil monetary fines, denying a facility new Medicare and Medicaid payments, mandating directed staff training on particular aspects of care, imposing a receivership arrangement to manage a facility, forcing the transfer of residents out of an offending facility, and, ultimately, decertifying a facility from (in other words, kicking it out of) participation in the Medicare and Medicaid programs altogether. Sanctions may be applied retroactively for the period since the last standard survey. CMS ordinarily accepts a state's recommendation for sanctions or other corrective actions but has the authority to modify those recommendations.

DISCUSSION QUESTIONS

1. Are American nursing homes regulated too much? Are they regulated too little? Are they regulated effectively?
2. What types of deficiencies would you suspect are most commonly found during nursing home inspections? *See* the Office of Inspector General's Memorandum Report, "Trends in Nursing Home Deficiencies and Complaints," *available at* http://oig.hhs.gov/oei/reports/oei-02-08-00140.pdf.
3. Does having available a wide range of possible sanctions for nursing home noncompliance give the states needed flexibility or does it allow states to avoid punishing errant facilities stringently enough?

Many state nursing home licensure laws impose detailed minimum staffing levels for registered nurses, licensed practical nurses, and nursing assistants. Such laws represent a structural approach—as opposed to an approach focusing more on process or outcomes—to health care quality regulation.

DISCUSSION QUESTIONS

1. Is it appropriate for a state legislature or administrative agency to delineate precise minimum staffing levels for nursing facilities?
2. If the states require certain minimum staffing levels, should those states be required to ensure adequate funding for nursing facilities to meet those levels?
3. Should there be any enforcement leeway when a nursing facility falls below state imposed minimum staffing levels despite diligent good faith efforts to comply?

A subject receiving particular attention in the federal regulations is that of involuntary transfer or discharge of a resident from or within a nursing facility. Federal regulations limit permissible grounds for transfer or discharge to the following situations:

- The resident agrees to the transfer or discharge
- Medical necessity
- Failure of the resident to pay for services provided or to cooperate in obtaining payment from a third party such as Medicaid
- The "resident's welfare or that of other patients"

The resident must be given advance notice of any proposed transfer or discharge, except in emergency situations.

The "medical necessity" exception to the general legal prohibition against forced relocations would include, for example, situations in which the resident requires acute care that can be provided properly only in a

DISCUSSION QUESTIONS

1. Why has the government imposed strict limitations on forced relocations from or within a nursing home? Do you believe that residents can really suffer from "transfer trauma"? *See O'Bannon v. Town Court,* 447 U.S. 773 (1980). How can nursing facilities minimize any effects of transfer trauma?
2. What are other situations that would justify use of the "medical necessity" exception?
3. Doesn't forced relocation of a resident who depends on government financing for care, based on a utilization review finding and without any opportunity to challenge that finding in court, violate that resident's right to Due Process under the Fourteenth Amendment of the U.S. Constitution? *See Blum v. Yaretsky,* 457 U.S. 991 (1982).

hospital environment. It also would encompass situations in which the government mandated utilization review process determines that, for a resident whose care is being financed by Medicare, Medicaid, or another third party, nursing facility level care is no longer medically necessary or appropriate.

Since congressional enactment of the Medicare and Medicaid health care financing programs in 1965 and the subsequent burgeoning of the modern American nursing home industry, there has been a keen interest in legal issues pertaining to nursing facilities as businesses. This interest has concentrated on, for example, such matters as incorporation, payment for services, program fraud, tax status, and employment-related obligations. Significant attention to legal issues pertaining to resident care and the provider–resident relationship, and specifically the quality of resident life, has developed only more recently.

The federal government began imposing requirements, including some sections on resident care (originally called Conditions of Participation), on Medicare- and Medicaid-certified nursing facilities in 1974. However, the so-called medical malpractice crises of the 1970s, 1980s, and 1990s were for the most part not very relevant to geriatrics generally and to institutional and home and community-based long-term care particularly. Liability insurance premiums for long-term care providers were relatively negligible, and policies were readily available for purchase (although underwriters sometimes had trouble setting premiums because there was so little litigation experience on which to base their rates). By contrast, the contemporary legal environment surrounding long-term care in the United States, especially nursing facilities, is markedly different.

In looking at the radically changed legal climate of nursing facility operation, there are two diametrically opposed perspectives on the question, "What went wrong?" According to the plaintiffs' personal injury bar and some of the other officially authorized and self-appointed advocates for nursing facility residents, the answer is "nothing." They view the recent increase in personal injury litigation against nursing facilities and their staffs as a much needed and perfectly legitimate correction for the civil justice system's years of neglect of substandard nursing home care. By contrast, nursing home providers and their defenders believe much has gone wrong today, with severe negative consequences for the availability, quality, and affordability of needed and desired services.

There are several potential explanations for the development of a legal climate that the nursing facility industry perceives to be onerous and counterproductive. One important factor is the changing nature of nursing facility consumers: Today's nursing facility residents, on the whole, are much more vulnerable, dependent, frail, and aged than was the earlier nursing facility population. Society generally has become increasingly consumer-oriented and rights-driven in virtually all aspects of life, which frequently translates into more litigation and other forms of uninvited external oversight and involvement. Clearly, nursing facilities are affected by this phenomenon.

The governmental interest has expanded as the public pays a larger and larger portion of the nursing home bill, through the Medicaid and Medicare tax-financed programs. Negative popular press generated by the acute health care system, such as news stories about medical errors or inappropriate breaches of confidentiality, exert a spillover effect to the long-term care sector. Moreover, the print and broadcast media seemingly have launched a continuous pitched battle against the nursing home industry specifically, focusing on gory allegations of abuse and neglect, and public office holders have figured out how to earn electoral goodwill by appearing to "get tough" with providers. The overwhelming involvement of for-profit corporations, particularly large chains, in the provision of nursing home care makes the American long-term care industry an even more inviting target for official condemnation, although the not-for-profit sector certainly is not immune from the negative effects of an intrusive legal climate. Finally, consumer advocacy organizations and the plaintiffs' personal injury bar have become increasingly aggressive, creative, and collaborative in targeting the industry that, ironically, takes care of their clients when no one else can or will.

Long-term care providers are chronically anxious and apprehensive because they feel engulfed by hostile forces. In many respects the current hodgepodge of legal oversight and involvement in the nursing home context clearly illustrates American society's present ambiguity and inconsistency about precisely what role(s) we expect nursing facilities to fill. Criticism and questioning of the continued value of a regulatory regime predicated on a police model ("catch the bad guys and punish them") of quality assurance (let alone quality improvement) has grown vociferous. Both the undeniably high costs and the arguably dubious benefits of such a regime have come under close scrutiny. As noted previously, much of this recent criticism and questioning has specifically focused on the adverse, indeed antitherapeutic, impact of an unduly adversarial regulatory environment (including medical malpractice litigation) on the quality of, and access to, decent nursing home services for vulnerable persons with no realistically viable long-term care options.

The Older Americans Act mandates, at 42 U.S.C. § 3027(a)(12)(A)(i), each state to operate a long-term care ombudsman program that provides an individual who will, on a full-time basis, investigate and resolve complaints by or on behalf of older individuals who are residents of long-term care facilities relating to action, inaction, or decisions of providers or their representatives of long-term care services, of public agencies, or of social service agencies, which may adversely affect the health, safety, welfare, or rights of such residents. The term "long-term care facilities" includes both nursing homes and nonmedical facilities such as assisted living and board and care settings.

The state long-term care ombudsman ordinarily oversees and provides technical support to local ombudsmen offices throughout the state. Most of the hands-on complaint investigations are conducted by volunteers recruited and supervised by the local offices. Under the Older Americans Act, the state is required to provide the ombudsmen's offices with access to facilities' and residents' records, which the ombudsman (and its employees and volunteers) are obligated to treat as confidential.

Different ombudsman programs have different personalities and orientations to their assigned advocacy role, ranging from very adversarial toward facilities to a much more consultative and conciliatory approach to cooperative problem solving, with many points in between. *See* Institute of Medicine, *Real People, Real Problems: An Evaluation of the Long-Term Care Ombudsman Programs of the Older Americans Act,* National Academies Press, Washington, DC (1995).

DISCUSSION QUESTIONS

Which orientation (adversarial versus consultative, or some variation between those extremes) is likely to make a local ombudsman program most effective in advocating for the health, safety, welfare, and rights of long-term care facility clients? Why? Should facilities envision their local ombudsman program as a feared adversary or as a partner?

For a variety of reasons, including the enactment of legislation in several states that literally invited lawyers to file personal injury claims against nursing homes, the increased availability of a cadre of willing expert witnesses, and a growing mood of financial generosity on the part of juries, the number of civil malpractice actions filed against nursing homes and staff has escalated tremendously. The plaintiffs' personal injury bar has discovered this potentially lucrative arena as a natural extension of the traditional elder law practice.

DISCUSSION QUESTIONS

1. Whose perspective on the changing legal environment for nursing homes is correct: the view of the plaintiff's personal injury bar that the increase in the number of lawsuits being brought against nursing homes is just a legitimate correction (i.e., making up for lost time) for the civil system being too lax with nursing homes in the past, or the view of nursing home providers that the present legal climate is unreasonably onerous and counterproductive?

2. Is the present legal climate for nursing homes ultimately therapeutic or antitherapeutic for residents and their families? What are the benefits and costs, and to whom, of the current legal overlay? Is the current legal state of affairs successful?

3. Should nursing homes be permitted to require entering residents or their families to sign an agreement to submit to binding arbitration of any disagreements with the facility, instead of retaining the right to bring a lawsuit in court? Under what circumstances, if any, should the courts enforce binding arbitration clauses? Nonbinding arbitration clauses? What are the advantages and disadvantages of binding arbitration of provider–client disputes in the nursing home context for the resident, the facility, and the public? *See* Nathan Koppel, *Nursing Homes, in Bid to Cut Costs, Prod Patients to Forgo Lawsuits,* Wall St. J. Apr. 11, 2008, at A1; www .arbitrator.com/arbstatutes.htm; *Hill v. NHC Healthcare/ Nashville, LLC,* No. M2005-01818-COA-R3-CV (Tenn. Ct. Appeals, Apr. 30, 2008), *available at* www.tsc.state .tn.us/opinions/tca/pdf/082/hillbopncorr.pdf (invalidating a mandatory, binding arbitration provision in a nursing home admission contract as unconscionable).

Exercises

Case 1

Mrs. R is a 70-year-old widow with one moderately attentive son who lives in a different city. She is a nursing home resident with mild dementia and many physical problems who was treated in a hospital for pneumonia and then readmitted to the nursing home. Two days after her return to the nursing home, Mrs. R began to deteriorate. She developed a slight fever as a remnant of her previous infection and seemed lethargic. The team discussed this case at its weekly meeting, which was attended by the licensed practical nurse and social worker involved in Mrs. R's care; the registered nurse was attending a continuing education program outside the building that day. One of the things discussed was Mrs. R's expression to several staff members that she did not want any "heroic efforts" to be used to keep her alive. Mrs. R died that night in her sleep.

Mrs. R's son informed the state survey and certification office about his mother's death. As part of the investigation report, the state surveyor (a retired police officer) noted that the facility had not immediately informed the physician or the son about significant changes in the resident's condition, as required by state statute and the federal regulations. When questioned about the absence of timely notification, a licensed practical nurse told surveyors about Mrs. R's explicit "no heroics" instruction.

Should the facility have notified the physician and the son about Mrs. R's rapid deterioration? What could the physician and/or son have done with that information in light of Mrs. R's expressed wishes about treatment? Is the facility's failure to notify properly just a technical violation of the law, or is it more substantive? Should the violation be excused under these circumstances? How should the staff members have documented this series of events?

Case 2

Mrs. T, an 82-year-old widow with no family and no advance directives, was admitted to a nursing home from a hospital after a bout of malnutrition, dehydration, and anemia. In the hospital, she had deteriorated mentally because of multi-infarct dementia and was unable to meet, and disinterested in meeting, her nutritional needs. Even though her decisional capacity was in doubt when she was admitted to the nursing home, because of cost and hassle factors no efforts had been made to adjudicate her incompetent and have a guardian appointed. The facility medical director was serving as Mrs. T's attending physician.

Mrs. T was a slight, short, frail woman who at admission to the nursing home weighed 95 pounds in a soaking wet bathrobe. She was pleasant but quiet, preferring to keep pretty much to herself. About a month after her admission, it was noted that she had dropped 5 pounds. She told the nurse she ate "some of the food here," but that she did not really like the way the nursing home served meals and usually was not very hungry anyway. The nurse told Mrs. T it was important for her to eat and pointed to another resident with a feeding tube, which elicited from Mrs. T a pained expression. The nurse noted in Mrs. T's chart that she was at danger of malnutrition. The nurse additionally ordered a dietary consult and requested that Mrs. T be offered calorie-rich snacks several times per day.

Not long thereafter, Mrs. T suffered a seizure and was unwilling to eat even though she was able to swallow. A neurological consultation revealed that she had had a minor stroke. A week later the nurse noted "dysphagia, weight loss, drooping mouth, taking 50% of meals by mouth." In consultation with the dietitian, the nurse ordered high-caloric shakes thinned with liquid and noted that Mrs. T would require coaxing from the staff to drink the shakes and eat the snacks to be offered to her all day. A month later there was further weight loss of a few pounds, and Mrs. T was still consuming only very small portions and only very slowly, requiring a lot of staff time and attention. The physician concluded that Mrs. T would require insertion of a feeding tube to ensure she received adequate nutrition and so notified the facility administrator. The administrator's chief concern was that Mrs. T's weight loss would be a "red flag" receiving special attention from the state surveyors at the next facility survey and that the facility might be cited by the regulators for neglecting a resident's nutritional status.

In light of this legitimate regulatory concern, what should be done? Should a feeding tube be inserted? Could a conscious choice not to insert a feeding tube, when the resident is steadily losing precious weight, be justified to the state surveyors? Is there a clash here between legal and ethical principles, on one side, and the facility's risk management incentives, on the other? If so, what is the best compromise?

Regulation and Resident Safety

For many individuals who enter a nursing home, the admission decision is made—either formally or *de facto*—by relatives when the person's care needs can no longer be met in a private home or a communal living setting. For relatives making the difficult decision to admit a loved one to a nursing home, often the primary consideration is their physical safety. Although this placement choice is almost always accompanied by regret and guilt, family members resigning themselves to the necessity of nursing home admission are able to tell themselves, "At least Mom will be safe there." Sometimes, however, family members are dreadfully wrong in making the assumption that the nursing home is a safe environment for its residents.

This discussion begins by outlining some of the safety concerns that persist in at least a portion of modern American nursing homes and the most serious practical impediments to alleviating those safety concerns more effectively. This is followed by an examination of how resident safety comprises only one part of the larger quality improvement picture in the nursing home context. Although the threat of negative legal repercussions may be necessary to address safety issues, a fuller concern about improving the quality of care and quality of life for nursing home residents also requires the development and implementation of a combination of positive incentives.

The safety of nursing home residents may be jeopardized by a variety of systemic errors or shortcomings occurring within a facility. Unsafe situations in this setting include adverse drug events, injurious resident falls, pressure ulcers, problems with tube feeding, faulty communications or other breakdowns when a resident is transferred to or from the hospital, and equipment breakdowns or mix-ups. Beyond these safety concerns, which are associated with institutional omissions or inadvertent mistakes, intentional abuse of residents by staff in some facilities has also been documented.

One important component of a successful strategy to address these safety problems is the encouragement of nursing home personnel to be more forthcoming in reporting and disclosing errors. However, many of the same factors that act as obstacles to the implementation of aggressive error reduction programs in hospitals and outpatient contexts apply with full, or even arguably greater, force in the case of nursing homes. Specifically, the pervasively adversarial—bordering on poisonous—legal, economic, political, and media environment surrounding the U.S. nursing home industry creates a set of powerful negative incentives that discourage nursing home personnel from openly admitting (as a prelude to attempting to rectify) resident safety problems in their own facility. Personnel have a widespread and quite reasonable apprehension that disclosing instances of unsafe resident care may well expose the facility, and staff members individually, to substantial regulatory sanctions, civil liability (and a resulting increase in the premium price of liability insurance coverage), and criminal prosecution. Further, there is a realistic anxiety that openly addressing safety problems is likely to subject a nursing home to negative publicity and hence damage the facility's ability to attract residents in an increasingly competitive marketplace.

Despite these barriers, families who admit their relatives to nursing homes understandably expect those facilities to do a better job of identifying and proactively addressing systemic problems that jeopardize the safety of residents. However, focusing on resident safety—no matter how important an aspect of care it is—cannot by itself ensure that nursing home residents will enjoy the high-quality experience that they deserve.

Public regulators and the private marketplace expect nursing homes—as long-term care providers in which most residents live until they die—to provide residents with a quality of care and quality of life that is not only medically and physically safe but also like home. In cultivating an environment that satisfies these legitimate quality expectations, maintaining resident safety is only a necessary, but far from sufficient, first step. To concentrate too exclusively on maintaining medical safety would represent an impoverished, minimalist approach, satisfied simply by avoiding harm, that neglects the nursing home's responsibility to maximize the well-being of its residents more holistically to the greatest extent feasible.

To illustrate the breadth of a nursing home's affirmative responsibilities, under the heading "Quality of Life" the Medicare/Medicaid certification regulations impose detailed requirements regarding, among other things, resident dignity, self-determination and participation, participation in resident and family groups, participation in the outside community, accommodation of individual needs and preferences, activities, private space, comfort, and comprehensive individual assessments and care plans. In addition, the regulations contain an extensive section devoted entirely to respect for, and promotion of, resident rights.

In a 1996 survey of nursing home administrators, directors of nursing, regulators, ombudsmen, and resident advocates, the most important quality items identified went far beyond resident safety. Under quality of care, respondents rated highest the general quality of care, maintenance of ADLs, and appropriate treatment of impairment in ADLs. The top three quality of life items were dignity, self-determination and participation, and accommodation of resident needs. The most important residents' rights items were to be able to exercise general rights, to be informed of one's condition, and to be free of reprisal when making complaints. A more recent ranking of nursing home quality indicators done by an expert panel similarly gave highest priority to items generally not associated with a focus on the absence of medical and nursing errors.

Regulatory and private expectations about a nursing home's affirmative obligations to foster quality of care and quality of life are not only not coextensive with a facility's more constrained duty to protect resident safety but in some circumstances may actually conflict with safety considerations. Providers overwhelmingly believe that paternalistic actions on their part (such as initiating guardianship proceedings that otherwise might have been delayed or avoided; see Chapter 4) are compelled by the providers' need to ensure resident safety as a matter of prudent legal risk management, even at the expense of other goals. Put differently, many nursing homes act—correctly or not—as though respecting the decisional rights of residents, especially decisions to take risks, will expose those residents to harm and therefore expose the provider to malpractice claims brought by family members or regulatory citations and sanctions at the hands of state surveyors or federal prosecutors if the risks should materialize. Providers are afraid to be flexible in deviating from the "rules," even at the request of the resident or family. When goals collide, protecting safety normally overrides the autonomy of the resident.

Despite the inconclusive evidence about its effectiveness, presumably a continued regulatory presence that threatens adverse consequences serves a useful function in strengthening the safety related efforts of nursing homes, to the benefit of at least the safety interests of residents. But if the pursuit of quality of care and quality of life is to be taken seriously, a regime of negative command and control regulation supplemented by private malpractice litigation will be inadequate to the task. Positive incentives to supplement the regulatory "stick" and promote quality beyond just resident safety are essential.

Such positive incentives may take a variety of forms. Modifying the methodology through which Medicaid and Medicare payments to nursing homes are computed to reward facilities for performance in providing a high quality of care and of life for their residents, based in large part on realistic outcome measures, would be one very valuable "carrot" to encourage desired provider behavior. Facilitating the collection and dissemination of information to the public regarding the quality of care and quality of life found in specific nursing homes can empower potential residents and their families to wield meaningful clout in an increasingly competitive environment for institutional long-term care consumers. Informed consumer choice, in turn, will compel nursing homes continuously to improve the quality of care and of life that they provide to attract residents to fill beds and keep the facility financially viable.

Nursing home personnel are well aware that long-term care "shoppers" have ready access to a substantial amount of information about nursing homes competing for their business. For instance, the On-Line Survey and Certification Assessment Reporting system is a computerized national database for maintaining and retrieving survey and certification data about nursing homes based on periodic state and federal Medicare and Medicaid certification inspections. "Nursing Home Compare" is another online federal government website that publicly disseminates information about conditions in individual nursing homes based on the Nursing Home Quality Initiative program of the CMS. Many states also place survey data about their own nursing homes on the Internet for the public and have it available in print form as well for consumers to use in comparing facilities. The need to make its publicly available profile as appealing as possible and more appealing than that of its competitors plays on the enlightened self-interest of a nursing home. As a result of this self-interest, the nursing home industry has introduced its own quality improvement initiatives (see Table 5.3).

A specific way in which the nursing home industry could improve quality of care and quality of life for residents is to enhance the communication network between the resident, family, and staff. Because the issue of rights and risks concerns all residents and their families, there is a need to develop philosophies of care in consultation with all affected stakeholders. Moreover, each facility's record-keeping system should reflect the usual

Table 5.3 Nursing Home Quality Improvement Initiatives

CMS, Nursing Home Quality Initiative, www.cms.hhs.gov/
NursingHomeQualityInits
American Association of Homes and Services for the Aging (AAHSA), Quality
First: A Covenant to Achieve Healthy, Affordable, and Ethical Long Term Care
Initiative, www.aahsa.org/qualityfirst
Wellspring Initiative Solutions, www.wellspringis.org
Eden Alternative, www.edenalt.org
Pioneer Movement, www.pioneernetwork.net

tripartite (resident, family, and nursing home staff) nature of decision making.

Voluntary self-initiated efforts aimed at changing the entire nursing home environment from the inside should be encouraged and supported as a supplement to regulatory strategies that concentrate on avoiding breaches of safety for residents. Indeed, "smart" regulations will work synergistically with industry efforts to facilitate a robust marketplace rather than replace it. Although the relationship between the amount of money spent by a nursing home and the quality of care and quality of life rendered to its residents is not direct, insufficient resources certainly hamper the ability of facilities to produce the desired results. If society truly aspires to an improved quality of care and quality of life for nursing home residents rather than resigning itself to accepting the more limited goal of just keeping residents safe, more financial support must be forthcoming.

Being kept physically safe, including safe from systemic errors that occur within the nursing home, is one important component of residents' lives. However, safety does not represent the entire expectations and preferences of residents concerning the quality of care and quality of life they hope to enjoy. To meet these expanded expectations and preferences will be a formidable task, calling for expansive thinking and ingenuity beyond simple compliance with the safety oriented boundaries established by command and control regulations.

Despite areas of apparent commonality, most of the lessons derived from patient safety initiatives in the hospital context cannot as a general matter be transposed simply and easily to the protection of persons in long-term care generally or to nursing facility residents specifically. The acute and long-term care arenas are distinct in significant enough respects to create different, special resident safety challenges in long-term care that call for original responses. The most salient of these distinctions are shown in Table 5.4.

First, most acute care rendered in hospitals is focused narrowly, indeed virtually exclusively, on the provision of medical interventions (chiefly the performance of technical procedures and the administration of medications) designed to manage or ameliorate discrete, immediate medical threats to patients as quickly and definitively as possible. The *raison d'être* for acute care is to make the patient better, or at least to control the immediate medical crisis sufficiently so the patient can be discharged from the hospital. By contrast, nursing homes are expected to

Table 5.4 Distinctions Between Hospitals and Nursing Homes Relevant to Resident Safety

1. *Hospitals* provide acute medical care. *Nursing homes* provide a broad constellation of health and social services.
2. *Nursing home* residents are generally older, sicker, poorer, more frail and disabled (physically and mentally) than *hospital* patients.
3. The organizational culture of *hospitals* focuses on meeting the medical needs of patients:

   · Institutional environment
   · Professional domination

   The organizational culture of *nursing homes* focuses on promoting the rights of residents:

   · Home-like social environment
   · Greater family involvement

4. *Hospitals* are primarily staffed with nurses and physicians. *Nursing homes* rely less on nurses and much less on physicians and more on certified nurse assistants
5. In *hospitals,* safety problems mainly concern

   · Botched medical procedures
   · Medication errors
   · Infections

   In *nursing homes,* safety problems mainly concern

   · Medication errors
   · Pressure ulcers
   · Resident falls
   · Wandering
   · Neglect and abuse

6. *Nursing homes* are even more extensively regulated by government agencies than are *hospitals.*

Reprinted with permission from Marshall B. Kapp, *Making Patient Safety and a "Homelike" Environment Compatible: A Challenge for Long Term Care Regulations,* 12 Widener L. Rev. 227–247 (2005).

make available to their resident population a much broader constellation of services. Besides acute medical treatment for immediate physical ailments, particular residents might also require a variety of ongoing medical, nursing, social, psychological, rehabilitative, supportive, and spiritual services not commonly falling within the province of acute care.

Engaging in these various kinds of long-term care activities may present risks to resident safety different from the acute care medical error risks that hospitals have begun to learn how to handle effectively.

Second, differences in the prevailing demographic, functional, health, and social characteristics of the modern American nursing facility resident population compared with the prevailing characteristics of typical hospitalized patients arguably create relevant distinctions between the two settings in terms of types and degree of risk exposure and effective strategies both to avoid the materialization of those risks in the first place and to remedy them when they occur. These population differences are manifold.

One major demographic characteristic of the nursing facility population is old age. Over 90% of nursing facility residents are over age 65 and almost half are over 85; the average age is more than 80. At age 95 an individual has about an equal chance of being cared for in a nursing facility or in the community. The geriatric population among hospital patients certainly is substantial, but not to the same extent present in nursing facilities. It can be concluded that institutional homes for the elderly constitute age-differentiated settings by the very way in which they are defined and organized.

Moreover, the percentage of nursing home residents with chronic, serious physical disabilities creating permanent dependence in terms of needing assistance with ADLs continues to escalate. Among nursing facility-dwelling Medicare recipients over age 65, in 2002 almost 65% had functional limitations requiring assistance with three or more ADLs. Although nursing home residents are not by definition passive, they are remarkably dependent. This development is attributable not only to the general aging of the population, but also to the constellation of private and public sector initiatives (fueled in large part by legal requirements) (*see Olmstead v. L.C. ex rel. Zimring,* 527 U.S. 581 [1999], holding that Title II of the Americans With Disabilities Act requires governmental units to provide publicly financed services to disabled persons in the most integrated, therefore the least institutional, appropriate environment) that have been markedly effective in helping even very frail and disabled older individuals to forestall nursing facility admission until an overwhelming degree of chronic disability has been reached. Because entry into a nursing facility rarely happens today unless and until reasonable, less drastic alternatives have been attempted and exhausted for an individual, the illness and disability acuity level among nursing facility residents is substantially higher, more complex, and more resistant to improvement than was previously the situation in long-term care settings. Increasingly, when individuals finally are admitted to nursing facilities, often it is with the expectation and plan that they will die there. This all carries potentially serious connotations for residents' vulnerabilities to risks of avoidable harm.

Special safety concerns also may be implicated by the very significant prevalence of serious, chronic mental disabilities among nursing facility residents. In many respects, "nursing homes have become the mental hospitals of our era." Dementia is the most common negative health condition among nursing facility residents, and most dementia-related deaths in the United States occur in nursing facilities. The prevalence of mental disability, coupled with the unfortunate reality that proper treatment for mental illness frequently is lacking in nursing facilities, constrains the ability of most nursing facility residents to oversee their own care and play much of a meaningful part in watching out for their own safety. By contrast, hospitalized and ambulatory patients have been advised to advocate for themselves in helping to prevent treatment errors. Additionally, the prevalence of serious cognitive impairment among nursing facility residents largely moots the potential, which has been discussed extensively in the hospital context, that communicating medical errors to patients can act as a useful component of a safety improvement strategy.

Much more so than their hospital counterparts, nursing facility residents are likely to be financially poor and therefore dependent on public benefit programs, with the added vulnerabilities that such a condition entails. Most people tend not to leave their own homes or assisted living facilities to enter nursing facilities until they have run out of money. They only reluctantly leave at that point because, in nursing facilities, "the impoverished, including middle-class men and women who have outlived their savings, are covered by Medicaid as they are not (except for a small percentage) in assisted living." (Jane Gross, "Under One Roof, Aging Together Yet Alone," N.Y. Times, Jan. 30, 2005, at 1, 27.) The overwhelming majority of nursing home beds are certified to participate in the Medicaid program.

Third, in many respects crucial to the issue of care recipient safety, the organizational culture of nursing homes diverges significantly from that permeating acute care generally and hospitals particularly. For starters, although both acute and nursing facility providers are concerned about responding to both the care needs and the legal and ethical rights of their consumers, they generally are driven by different priorities. In acute care, a focus on the *needs* of the *patient* ordinarily clearly predominates, whereas the nursing facility culture for the most part revolves around the *rights* of *residents*. This means that the fundamental goals of nursing facility care frequently may be multiple and internally inconsistent. As noted by one set of authors, "An overriding issue in quality assurance for long-term care is how to balance pursuit of safety versus respect for individual freedoms, and what to do with the bad results."

In addition to pursuing health and safety for its residents (certainly the chief objective of hospitals and ambulatory care providers for their patients), nursing homes are concerned about maximizing respect for, and supporting the effectuation of, their residents' autonomous decision-making (including risk-taking) prerogatives. The impetus for moving conceptualization of the nursing facility's mission in this direction, and the potential philosophical and practical tensions between the goals of resident safety on one hand and autonomy on the other, is reflected in contemporary criticisms of nursing facilities that still supposedly foster dependency by keeping residents well cared for, safe, and virtually powerless. At best, the push for resident autonomy, both externally and internally generated, may act as a powerful source of distraction from, if not an outright enemy of, the nursing facility's attempt to ensure resident safety. To afford residents more control over their own lives inevitably entails the possibility that they may make risky, even foolish, choices. It should not be surprising, therefore, that nursing facility providers often suffer from cognitive dissonance in trying to figure out how to behave.

Another mission-related cultural distinction pertains to the "home-like" or social environment that nursing facilities are expected to create and maintain, as compared with the more narrowly constrained institutional, medically driven character of hospitals and ambulatory care centers. Most nursing facility residents remain nursing facility residents for a relatively long, indeterminate period of time; hence, the facility should mimic the individual, family, and social expectation of an emotionally warm environment and that of a happy personal home set in a friendly community, even while the facility is being regulated closely by the government as a health care institution.

As the Committee on Improving Quality in Long-Term Care of the Institute of Medicine noted:

> [L]ong-term care is both a health program and a social program. For the health services component, judgments about quality emphasize medical and technical aspects of care, and such judgments are generally based on achieving desired health and functional outcomes and on adherence to correct processes of care. For the social services aspect, judgments about quality place more emphasis on the opinions and satisfaction of consumers (or their surrogate agents).

The problem is the impossibility of maintaining the same level of safety against risks of harm in a home-like nursing facility environment, with the personal freedom of action for residents and families that such an environment encompasses, that ought to be reasonably achievable in an acute care environment. In the acute care setting, the provider retains the power to exercise control over virtually all foreseeable matters (down to limiting what items families can bring into the hospital and the coming and going of patients) that might endanger patients' safety. By contrast, the home-like environment imperative of nursing facilities, which recognizes ideal safety precautions are not always synonymous with residents' ideas about acceptable levels of quality of life, restrains nursing facility providers much more in exercising control over risks.

Essentially by definition, the respective time frames of acute and long-term care are rather distinct. The longer time period during which residents remain within nursing facilities is relevant in terms of opportunities for various risks of harm to develop and materialize. To achieve greater safety in nursing facilities, it is more important to concentrate on the general patterns of behavior a home follows to ensure safety than it is to focus just on discrete problematic incidents as most homes do.

The legal and ethical doctrine of informed consent for specific medical interventions (see Chapter 2) notwithstanding, professional domination is the prevailing modus operandi in acute care settings. In the patient care sphere, the medical staff basically is in charge of pursuing the hospital's fundamental goal of making the patient well and achieving an expeditious discharge. In nursing facilities, by contrast, there usually is a much greater effort made to include the collective voice of the resident population in shaping many of the facility policies that affect the quality of residents' collective and individual lives. For example, residents' councils are common in nursing facilities as formal structures allowing residents to meet and air opinions about various aspects (for example, regarding food served or activities planned) of facility operations. Facilitating opportunities for resident participation enhances resident autonomy but may result in facility situations that carry the seeds of peril to residents' safety.

In the hospital environment, families (defined broadly) often constitute an important part of the organizational culture in the sense of accompanying patients, visiting and running errands for them, advocating for them regarding specific medical treatments, acting as an intermediary between patient and health care providers, emotionally and spiritually supporting patients, overseeing insurance and other financial matters pertaining to the hospital stay, and helping to formulate and ultimately implement discharge plans for posthospital care. In the nursing facility context, families are involved in the same way but often in a much more intense, often burdensome, way and for a longer duration. Caregivers often become the "hidden clients" of nursing homes. Over time, continuing personal relationships often develop between a resident's family members and facility management and staff, other residents and/or their families, ombudsmen, and, sometimes, the agencies that regulate the nursing facility. Many nursing facilities establish family councils to give administration and staff input. Family members may take on particular tasks connected to the care of their loved ones, such as the adult child or spouse who always comes to the facility at mealtime to help feed the resident. Additionally, families ordinarily are closely involved in the initial decision to admit a loved one to the nursing facility and in the process of selecting a particular facility.

Another cultural aspect of family involvement in nursing facilities with implications for the effective pursuit of resident safety is the personal guilt many relatives experience, because they blame themselves for not being able to continue caring for their older loved one in a private home or community setting. Family members thus may believe they have abandoned their loved one to a nursing facility. Relatives' guilt and grief are often manifested as anger directed at nursing home staff. Additionally, other attitudinal barriers can obstruct good communication between relatives and nursing home staff.

The cultural atmosphere of nursing facilities within which resident safety initiatives must be pursued also is influenced heavily by continuing negative public perceptions about, and attitudes toward, nursing facilities generically. For the most part, the nursing facility industry still carries a terrible public reputation, fueled by a constant stampede of adverse publicity about scandalously inadequate care appearing regularly in the popular media. The dominance of proprietary ownership, including a number of for-profit chains with extended corporate structures, also contributes to the industry's negative public image (although not-for-profit facilities usually are held in low regard too). Because of negative public perceptions and attitudes, sincerely motivated safety initiatives often are greeted with skepticism and are not enthusiastically supported. This problem, and the resulting dampening of enthusiasm for bold and needed systemic improvements in nursing facilities, is exacerbated by a generally hostile political climate in which holders and seekers of public office understand the significant political advantage of being portrayed in the media as "tough" on nursing homes.

Fourth, staffing patterns are important to the issue of patient safety, because modern health care delivery is carried out by a complex web of participants. In hospitals, most direct patient care is provided by registered and licensed practical nurses. Nurses are the central building block of nursing facility staffs. However, in nursing facilities, registered nurses and licensed practical nurses frequently function in supervisory, rather than direct care, positions. In nursing facilities, unlike hospitals, the bulk of hands-on resident care depends on certified nurse assistants, who lack degrees and are poorly paid at or near the minimum wage. In addition to the difference in educational qualification levels between hospital and nursing facility direct care staff, nursing facilities, as a group, overwhelmingly experience more extensive staff turnover at all levels than generally would be observed in hospitals.

The difference in staffing mix between hospitals and nursing facilities is understood further by considering the role of physicians in each care setting. The physician's presence in most nursing facilities is considerably less robust than that ordinarily evident in hospitals. According to the

American Geriatrics Society, physicians still do not spend significant amounts of time caring for nursing home residents. Each Medicare- and Medicaid-certified nursing facility must contract with a licensed physician to serve as the facility medical director, with administrative responsibility regarding the quality of medical care provided therein, but the medical director is allowed to (and in all but the largest facilities does) function in this role on a less than full-time basis. Federal regulations mandate each nursing facility admission be approved in writing by a physician and every nursing facility resident remain under a physician's care. Otherwise, physician contact with nursing facility residents usually takes the form of issuing telephone orders and/or sending the resident to the hospital emergency department in response to a nurse's phone call reporting a problem or treating a resident who has been brought to the physician's private office. Moreover, few nursing facilities are affiliated with medical schools; hence medical students and postgraduate medical trainees (residents and fellows) rarely are available to contribute to resident care. The very limited physician involvement as an integral part of a nursing facility's daily life poses obvious problems for conducting effective resident safety improvement projects in nursing facilities.

Fifth, there is the issue of safety concerns in hospitals and nursing homes. In hospitals, iatrogenic and nosocomial dangers ordinarily are connected to botched medical procedures, medication errors, and infections. Hospital safety strategies largely are efforts to respond to those specific dangers. Nursing facilities share hospitals' concern about medication errors. A substantial amount of prescription and over-the-counter drugs are ordered and dispensed every day in the nursing facility setting, presenting abundant opportunities for medication errors to take place. There is a high incidence of serious and often preventable adverse drug events emanating from medication use in nursing facilities. Even worse, published studies actually may, if anything, underestimate the real extent of adverse drug events in nursing facilities. When an adverse drug event occurs in a nursing facility, the risk of harm, or even fatality, to the resident is substantial.

Among the identified causes of medication errors in nursing facilities are the following: faulty communications when a person is transferred from a hospital to the nursing facility, excess dosage, drug interactions, mistaken drug selection, failures in baseline or continuing monitoring, not acting in response to relevant information, contraindicated drug use, confusing abbreviations, sound-alike and look-alike drugs, and sloppy order writing. The JCAHO listed among its 2005 Long Term Care National Patient Safety Goals the following: "improve the safety of using medications" and "accurately and completely reconcile medications across the continuum of care."

In nursing facilities, the most prevalent safety concerns other than medication errors tend to revolve around dangers different than those that predominate in hospitals (although all of these dangers certainly exist in hospitals). The situation necessitates the implementation of more specific nursing facility–oriented safety interventions. An especially prevalent and severe problem in the care of nursing facility residents is the development of pressure ulcers, also known as pressure sores, bedsores, and decubitus ulcers. These are localized areas of skin tissue damage or necrosis that develop because of sustained pressure over a bony protrusion such as the hips, buttocks, elbow, or heel. Major risk factors include immobility, friction, shear, incontinence, and poor nutritional status, all dangers to which nursing facility residents are exposed disproportionately. Potential morbid complications of untreated pressure ulcers are cellulitis, osteomyelitis, and sepsis (infection). Extreme cases can be fatal.

There is professional debate about whether pressure ulcers are totally avoidable for nonambulatory individuals. Some take the negative position, pointing to the 2004 death of actor Christopher Reeves due to a pressure ulcer–caused infection despite impeccable personal nursing attention. Nonetheless, there is a strong consensus among professional experts in the aging arena that severe pressure ulcers should rarely, if ever, materialize in nursing facility residents who have been afforded competent, attentive medical and nursing preventive care. Such care would include regular turning and/or repositioning, skin inspection, ensuring adequate nutritional intake, and the use of pressure-relief surfaces where possible. From this perspective, the occurrence of pressure ulcers in a nursing facility resident indicates the presence of errors or inexcusable shortcomings in delivering quality care. Thus a virtual mantra among plaintiffs' attorneys is, "In cases of preventable pressure sores occurring in nursing homes, neglect should always be considered as a possible cause."

Pressure ulcers are one indicator of safe, quality care measured by nursing facilities as part of the mandatory minimum data set. The minimum data set is required for participation in the Medicare and Medicaid programs. Part of the minimum data set evaluation includes the required resident assessment instrument, which is useful as a comprehensive guide to assess all facets of resident care, including pressure ulcers.

Another significant safety concern in nursing facilities is the prevalence and severity of resident falls. A fall is defined as "unintentionally coming to rest on the ground, floor, or other lower level, but not as a result of syncope or overwhelming external force." Approximately half of all nursing facility residents fall at least annually, with serious (sometimes even fatal) injury occurring in about 10% of residents. Complications may include bone fractures, injury to the soft tissues, increasing functional dependence, and the fear of falling again—which itself can be debilitating. Falls among hospitalized patients also are a persistent problem, but the old age and frailty profile of nursing facility residents makes them especially vulnerable to serious injury when falls occur.

The 2005 Long Term Care National Patient Safety Goals of the JCAHO included a reduction of the risk of resident harm resulting from falls. Specifically, this document directs nursing facilities (1) to assess and periodically reassess each resident's risk of falling, including the potential risk associated with the resident's medication regimen, and take action to address any identified risks, and (2) to implement a fall reduction program, including a transfer protocol, and evaluate the effectiveness of the program.

Despite the fact that much can be done in the realm of effective prevention, some resident falls in nursing facilities may be inevitable. Certainly, enhancing resident freedom of choice and movement carries the possibility of increased risk. Accepting a certain risk of falls is preferable to continuing the practice, commonplace in the industry before congressional enactment of the Nursing Home Reform Act (as part of OBRA) in 1987, of continuously physically and/or chemically restraining large numbers of residents, purportedly to prevent falls. Although there still is work to be done in this arena, significant progress has been achieved since the late 1980s in reducing the routine use of restraints in nursing facilities, with corresponding benefits to residents' sense of autonomy.

Another risk area that may be affected by an enhanced institutional respect for resident autonomy involves the constellation of potential harms that may happen to a cognitively impaired resident who physically wanders away from the nursing facility. Most of the strategies available to nursing facilities to deal effectively and proactively with this common problem entail some degree of intrusion on residents' freedom of movement and consequently conflict with a culture that puts a premium on maximizing the home-like nature of the residents' long-term living environment.

An extremely important risk area affecting nursing facility residents with dismaying frequency, but ordinarily affecting hospital patients only very rarely, concerns patterns of neglect or, in extreme cases, abuse. Neglect and abuse may take a variety of forms and almost always emanate from a pattern of systemic, as opposed to individual, errors and omissions unfolding without correction over a sustained period of time and requiring systemic remedial and preventive strategies different than those usually developed and implemented in hospitals to address their own, different kinds of safety shortcomings.

Finally, there is the matter of different legal environments. Hospitals are subject to extensive legal and quasi-legal (for instance, voluntary accreditation-related) regulation designed to ensure the quality and safety of medical care rendered to patients. Compared with nursing facilities, though, hospital regulation may seem almost minimal. The extent to which nursing facility personnel in the United States today function within a cultural environment constantly threatening them with external, punitive oversight and intervention is a distinguishing feature of institutional long-term care that carries substantial implications for attempts to implement effective resident safety strategies.

Negative media coverage of the nursing facility industry and high malpractice insurance premiums, or difficulty in obtaining malpractice insurance at all, create to some degree the providers' aura of apprehension. Such media coverage includes provocative advertisements to potential plaintiffs by personal injury attorneys, advertisements sent to nursing facility personnel for risk management products portrayed as desperately needed, discouraging messages about colleagues' conflicts with regulators or the courts transmitted through the professional "grapevines" and "rumor mills," and adverse personal experiences in dealing with the regulatory or judicial systems.

The regulatory environment engulfing contemporary nursing facility operations includes, among other components, provider anxieties about Medicaid certification and state licensure surveys, criminal prosecutions initiated by local prosecutors and state attorneys general charging facility ownership and staff with abuse and neglect of residents (and, in the case of dead residents, homicide), criminal prosecutions brought by the U.S. Attorney's Office and the federal DHHS Office of Inspector General (OIG) on Medicare/Medicaid program fraud and abuse theories for billing the government for inadequate care, and criminal prosecutions and/or professional disciplinary actions for overuse or improper use of controlled substances. Government regulators are aided in their enforcement activities by state long-term care ombudsman programs, whose representatives enjoy the legal power to enter a nursing home at any time to investigate complaints or otherwise communicate with residents. Besides being subject to mandatory government standards of behavior, an increasing percentage of nursing facilities are being economically forced by the pressures of a competitive marketplace to participate in private, theoretically voluntary accreditation programs administered by bodies such as the JCAHO.

All of this contributes to an intrusive regulatory climate. This climate fosters an aura of apprehension among nursing facility administrators and staff that intensely discourages active, open, enthusiastic cooperation in identifying and ameliorating safety problems, when the safety short-comings identified and addressed may turn out to be discoverable and admissible in legal proceedings as evidence to support adverse actions taken against safety-seeking facilities and individual staff members. Additionally, nursing facility care providers are legitimately concerned about potential civil malpractice lawsuits being brought against them by, or on behalf of (usually by family members), injured residents. For most of these providers, litigation-related fears mainly revolve around the hassle, emotional trauma, and damage to professional reputation associated with being sued. The ultimate winning or losing disposition of a lawsuit is almost irrelevant, especially in light of the financially insulating effect of liability insurance. Rather, provider anxieties grow out of the media feeding frenzy that invariably accompanies litigation against nursing facilities alleging transgressions in resident care quality and safety. Apprehension that preventive or remedial safety initiatives may be interpreted by the fact-finder in a subsequent litigation context as an admission of legal fault provides further disincentives to nursing facility administrators and staff from acting expeditiously and effectively when safety problems become apparent.

Patient safety lessons generated in the hospital context, although valuable, cannot automatically be transposed successfully in the nursing facility sphere. Instead, more particularized, targeted strategies that focus on nursing facilities' unique resident population, cultural context, and types of risks involved must be developed and implemented. These strategies must include, among other things, much more research on the extent, nature, and causes of threats to resident safety particular to nursing facilities, funded demonstration projects testing targeted safety interventions, and the appropriation of adequate public and private resources to properly address the challenges, for example, by significantly increasing the wages of the certified nurse assistants who provide the bulk of direct care to nursing facility residents. Developing an improved working climate is also essential to reducing staff turnover and the safety concerns accompanying lack of stability in the workforce.

Part of any effective resident safety strategy must address head-on the powerful and counterproductive disincentives to cooperation now fostered by what is perceived by the nursing facility industry to be an adversarial, antagonistic legal environment. In a development creating hope in this regard, the regulatory paradigm for nursing facilities is beginning to shift away from primary reliance on a rigid command and control approach, at least at the federal level. Although aggressive command and control regulation still retains some vigorous proponents, questioning of the continued value of a police model built on apprehending and penalizing offenders has grown more vocal. Hence, in large measure the long-term care policy energy has turned away from blaming and shaming miscreants toward coming up with workable legal and nonlegal strategies (for example, behavioral incentives supplied by a competitive economic marketplace) to supplement or replace the heretofore prevailing regulatory and litigation approaches to ensuring and improving both quality and safety.

In sum, by concentrating on the factors specially shaping the provision of nursing facility care in the United States at this time, we may create and/or take advantage of valuable opportunities to improve the safety of nursing facility residents. We must work diligently to make the most of these opportunities. At the same time, however, the unique characteristics of American nursing facilities call for a heavy dose of realism in the expectations of residents, families, the public, the media, and—perhaps most importantly—the legal system concerning not only the possibilities but also the limits of resident safety strategies. In general, nursing homes are not insurers of safety for their residents. Ultimately, the goal of resident safety must be continually balanced in practical ways against competing social objectives such as enhancing resident autonomy. Accepting compromises reflecting differing values may need to be made. Guaranteeing the absence of resident injuries may well turn out to be partially incompatible with the full fostering and flourishing of a home-like living environment for the frailest and most dependent of our fellow citizens.

DISCUSSION QUESTIONS

1. Do you agree that physical safety of their loved one ordinarily is the highest priority goal for family members of a nursing home resident? Why do you believe it is their highest priority? If you disagree, what higher priorities do families want to achieve? Are the safety expectations of families reasonable under the circumstances?

2. Do you believe that nursing homes are fundamentally safe places for their residents? Why or why not? Do you believe that legal regulation makes nursing homes more or less safe for residents?

3. Should nursing home personnel openly admit and try to correct safety problems within the nursing home? Why or why not should this be done openly?

4. Can nursing homes realistically maximize residents' full potential for enjoying and experiencing life while simultaneously keeping those residents as safe from injury as possible? From a practical perspective, are the two goals compatible? Is it fair and productive to impose on nursing homes both affirmative obligations to foster residents' quality of care and quality of life and negative obligations to protect residents against harm?

5. Are the anxieties of nursing home personnel about potential negative legal repercussions if their respect

for resident and family choice results in injury to the resident reasonable and accurate or unreasonable and exaggerated? Do providers' risk management concerns represent a rational appraisal of the legal climate or an exercise in undue legal paranoia?

6. If a choice must be made between respecting the autonomous choices of residents and families, even if those choices entail certain risks, on one hand, and paternalistically protecting the resident against risk of harm, on the other, which direction should be taken? Which goals of nursing home care ultimately should triumph? Do you agree or disagree with the perception that both the rights and safety models assume the nursing facility is an untrustworthy adversary to be monitored and controlled by the consumer and/or regulator, rather than as a possible partner with which to collaborate?

7. What public policy strategies do you believe are most likely to be effective in encouraging nursing homes to promote quality of care and quality of life beyond just resident safety? What is the proper balance of government regulation and private industry initiatives?

8. How much faith do you place in the power of informed consumer choice operating in a competitive long-term care marketplace to change nursing home culture such that facilities pursue resident safety, but not at the expense of other facets of quality of care and quality of life? How can health care and human services professionals best assist older persons and their families to access, understand, and utilize publicly available information about particular nursing homes in making their own difficult choices?

9. How can you help relatives of nursing home residents to reduce the feelings of guilt and grief that are often manifested as anger (and sometimes legal claims) toward facility staff?

10. What can be done to improve public perceptions about, and attitudes toward, nursing homes?

11. For nonambulatory nursing home residents, are pressure ulcers completely avoidable? With proper care, should pressure ulcers never occur, such that their occurrence automatically proves negligence on the part of the caregivers?

12. Are resident falls in nursing homes avoidable or inevitable? What, if anything, does a resident fall prove about the nursing home's quality of care or its negligence? Do you agree with the previous statement that "accepting a certain risk of falls is preferable to continuing the practice of continuously physically and/or chemically restraining large numbers of residents"?

13. Do you agree with the statement that "in general, nursing homes are not insurers of safety for their residents"? Should they be?

According to the Chief Counsel to the HHS Inspector General:

In addition to promoting financial integrity, [the OIG] has made improving the quality of care a top priority for OIG, because behind every claim for reimbursement is a program beneficiary. In particular, OIG has long been concerned with the quality of care rendered in nursing facilities. OIG's efforts to improve quality of care in nursing homes involves three strategies: (1) the evaluation of the systems used to oversee quality of care, (2) the investigation and prosecution of cases of egregiously substandard care, and (3) the provision of guidance to the long term care industry in order to encourage program compliance and high quality care. Lewis Morris, In the Hands of Strangers: Are Nursing Home Safeguards Working? *Testimony before the Subcommittee on Oversight and*

Investigations, Committee on Energy and Commerce, U.S. House of Representatives, Washington, DC, May 15, 2008.

On April 16, 2008 the DHHS OIG published a Draft Supplemental Compliance Program Guidance for Nursing Facilities, 73 Fed. Reg. 20680-96. This proposal sought comments from interested parties on a draft supplemental compliance program guidance for nursing facilities that would supplement OIG's prior (2000) compliance program guidance for nursing facilities. The 2008 proposal took "into account Medicare and Medicaid nursing facility payment systems and regulations, evolving industry practices, current enforcement priorities (including the Government's heightened focus on quality of care), and lessons learned in the area of nursing facility compliance." On September 30, 2008, the OIG published, 73 Fed. Reg. 56832, the final version of the supplemental compliance program guidance for nursing homes.

The OIG defined the benefits of a compliance program as follows:

A successful compliance program addresses the public and private sectors' common goals of reducing fraud and abuse, enhancing health care providers' operations, improving the quality of health care services, and reducing their overall cost. Meeting these goals benefits the nursing facility industry, the government, and residents alike. Compliance programs help nursing facilities fulfill their legal duty to provide quality care; to refrain from submitting false or inaccurate claims or cost information to the federal health care programs; and to avoid engaging in other illegal practices.

DISCUSSION QUESTIONS

Are these stated goals for a nursing facility compliance program realistic, or overly optimistic? Is a formal corporate compliance program necessary to accomplish these goals? Are there better ways to pursue these goals?

The proposed compliance program guidance states the following:

> *OIG does not intend this supplemental CPG [compliance program guidance] to be a "one-size-fits-all" guidance. OIG strongly encourages nursing facilities to identify and focus their compliance efforts on those areas of potential concern or risk that are most relevant to their organizations. Compliance measures adopted by a nursing facility to address identified risk areas should be tailored to fit the unique environment of the facility (including its structure, operations, resources, the needs of its resident population, and prior enforcement experience). In short, OIG recommends that each nursing facility adapt the objectives and principles underlying this guidance to its own particular circumstances.*

Restraint Use in Nursing Homes

On its face, the current law and public policy in the United States regarding the use of restraints in nursing homes is excellent. The employment of physical or mechanical restraints in nursing homes is a subject addressed extensively in the Nursing Home Quality Reform Act provisions of OBRA of 1987, Public Law No. 100-203, codified at 42 U.S.C. §§ 1395i(3) (a)–(h) and 1396r(a)–(h), and implementing regulations. These legal provisions quite clearly convey legislative and executive branch intentions to reduce significantly the unnecessary and inappropriate utilization of physical restraints in nursing homes. (OBRA 87 also included corresponding provisions relating to the use of drugs as chemical restraints.) The sort of

DISCUSSION QUESTIONS

You are made head of the team assigned to write a compliance program for the specific nursing home in which you work. How do you begin this task? What questions would you ask? How would you find the answers to those questions?

misuse of restraints in nursing homes targeted by the legal revolution of 1987 was, at the time of OBRA's enactment, very prevalent nationally.

Defined intentionally broadly by the federal CMS as any manual method or physical or mechanical device, material, or equipment attached or adjacent to the resident's body that the individual cannot remove easily which restricts freedom of movement or normal access to one's body, physical restraints have been a regular part of the American institutional long-term care climate for centuries. It was a considerable time before a professional and public appreciation that the use of physical restraints in nursing homes frequently is unnecessary, improper, and even abusive resulted in federal and state regulations setting firm parameters for such use.

Federal law provides that the resident has the right "to be free from any physical restraints imposed for purposes of discipline or convenience, and not required to treat the resident's medical symptoms" as documented in the resident's chart and incorporated into the resident's assessment and care plan, 42 U.S.C. 1396r(c)(1)(A)(ii) and 1395i-3(c)(1)(A)(ii) and 42 C.F.R. § 483.13(a). CMS encourages state surveyors to take an aggressive stance in enforcing these regulatory limits on nursing facility prerogatives. This vigorous enforcement posture is consciously intended to be consistent with the resident outcome orientation characterizing the nursing home survey and certification system in operation since the enactment of OBRA 87. Besides being attentive to CMS regulations connected to a nursing facility's participation in Medicare and Medicaid, providers also must be aware of potential civil liability associated with the regulation of physical restraints as medical "devices" by the U.S. Food and Drug Administration. Furthermore, every single state, as part of its own respective legislated resident bill of rights, guarantees nursing facility residents the right to be free from unnecessary physical restraints. These state provisions are in agreement with both the spirit and letter of the federal requirements.

Contrary to a still popular strain of public opinion, the governmental provisions constraining the permissible use of physical restraints do not unduly increase the potential negligence (malpractice) liability exposure of nursing homes or their staffs based on the occurrence of resident falls or wandering. In fact, the very opposite is true. Judgments holding providers liable for failure to impose restraints on unwilling residents are far eclipsed by the rate of litigation brought on the basis of inappropriate ordering of restraints, failure to monitor and correct restraints' adverse effects on residents, or mistakes in the mechanical application of the restraint. The courts have held, "The duties imposed upon nursing homes...obviously require them to maintain a delicate balance between residents' freedom from restraint and the need for protective restraint of impaired residents. The exercise of such competing duties necessarily should be subject to professional standards of skill and care." In other words, the courts have backed up the regulators by overwhelmingly taking the position that nursing facility residents should not be restrained unless doing so is dictated as a matter of considered, documented medical judgment in the particular situation and not for the previously accepted, virtually automatic purposes of administrative convenience and behavior control. Moreover, among many knowledgeable people, the widespread, inappropriate employment of physical restraints acts as a proxy indicator for poor care generally. As explained by one geriatrician:

> *I would certainly prefer to be in a facility that recognizes that tying people down is an attack on their dignity and does not even have the desired effect of protecting them from falling. A facility that continues to use a lot of restraints, despite the federal law restricting their use that went into effect in 1987 and despite the adverse publicity associated with them, is probably benighted in other ways as well. The use of restraints is a likely indication of other kinds of unfortunate attitudes and behaviors on the part of staff and administrators.*

It appears that, as a general matter, the wisdom of physical restraint reduction is no longer a proposition open for debate among reasonable participants in public policy forums. Indeed, in this sphere acute care hospital regulation (in the multiple forms of private accreditation standards, government command and control edicts and guidance documents, civil litigation, and organizationally developed clinical practice parameters) has followed and built on lessons derived from the nursing facility world.

Instead of dwelling on the, by now, well-established medical, psychological, and social rationales for restraint reduction, people interested in nursing facility resident well-being should focus today on implementation issues. In actual practice, improvements regarding the use of physical restraints in nursing homes (as is also true in hospitals) have varied considerably among specific homes and have fluctuated over time. Although important strides have been made in reducing restraint use in the post-OBRA 87 era, the presence of physical restraints continues to persist in many inappropriate situations. There is broad consensus in the policy and practice communities that constant efforts are necessary to keep up positive momentum and prevent clinical backsliding. Nursing homes must be further motivated (through revised payment mechanisms, among other means) and empowered to develop and carry out internal policies and procedures to comply with all applicable legal requirements in this arena. Less restrictive alternatives to the use of restraints, including both environmental and administrative changes in the facility if needed, must be explored fully and explained to staff, residents, and families.

DISCUSSION QUESTIONS

1. Is the widespread use of restraints in a particular nursing home necessarily a proxy indicator for poor quality care generally? Is it fair to judge individual facilities based on their restraints statistics? *See* Amie E. Schaadt, *Applying the False Claims Act to Chemical and Physical Restraint Cases: Is the Government Going Too Far?*, 68 U. Pitt. L. Rev. 763–783 (2007).

2. Is it realistic and/or desirable to insist on restraint-free nursing homes? Are there legitimate uses for restraints? Are they currently overused or underused?

3. As a matter of practice, what can be done to reduce the use of restraints in nursing homes? *See* Elizabeth Capezuti et al., *Consequences of an Intervention to Reduce Restrictive Side Rail Use in Nursing Homes*, 55 J. Am. Geriatr. Soc'y 334–341 (2007). Identify some less restrictive or intrusive alternatives that might be utilized in place of restraints.

In recognition of the continual challenge to wean nursing homes away from their historical dependence on the use of physical restraints, the Nursing Home Quality Initiative launched in November 2002 by CMS to assist homes to improve the quality of care and quality of life for all residents includes a large component aimed at enabling the federally funded Quality Improvement Organizations (www.cms.hhs.gov/QualityImprovementOrgs) to work closely with individual homes on restraint reduction efforts. Among other things, the Quality Improvement Organizations use the percentage of residents who are physically restrained as one of their quality measures for assessing the overall performance of Medicare-certified nursing homes.

42 C.F.R. § 483.25(h) provides the following:

> *The facility must ensure that*
> *(1) The resident environment remains as free from accident hazards as is possible; and*
> *(2) Each resident receives adequate supervision and assistance devices to prevent accidents.*

Guidance to Surveyors for Long Term Care Facilities interpreting this provision was issued by CMS in CMS Manual System, Pub. 100-07, State Operations Provider Certification, Transmittal 27 (Aug. 17, 2007). The Definitions section of this Guidance states the following:

> *"Accident" refers to any unexpected or unintentional incident, which may result in injury or illness to a resident. This does not include adverse outcomes that are a direct consequence of treatment or care that is provided in accordance with current standards of practice (e.g., drug side effects or reaction).*
> *"Avoidable Accident" means that an accident occurred because the facility failed to:*
> *—Identify environmental hazards and individual resident risk of an accident, including the need for supervision; and/or*
> *—Evaluate/analyze the hazards and risks; and/or*
> *—Implement interventions, including adequate supervision, consistent with a resident's needs, goals, plan of care, and current standards of practice in order to reduce the risk of an accident; and/or*

–Monitor the effectiveness of the interventions and modify the interventions as necessary, in accordance with current standards of practice.

"Unavoidable Accident" means that an accident occurred despite facility efforts to:

–Identify environmental hazards and individual resident risk of an accident, including the need for supervision; and

–Evaluate/analyze the hazards and risks; and

–Implement interventions, including adequate supervision, consistent with the resident's needs, goals, plan of care, and current standards of practice in order to reduce the risk of an accident; and

–Monitor the effectiveness of the interventions and modify the interventions as necessary, in accordance with current standards of practice.

"Fall" refers to unintentionally coming to rest on the ground, floor, or other lower level, but not as a result of an overwhelming external force (e.g., resident pushes another resident). An episode where a resident lost his/her balance and would have fallen, if not for staff intervention, is considered a fall. A fall without injury is still a fall. Unless there is evidence suggesting otherwise, when a resident is found on the floor, a fall is considered to have occurred.

The CMS Guidance also presents an Overview, which states in part as follows:

Numerous and varied accident hazards exist in everyday life. Not all accidents are avoidable. The frailty of some residents increases their vulnerability to hazards in the resident environment and can result in life threatening injuries. It is important that all facility staff understand the facility's responsibility, as well as their own, to ensure the safest environment possible for residents.

The facility is responsible for providing care to residents in a manner that helps promote quality of life. This includes respecting residents' rights to privacy, dignity and self-determination, and their right to make choices about significant aspects of their life in the facility.

For various reasons, residents are exposed to some potential for harm. Although hazards should not be ignored, there are varying degrees of potential for harm. It is reasonable to accept some risks as a trade-off for the potential benefits, such as maintaining dignity, self-determination, and control over one's daily life. The facility's challenge is to balance protecting

Exercise

Mr. X, an 80-year-old wheelchair-bound man, is a resident in a nursing home. He has fallen several times in the past and is currently deemed to be at high risk to fall and suffer significant injury. The facility, with the family's reluctant agreement, has implemented different types of physical restraints, including lap belts and a tray attached to Mr. X's wheelchair, and has positioned Mr. X in the common area where he is more visible to staff. Mr. X is extremely resistant to these interventions and gets quite agitated. He just wants to be left alone in his room to look at magazines or watch television. He is moderately to severely demented. If permitted to do so, he is likely to get out of the wheelchair and fall again. The medical director and nursing staff perceive Mr. X will probably suffer physical injury if not restrained or serious emotional injury if he is restrained.

How should the facility and its staff handle this situation? With each of the potential courses of action, what are the possible risks regarding civil liability, regulatory sanctions for violating the resident's rights, and sanctions for violating the regulatory provisions regarding accident prevention? Is it realistically feasible for the facility to successfully "balance protecting the resident's right to make choices and the facility's responsibility to comply with all regulations"? In a case like this, is the best risk management strategy also the best ethical solution?

the resident's right to make choices and the facility's responsibility to comply with all regulations.

The responsibility to respect a resident's choices is balanced by considering the potential impact of these choices on other individuals and on the facility's obligation to protect the residents from harm. The facility has a responsibility to educate a resident, family, and staff regarding significant risks related to a resident's choices. Incorporating a resident's choices into the plan of care can help the facility balance interventions to reduce the risk of an accident while honoring the resident's autonomy. Consent by resident or responsible party alone does not relieve the provider of its responsibility to ensure the health, safety, and welfare of its residents, including protecting them from avoidable accidents. Although federal regulations affirm the resident's right to participate in care planning and to refuse treatment, the regulations do not create the right for a resident, legal surrogate, or representative to demand the facility use specific medical interventions or treatments that the facility deems inappropriate. The regulations hold the facility ultimately accountable for the resident's care and safety. Verbal consent or signed consent forms do not eliminate a facility's responsibility to protect a resident from an avoidable accident.

In November 2007, CMS for the first time published a list of what the agency, on the basis of repeated inspections, calls "poor-performing nursing homes" or "special focus facilities." Each nursing home on this list is identified by name and full address. The list is available at http://www .cms.hhs.gov/certificationandcomplianc/downloads/SFFList.pfd and also at www.NHCompare.gov (maintained by CMS).

DISCUSSION QUESTIONS

What, if anything, would you conclude about a particular nursing home from the fact that it is listed on the CMS list of "poor performing nursing homes"? What would you tell a patient/client or families about the significance of being on this list?

NONPROFIT NURSING HOMES

With a few notable exceptions, most of the public discussion and debate regarding the present status and future prospects of the nursing home industry in the United States has been conducted in rather politicized, adversarial language. Opinions expressed and policy prescriptions recommended vary greatly depending on the particular, generally self-interested, perspective of whoever is the speaker at the time. Sides have been chosen (or assigned), and real or perceived enemies demonized.

Most of the factors that have converged in the last few years to create a contemporary nursing home "crisis" affect individual nonprofit nursing homes as seriously as they impact the proprietary sector of the industry. The majority of nonprofit nursing homes that are being challenged today to make difficult choices with potentially far-reaching consequences, and to operate radically differently in many respects than they have traditionally functioned, really are benevolent and mission-driven because of their community ownership and the sense of altruistic commitment and responsibility ordinarily present on the part of their governing bodies.

Although this is an especially demanding time to be operating a nursing home, either proprietary or nonprofit, from a broad social policy viewpoint several aspects of the current "crisis" are positive. The major conundrum is finding effective ways to enhance and exploit those salutary developments without inadvertently mortally wounding or destroying those parts of the traditional institutional long-term care system—in this instance, the valuable contributions of nonprofit nursing homes in humanely serving older and disabled persons in need—that ought to be preserved and even bolstered as a matter of the public's welfare.

The lion's share of the public commentary expressed thus far regarding the challenging circumstances confronting modern American nursing homes has focused on the roughly three-fourths of the industry characterized by investor, or proprietary, for-profit ownership. At its most vituperative, this commentary consists essentially of consumer advocates reflexively condemning anything connected to a capitalist marketplace approach to health and human services, accusing nursing home corporations of purposefully sacrificing quality of resident care to maximize short-term shareholder profits, and the proprietary sector of the industry indeed focusing its energies and complaints mainly on payment rates, malpractice insurance premiums, the costs of regulatory compliance, and other matters pertaining to the industry's own economic bottom line.

A vital factor that has been largely overlooked amidst the barrage of complementary insults and accusations flowing between consumer advocacy groups and the proprietary trade associations is the real and potential impact of financial, regulatory, and legal pressures on the continued vitality and viability of nonprofit nursing homes. In light of the proliferation of HCBLTC alternatives and assisted living facilities that enable persons to avoid or substantially delay entry into a nursing home, nonprofit nursing homes feel the financial pinch of vigorous competition just as painfully as does the proprietary sector. Older and disabled individuals are no more anxious to be admitted to a nonprofit nursing home than a proprietary one if there is another real choice. Moreover, nonprofit facilities generally do not have available to them the marketing budgets that most proprietary chains expend to pursue their scramble to find and enroll new residents.

The federal, state, and local regulatory environment affects nonprofit and proprietary nursing homes in exactly the same ways. Neither the survey and certification nor licensure processes, local prosecutors, nor the OIG give any special favorable consideration or advantage to nonprofit facilities; the same substantive rules and administrative procedures apply with full force regardless of a facility's ownership status. Similarly, neither tort doctrine, plaintiffs' personal injury attorneys, nor professional liability insurance underwriters draw any distinction between nonprofit and proprietary nursing homes (although it is conceivable that juries might take a nursing home's ownership status into account in considering whether, and to what extent, to award damages).

Likewise, minimum staffing requirements do not offer any dispensation for nonprofit status, and recruiting and retaining qualified staff is no easier for nonprofit than proprietary nursing homes. Few, if any, current or potential nursing home employees are swayed in their job choice by a facility's ownership status. Further, nonprofit nursing homes are by no means exempted from negative media attention, and their reputations and morale levels are tarnished by such reports to at least as great a degree as occurs in the case of proprietary facilities. Finally, Medicare and Medicaid payment rates are no more generous for nonprofit nursing homes than for their proprietary counterparts, and there is no evidence that residents of nonprofit nursing homes are especially likely to have purchased private long-term care insurance policies.

The fact that the nonprofit sector of the nursing home industry joins its proprietary counterpart in experiencing many aspects of the current crisis ought to matter deeply to those who purport to be concerned about the quality of care and quality of life available to older and disabled persons who need long-term care services. Assuming that one accepts a continuing need for the availability of *some* institutional long-term care options, most nonprofit nursing homes ought to be recognized and supported as valuable participants who represent an essential middle ground between an arguably excessive financially driven proprietary industry, on one hand, and the nihilistic service vacuum that would neglect and imperil the most vulnerable members of society, on the other, if nursing homes ceased to exist altogether.

The ultimate irony is that the combination of growing competitiveness for residents, an unfriendly regulatory and litigation environment, the severe shortage of qualified labor, hostile media treatment, and a very cost-conscious third-party payer climate is, probably too frequently, compelling nonprofit nursing homes to behave in a more businesslike and less benevolent fashion and thus to become less and less distinguishable from their proprietary counterparts on both a strategic and an everyday activities basis.

Certainly, a number of the factors contributing to the current nursing home crisis have brought about positive ramifications. Keeping people out of nursing homes—proprietary or nonprofit—as long as possible is an accomplishment to be broadly applauded and encouraged, as long as the individuals being diverted from long-term care institutions are receiving the help they need and are not simply being neglected. Society ought to support expansion of HCBLTC options, particularly those based on the principle of maximizing consumer choice and control over the service package.

Nonprofit agencies and their community owners should be in the forefront of this diversification, not just because new product lines and profit centers are needed for financial survival, let alone prospering (although financial viability is both a relevant and legitimate consideration), but because HCBLTC options respond to what members of the communities that nonprofit agencies exist to serve prefer in their lives. The major trade association representing nonprofit long-term care providers has suggested, "providers will also want to examine ... new opportunities ... for expanding their home and community-based services or for starting an HCBS program. This type of community outreach offers prospects for providers on many levels."

There is another positive note to the current situation. Real fraud, abuse, and waste do take place in public payment programs, and it is difficult to criticize aggressive attempts by the government to eliminate their negative effects.

Those salutary developments notwithstanding, the present crisis places the United States at a crossroads in terms of deciding what role, if any, the populace expects nursing homes to play in the larger national long-term care marketplace/system in the future. The answer that probably is not viable, and assuredly is not desirable, is a continuation of the current process of slow demise, confusion, and uncertainty being experienced by both the proprietary and nonprofit sectors of the nursing home industry. The more feasible policy alternatives divide into two basic approaches.

Under one approach, we could decide to discontinue allowing nursing homes to participate in Medicare and Medicaid programs or to otherwise receive public (e.g., Department of Veterans Affairs) payments for providing nursing home services. Any nursing home remaining in business would have to survive on a combination of private pay residents, private long-term care insurance, and charitable donations. In such a scenario, it is likely that most remaining nursing homes would be proprietary and even more focused on bottom line financial returns. Absent involvement of governmental purse strings, the legal justification for regulatory intrusion into nursing home operations would be greatly diminished. Prohibiting nursing homes that do not participate in public financing programs from discriminating in resident admissions and retention on the basis of ability to pay, even if legally permissible, surely would—whether consciously intended to do so or not—put a quick and complete end to the American nursing home industry.

If a vast reduction in the number, if not total elimination, of nursing homes is the desired practical outcome, the nation had better be exceedingly committed to accomplishing the following: infusing substantial financial resources into expansion of HCBLTC options and assisted living; administering those noninstitutional or quasi-institutional service programs soundly and efficiently; developing, finding, cultivating, and retaining suitable workers for those programs; and accepting the inevitability that some long-term care clients will be at substantial risk of undetected neglect or even abuse and exploitation when relying on services provided in relatively ineffectively monitored home and community-based or assisted living environments.

Each of the approximately 1.6 million persons who presently reside in around 17,000 nursing homes would need to be cared for somewhere, by someone; more than four-fifths of these individuals require help with three or more ADLs, such as bathing, dressing, toileting, transferring from a bed or chair, feeding, and mobility. As one leading geriatrician has put it, "In this day of 'sicker and quicker' transfer of patients from hospitals to nursing homes, it is rare to find a nursing home resident who does not need nursing home care. I have never met a malingerer living in a nursing home." In the idealistic scenario posited here—a world without nursing homes—nonprofit, mission-driven organizations should be given financial and other kinds of incentives to be even more active competitors in the HCBLTC and assisted living marketplaces to help them meet the challenge. Otherwise, we may be fated to see repeated some version of the massive social problems created by deinstitutionalization of the seriously, chronically mentally ill from large public institutions in the 1960s and 1970s without an accompanying widespread commitment to support adequate community treatment and housing entities to serve that dependent population.

A different vision of the future of long-term care in the United States would entail a public policy of bolstering nursing homes and making them more economically and programmatically viable entities than they are today. As subissues to be considered under this general vision, the nursing home industry could be larger, smaller, or the same size as it is presently and could consist of either the current mix of proprietary and nonprofit facilities or a different ownership profile. One option might be a much smaller role for nursing homes in a total long-term care system that is more (but not completely) reliant on home and community-based alternatives, in which the institutional role is fulfilled exclusively by nonprofit facilities.

Successfully pursuing a policy of fostering more viable nursing homes for those who need them, regardless of the eventual size and ownership status of those facilities, would necessitate serious reexamination of the status quo in at least two areas. First, there would need to be a thorough and open-minded reassessment of the actual effectiveness and value (including the cost-to-benefit ratio) of present regulatory and litigative approaches to ensuring acceptable levels of quality of care and quality of life in nursing homes. Second, the ways in which we pay nursing homes for caring for residents must be critically rethought. This inquiry ought to address not just the technical, tortuous aspects of Medicare and Medicaid payment methodologies but also fundamental questions regarding the proper mix of public and private responsibility for financing long-term care (including the role to be played by the private long-term care insurance industry) and the desirable ratio of spending between institutional and noninstitutional long-term care.

DISCUSSION QUESTIONS

1. Do you agree with the claim that most nonprofit nursing homes really are benevolent and mission-driven, with a sense of moral responsibility to their respective religious or secular communities, in a way that fundamentally distinguishes them from for-profit or proprietary facilities? Or, do most nonprofit facilities—either out of choice or practical necessity—behave essentially just the same as their for-profit counterparts?

2. Are you suspicious of the motivations and performance of for-profit long-term care providers? Should long-term care providers be allowed to make a profit from their care of older persons who need their services? Should we legally ban for-profit long-term care providers? See *Culture Change in a For-Profit Nursing Home Chain: An Evaluation, available at* www.commonwealthfund .org/publications/publications_show.htm?doc _id=668880. Should we at least ban or restrict proprietary chains that own multiple individual providers?

3. Does American society even need a nonprofit sector of the nursing home industry? Should our regulatory system somehow favor nonprofit providers? How could we do so? Should nonprofit providers be held to a lower (or at least different) standard of care in the tort system than we hold for-profit providers? Should we limit the damages that can be awarded in a malpractice lawsuit against a nonprofit provider? Should liability insurers differentiate in calculating premiums based on the ownership status of a provider applicant? Should they be legally required to charge nonprofit providers' lower premiums?

4. Is it a positive or negative development that nursing homes now need to compete vigorously for residents to keep their beds full and their financial bottom lines healthy?

5. In pursuing your own career opportunities, would you be swayed by a potential employer's ownership status (i.e., whether or not the potential employer was for-profit or nonprofit)? Why or why not would this factor make a difference to you?

FINANCING LONG-TERM CARE

The Need

It is estimated that the number of people aged 65 and older in the United States will double between 2000 and 2030; by 2050, the share of the American population comprising people of that age will be 21.5%, up from 12.4% in 2000 and 8.1% in 1950. The largest growth spurt will be among the so-called oldest old, those aged 85 and greater, whose share of the population will reach 5.2% by 2050.

There is some evidence that the level of functional impairment among the American aged, as measured by losses in the ability to perform ADLs, has declined over the past century. Nonetheless, as Americans live longer, they are more likely to develop age-related disabilities that limit their autonomy and ability to live independently. At that point, some type of long-term care becomes necessary. Estimates suggest that the number of disabled elderly who cannot perform basic ADLs without assistance may as much as double from 2000 through 2040.

Individuals with chronic disabilities seriously interfering with the performance of basic ADLs without assistance usually require long-term care of various kinds. It is estimated that of the more than 10 million Americans needing long-term care, approximately 17% are nursing home residents, 47% are persons aged 65 or over who receive services in their own homes or assisted living facilities or continuing care retirement communities, and 36% are community dwelling residents under age 65.

Medicaid and Nursing Home Care

The combination federal–state (i.e., supported in part with federal dollars but implemented by the individual states in compliance with federal regulations) Medicaid program established in 1965 as Title 19 of the Social Security Act now foots the bill for almost half of the paid long-term care provided in the United States. Until relatively recently, almost all of the Medicaid dollars devoted to long-term care went to pay for nursing home services. Over the last decade or so, however, a strong combination of consumer preferences and legal edicts based on the integration mandate of the Americans With Disabilities Act has resulted in more Medicaid funding becoming available, primarily through a variety of Medicaid waivers granted to individual states by DHHS, to pay for formal long-term care services delivered in home- and community-based settings. The bill for long-term care is substantial, in 2003 totaling about $183 billion for persons of all ages, and expenditures continue to rise dramatically. Per capita, Medicaid spending for long-term care varies widely among the states, ranging in fiscal year 2000 from $73 per year in Nevada to $680 in New York.

Eligibility for coverage under the Medicaid program is means tested, that is, dependent on proof that the prospective beneficiary lacks the financial means or wherewithal (in the form of assets and income) to pay for covered services without government assistance (i.e., the applicant is "categorically" or "medically" needy). This fundamental feature of the Medicaid program creates a powerful incentive for individuals to arrange their finances in such a way that, at a future date when they might apply for Medicaid coverage of their long-term care, they will be able to satisfy the financial means test of the program. Put most bluntly, individuals contemplating a future Medicaid application may be motivated to make themselves "poor on paper."

Professional advisors—including attorneys, financial planners, accountants, and insurance agents—may counsel clients to engage in a variety of planning activities to protect assets while still qualifying in the future for Medicaid eligibility if long-term care is necessary. These legally permissible sheltering techniques are listed in Table 5.5.

Congress and the DHHS have reacted negatively to the specter of professionals advising about, and older persons engaging in, these various forms of financial planning for purposes of maximizing future Medicaid eligibility in case long-term care is eventually needed. A perception exists that instead of spending down one's own assets until financial eligibility for Medicaid has been reached legitimately, a large number of Medicaid applicants (especially the most wealthy segment of the older population) engage in "legerdemain" or "gaming the system" by voluntarily impoverishing themselves through gratuitous transfers of assets to children, grandchildren, or others. According to DHHS, "Not surprisingly, a web search on 'Medicaid estate planning' yields thousands of results offering advice on a variety of strategies to qualify for Medicaid while preserving assets and savings for heirs."

In response to apprehension about this sort of beneficiary abuse of the Medicaid program (the exact factual extent of which has been the subject of serious dispute), the federal government has established a set of "lookback period" rules, *see* 42 U.S.C. § 1396(c). Subject to certain complex exceptions (most importantly provisions designed to minimally protect

---

Table 5.5   Medicaid Planning Techniques

- Gifting away assets to family members
- Placing assets in trust
- Investing in improvements for one's home and contiguous property
- Investing in a family business
- Using assets to purchase home furnishings
- Purchasing a prepaid burial plot
- Purchasing a car

the healthy spouse, or "community spouse," from being impoverished by the long-term care costs of the spouse needing long-term care) these rules contained in OBRA of 1993, Public Law No. 103-66, 107 Stat. 312 § 13611(e), impose periods of Medicaid ineligibility based on the dollar value of those gratuitous transfers that occurred during the look-back period. The general look-back period had been 36 months and 60 months for transfers to a trust, 42 U.S.C. § 1396p(c)(1)(B)(i). In the Deficit Reduction Act of 2005, Public Law No. 109-171, Congress attempted to tighten Medicaid eligibility for long-term care by, among other things, increasing penalties on individuals who transfer assets for less than fair market value to qualify for long-term care and setting a limit on the amount of home equity that can be excluded from consideration of a Medicaid applicant's available assets.

Arguments regarding the social policy wisdom of government restrictions on the use of voluntary impoverishment and/or the conversion of counted assets to excluded assets as techniques within a Medicaid long-term care eligibility planning strategy do not often explicitly entail resort to ethical reasoning. Nonetheless, these arguments, even though thoroughly driven by political ideology and the economic self-interests of the respective advocates, are fully susceptible to ethical analysis and characterization.

Opponents of legal restrictions on the freedom of individuals to manage their own assets so as to position themselves for eventual Medicaid eligibility appeal to the ethical principle of autonomy (self-determination), embodied in the legal concept of liberty, in the sense of respecting the right of individuals to manage their own affairs free of unwanted external interference. Moreover, proponents of unfettered opportunities for Medicaid planning contend that congressionally imposed planning restrictions disrespect the dignity interests of applicants by requiring them to spend down their hard-earned, hard-saved assets until they are truly and publicly impoverished to qualify for governmental long-term care support. In addition, reliance on the ethical precept of social or distributive justice really undergirds the argument that Medicaid, as a social welfare program, ought to be widely (if not universally) available as a method to fairly or equitably redistribute, and thereby share, society's (i.e., the general population's) resources as needed to help people who have permanently or temporarily suffered the adverse effects of life's cruel contingencies (for instance, the need for long-term care) through no fault of their own. Under this view, the social justice principle demands that the people collectively, acting through the agencies of representative government, should always be prepared to act as the ultimate, safety net risk manager to ensure individuals against the ravages of those vicissitudes that might imperil them.

Proponents of strict legal restrictions on the ability of individuals to voluntarily divest themselves of financial assets or move them from counted into excluded form, in anticipation of applying at a future time for Medicaid eligibility, depend on (generally without explicitly citing by name) the same ethical principles just discussed in support of their own position. However, they reason from those ethical principles to very different conclusions. Supporters of strong federal look-back rules contend, in effect, that the autonomy principle and the government's duty to respect the personal dignity interest of persons supports reliance on individual responsibility to the maximum extent that each individual is able to shoulder his or her respective burden rather than unnecessarily abdicating responsibility and the control that cannot be uncoupled from responsibility, to a detached, paternalistic, overly intrusive "nanny state."

This perspective is bolstered by evidence that knowledge about the availability of Medicaid to pay for long-term care operates as a significant disincentive for individuals to personally prepare financially for future long-term care expenses by engaging in strategies such as the purchase of private long-term care insurance or putting aside adequate personal savings. Few Americans expect to have enough money saved to personally finance their potential long-term care needs as they age.

Additionally, the arguments by critics of Medicaid planning techniques that allowing wealthy persons and their professional planners to take advantage of these techniques has the immoral consequence of depriving truly (rather than artificially) needy potential long-term care consumers of receiving their equitable share of beneficial but limited public resources are an interpretation and application of the social or distributive justice principle. So, too, is the contention that Medicaid planning constitutes an unfair use of the state's inherent police power authority to coerce taxpayers to sacrifice their own legitimate and socially valuable property rights in order to (1) subsidize the long-term care of individuals who could and should be exercising personal responsibility for their own welfare and hence (2) insure with public dollars the unimpeded passing of private property to those individuals' usually already affluent heirs, that is, convert Medicaid into an inheritance insurance program.

Limits on Medicaid

Ever since the beginning of the Medicaid program, the states have been permitted, but not mandated, to recover their long-term care expenditures from the estates of deceased Medicaid recipients who (1) were over the age of 65 when they received benefits and (2) had no surviving spouse, minor child, or adult disabled child. The Medicaid statute also allowed states, on a discretionary basis, to impose liens on property held within the estates of deceased Medicaid recipients. The function of postmortem liens is to prevent an estate from being settled, with the property distributed to the Medicaid beneficiary's heirs, before all claims against the estate, including the state's Medicaid claim, have been satisfied.

In response to anxiety about planning techniques to "game" the Medicaid eligibility determination process, Congress included in OBRA 1993 a provision requiring—not just permitting any longer, but instead mandating—every state to implement a Medicaid estate recovery program. Recoveries may be made only from the estates of deceased Medicaid beneficiaries who (1) were 55 or older when they received Medicaid benefits or (2) regardless of age were permanently institutionalized. A state may either use a narrow definition of "estate" to mean only those assets that pass through probate at death or adopt a broader definition that enables the state to recover also from some or all property that bypasses probate, including such items as assets that pass directly to a survivor through joint tenancy (joint ownership), living trusts, annuity remainder payments, or life insurance payouts. At a minimum, states are supposed to recover amounts spent by Medicaid for long-term care, whether the care consisted of institutional or home- and community-based services and related drug and hospital services. States have the option of recovering all Medicaid costs paid on a now-deceased beneficiary's behalf, regardless of service venue. States continue to have the power, as long as it is consistent with their own respective constitutions and statutes, to impose liens on a beneficiary's property to secure later recovery of costs, but "it is important to understand that the right [of a state] to recover [its Medicaid expenditures] can exist whether or not an actual lien is asserted." One state challenged Congress' constitutional authority to impose an estate recovery requirement on the states, but the federal courts rejected the state's challenge.

Under OBRA 93, states may waive estate recovery on a case-by-case basis when an attempt to recover would not be cost-effective. States also maintain discretion to waive estate recovery efforts in particular situations where enforcement would work an undue hardship on survivors of the Medicaid beneficiary. The federal law additionally obligates states to notify applicants about the estate recovery program during their initial application for Medicaid eligibility and the annual redetermination process. Further, the state must notify affected survivors about the initiation of estate recovery and give them an opportunity to claim an exemption based on undue hardship.

No other health insurance or social welfare program has similar estate recovery procedures, making Medicaid long-term care benefits unique in this regard. The uniqueness of this feature of Medicaid contributes to the ambiguity and confusion that surrounds contemporary long-term care financing in the United States.

Proponents of vigorous state estate recovery efforts make essentially the same points (often without framing their contentions explicitly in the vocabulary of ethics) that are made in support of tough restrictions on voluntary impoverishment as part of the process of Medicaid planning. That is, they mainly rely (without ordinarily stating it as such) on a social or distributive justice rationale, namely, that allowing the state to recover monies from the sale of property owned by now deceased former Medicaid beneficiaries gives the state more resources with which to provide benefits to people currently in need.

By contrast, the opponents of estate recovery as a component of the Medicaid program contend that estate recovery laws offend the ethical principles of beneficence (doing good for others) and nonmaleficence (preventing harm to others). The violation of these principles takes two forms under this position. First, putative heirs of deceased Medicaid beneficiaries who see their inheritances removed or greatly diminished by estate recovery efforts may be deprived of adequate resources— which they had reasonably depended on having—to take care of their own needs. Second, anxiety about eventual estate recovery may act as a strong disincentive for Medicaid-eligible individuals with substantial ADL impairments to accept available, potentially beneficial forms of long-term care services; there is evidence that some people choose to decline participation in the Medicaid program, at great sacrifice to their own health and well-being, to preserve their property as a legacy to be passed unencumbered after death to family members or other designated heirs. (The counterargument to the last contention is that the decision by potential Medicaid beneficiaries to forgo certain services that could be paid for by Medicaid funding to preserve their estates for distribution upon death is not an antibenevolent and malevolent consequence of estate recovery laws but instead a valid voluntary, informed exercise of personal autonomy by the involved individuals.)

Another ground for opposition to estate recovery is the argument that, in practice, enforcement of this tactic violates the ethical premise that, to be fair, like individuals should be treated alike. A violation of this principle occurs, it is argued, because implementation of estate recovery programs exerts a differential impact on nontraditional families whose members are denied asset protections that the Medicaid program affords to spouses and children in traditional family arrangements. At the least, advocates of this viewpoint suggest that fairness requires the recognition of a special hardship exemption from estate recovery for nontraditional family members who would be particularly disadvantaged if estate recovery were enforced. Some advocates for unencumbered availability of the Medicaid program go so far as to dispute the general public and professional understanding that Congress always intended for the program to apply only to people who are poor. These advocates have argued, for instance, that Medicaid should be treated—openly and without apology—not as a welfare program but instead as an entitlement for middle-class citizens who have planned wisely to take proper advantage of this source of government-financed long-term care.

Even some forceful advocates of personal, rather than governmental, financial responsibility for one's own long-term care find fault with Medicaid estate recovery on pragmatic grounds. It has been noted: "In theory, once [Medicaid beneficiaries] die the government could recover Medicaid costs from their estates. In practice, most of this wealth disappears, often in gifts to family members." Moreover, "estate recovery...has not worked well because it is punitive, after-the-fact, and politically sensitive." If a public policy fails to yield beneficial outcomes or consequences that outweigh the detriments imposed by that policy, it is very difficult to sustain ethical support for it.

To the extent that Medicaid planning and estate recovery both are problematic, ethically and otherwise, more acceptable alternatives for dealing with the challenge of adequately but fairly financing long-term care for a rapidly growing older population must be identified and sought. As one scholar has acknowledged, "If aspects of the [Medicaid] program must be cut, there is some logic to targeting asset transfer rules." Nonetheless, "alternatives to reforms advocating more aggressive impoverishment are appropriate and available...[and]...offer the promise of Medicaid budget relief without the pain of impoverishment for seniors."

There has been no shortage of ideas proposed over time for improving how we react to this complicated but essential task. Some of these ideas are enumerated in Table 5.6. A full discussion of the various potential long-term care financing alternatives that must take place at the public policy level necessarily needs to include consideration of many different but related factors, as enumerated in Table 5.7.

Table 5.6 Potential Long-Term Care Financing Alternatives

- Encourage individuals to purchase private long-term care insurance policies
- Tax incentives
- State/private long-term care insurance partnerships that permit insurance purchasers to receive Medicaid benefits if needed and still protect some or all of their assets from subsequent estate recovery
- Expand Medicare coverage for long-term care
- Eliminate the need for a preceding hospital stay
- Eliminate the skilled care requirement
- Change the duration-of-stay limitation

Table 5.7 Factors to be Considered in the Public Policy Discussion of Long-Term Care Financing

- Societal versus individual responsibilities
- Potential role of social insurance
- Role of the public sector in encouraging personal preparedness for the eventuality that long-term care will be needed
- Benefits, burdens, and costs of informal caregiving
- Balance of federal and state responsibilities to ensure adequate and equitable satisfaction of needs
- Effective and efficient implementation and administration of reforms
- Developing financially sustainable public commitments

Medicaid pays health care providers for rendering specified health-related services to specified groups of people who satisfy a financial means test. Federal rules entitle older and disabled people to Medicaid benefits if their incomes and assets are low enough to qualify them for the federal Supplemental Security Income cash assistance program. In addition, many states allow people to become eligible under a "medically needy" category if they "spend down" their income and assets on care. Title 19 requires that every state Medicaid program offer nursing home care among its basic services.

DISCUSSION QUESTIONS

1. Should it be legal for professional advisors to counsel clients on how to protect their assets while still qualifying in the future for Medicaid eligibility (i.e., on how to "look poor on paper") if long-term care is necessary? Wouldn't a legal restriction on such counseling act as an abridgment of the professional's First Amendment right to freedom of speech? See *New York State Bar Association v. Reno,* 999 F. Supp. 710 (N.D.N.Y. 1998).

2. Is such professional practice ethical? Is it ethical for the client to seek out and follow such advice? Is it ethical for the family who stands to inherit the client's assets to initiate and/or participate in the Medicaid estate planning process?

3. How widespread do you believe is the practice among wealthy or middle class older Americans of voluntary impoverishment for Medicaid eligibility purposes? Has Medicaid become an inheritance insurance program for the children and grandchildren of wealthy and middle class older Americans? Why would such a development be bad?

4. Is it good public policy for the federal government to require every state to implement a Medicaid estate recovery program? Why or why not? In their respective

estate recovery programs, should states adopt a narrow or broad definition of the deceased's "estate" from which financial recovery may be sought?

5. In deciding whether to use its discretion to waive or forgo estate recovery efforts in a particular case, what specific factors should a state Medicaid agency consider? How can the federal government prevent abuse of this discretion by a state?

6. If you have a client who is applying for Medicaid eligibility, is informed (as required by law) about the state's estate recovery program that will sell his property after his death to reimburse the state for its Medicaid expenditures made on his behalf, and says to you, "I cannot afford to pay for the long-term care I need now but I also really want to leave my house to my grandchildren as my legacy when I die," what do you advise that client to do?

7. Is it fair that Medicaid long-term care benefits are the only public health insurance or social welfare program subject to an estate recovery program? Why do Congress and the states treat Medicaid long-term care benefits uniquely in this regard?

8. For long-term care financing purposes, should we treat Medicaid as a social welfare program for the poor or as a middle-class entitlement program? What are the financial and behavioral ramifications of each approach? *See* Diane L. Dick, *Tax and Economic Policy Responses to the Medicaid Long-Term Care Financing Crisis: A Behavioral Economics Approach,* 5 Cardozo Pub. L. Pol'y & Ethics J. 379–423 (2007).

9. Do you agree with the quoted observation that, "If aspects of the [Medicaid] program must be cut, there is some logic to targeting asset transfer rules"?

10. Referring to Tables 5.5 and 5.6 and other ideas you have encountered, what would you change about

the current American system of financing long-term care? *See* Lawrence A. Frolik, *An Essay on the Need for Subsidized, Mandatory Long-Term Care Insurance,* 21 Notre Dame J.L. Ethics & Pub. Pol'y 517–535 (2007); Richard L. Kaplan, *Retirement Planning's Greatest Gap: Funding Long-Term Care,* 11 Lewis & Clark L. Rev. 407–450 (2007). For you, what are the most important ethical and policy considerations in arriving at an opinion on this matter? For further reading on the intricacies of health care and long-term care financing for the aged in the United States, *see* Lawrence A. Frolik, *The Law of Later-Life Health Care and Decision Making* (pp. 1–41, 93–154), Chicago: American Bar Association Publishing (2006); Lawrence A. Frolik & Richard L. Kaplan, *Elder Law in a Nutshell* (3rd ed., pp. 57–151, 157–158), St. Paul, MN: West Publishing (2003).

NOTES

Sections of this chapter were originally published in Marshall B. Kapp, *Consumer Direction in Long-Term Care: A Taxonomy of Legal Issues,* 24 Generations 16–21 (Fall 2000); Marshall B. Kapp, *Altering the Home Care Agency/Client Relationship: Notice Requirements,* 5(3) J. Long-Term Home Health Care 131–137 (Fall 2004); Marshall B. Kapp, *Consumer-Driven Long Term Care: Shaping the Government's Role,* 8(2) Marquette Elder's Advisor 199–214 (Spr. 2007); Marshall B. Kapp, *Nursing Home Reform Act, in* The Encyclopedia of Elder Care (2nd ed., pp. 563–564) (Elizabeth A. Capezuti et al., eds. 2008); Marshall B. Kapp, *Improving the Quality of Nursing Homes: Introduction to a Symposium on the Role of Regulation,* 26(1) J. Legal Med. 1–8 (March 2005); Marshall B. Kapp, *"At Least Mom Will Be Safe There": The Role of Resident Safety in Nursing Home Quality,* 12 Qual. & Safety in Health Care 201–204 (2003); Marshall B. Kapp, *Making Patient Safety and a "Homelike" Environment Compatible: A Challenge for Long Term Care Regulations,* 12 Widener L. Rev. 227–247 (2005); Marshall B. Kapp, *Resistance to Nursing Home Restraints Reduction Revisited: Introduction to a Symposium,* 20(3) J. Aging & Soc. Pol'y 279–285 (Summer 2008); Marshall B. Kapp, *The Nursing Home Crisis: Views from a Trustee in the Nonprofit Sector,* 4 J. Health Care L. & Pol'y 308–324 (2002); Marshall B. Kapp, *Medicaid*

Planning, Estate Recovery, and Alternatives for Long-Term Care Financing: Identifying the Ethical Issues, 7(2) Care Mgt J.: J. Long-Term Home Health Care 73–78 (2006); Marshall B. Kapp, *Family Caregivers' Legal Concerns,* 27(4) Generations 49–55 (Winter 2003–04); and Marshall B. Kapp, *Resident Safety and Medical Errors in Nursing Homes: Reporting and Disclosure in a Culture of Mutual Distrust,* 24(1) J. Legal Med. 51–76 (March 2003).

Older Individuals and the Right to Privacy

In the course of providing care, health care (and human services) professionals routinely learn very sensitive information about their patients. Professionals begin with a fiduciary, or trust, obligation to hold in confidence all intimate patient information entrusted to them. This ethical obligation, based on the patient's important interest in maintaining personal privacy and avoiding the social stigma and potential discrimination that a breach of one's medical privacy might entail, is enforced legally through civil damage suits based on both statutory and common law (judge-made precedent) and is embodied in the licensing provisions of virtually all state professional practice acts and accompanying regulations.

Federal regulations that became effective in 2003 (45 C.F.R. pts. 160 and 164) to implement the Health Insurance Portability and Accountability Act (HIPAA) of 1996 (Public Law No. 104-191, title XI, Part C) impose very specific requirements on covered health care entities and their business associates regarding the handling of personally identifiable medical information contained in patient records. These regulations impose severe criminal and civil sanctions for unauthorized disclosures of protected health information.

However, there are numerous exceptions to the general confidentiality rule and the state and federal statutes supplementing it (see Table 6.1). One exception occurs when a patient voluntarily and knowingly waives, or gives up, the right to confidentiality of particular information. Such waivers are done daily to make information available to third-party payers

Table 6.1 Exceptions to the General Confidentiality Requirement

Patient waiver of confidentiality
Danger to innocent third parties
Mandatory reporting laws
Legal process (court order)
Sharing information among health care team members

(e.g., Medicare claims processors and private health insurers), quality of care auditors (such as surveyors of the Joint Commission on Accreditation of Healthcare Organizations), and other public and private entities (like health care proxies authorized to make medical decisions under a patient's durable power of attorney). In addition, the usual confidentiality obligation may be outweighed in circumstances of jeopardy to innocent, vulnerable third parties, which happens when a patient with serious sensory or cognitive impairments insists on driving a motor vehicle or a dangerous psychiatric patient threatens to harm a specific victim and appears to have the present ability to carry out that threat. State statutory and case law varies regarding the health care provider's obligation to report a believable threat of harm to public health or law enforcement authorities.

The patient's expectation of privacy must yield when the health care provider is mandated by state statute to report to specified public health or law enforcement authorities the health care provider's reasonable suspicion that certain conditions or activities (e.g., elder mistreatment or neglect [*see* Chapter 8], domestic violence, infectious diseases, births, and deaths) are present or have occurred. Mandatory reporting statutes embody the state's exercise of its inherent police power to protect the general health, safety, welfare, and morals or its *parens patriae* authority to protect individuals (such as severely cognitively or emotionally impaired persons) who are not capable of protecting themselves.

Further, a health care professional may be compelled to reveal otherwise confidential information about particular patients by the force of legal process, that is, by a judge's issuance of a court order requiring such release. This is a possibility in any lawsuit involving a factual dispute about a patient's physical or mental condition. A court order (as opposed to a subpoena or subpoena *duces tecum,* which are issued simply as an administrative matter by the court clerk rather than by a judge) compelling one to produce personally identifiable patient information may overrule the state's provider–patient testimonial privilege statute. Every testimonial privilege statute provides for court-compelled testimony by the health care provider when, for instance, the patient has placed his or her own health condition and medical treatment in issue in a lawsuit.

Because the modern delivery of health care frequently is a team endeavor, each patient implicitly gives permission for the sharing of certain otherwise private information among the members of the treatment team. Information sharing of this nature is essential to optimal care. However, only information that is directly relevant and necessary to facilitate the contribution of each team member should be available to the various team members. Moreover, each team member who is privy to identifiable patient information is bound fully by all applicable legal and ethical constraints on the inappropriate revelation of such information.

ORGANIZATIONAL PRINCIPLES

The American Medical Association (AMA)'s Principles of Medical Ethics provide the following:

> *A physician shall respect the rights of patients, of colleagues, and of other health professionals, and shall safeguard patient confidences within the constraints of the law.... The patient has the right to confidentiality. The physician should not reveal confidential communications or information without the consent of the patient, unless provided for by law or by the need to protect the welfare of the individual or the public interest.*

The American Nurses Association's Code for Nurses With Interpretive Statements § 3.2 provides the following:

> *Associated with the right to privacy, the nurse has a duty to maintain confidentiality of all patient information. The patient's well-being could be jeopardized and the fundamental trust between patient and nurse destroyed by unnecessary access to data or by the inappropriate disclosure of identifiable patient information. The rights, well-being, and safety of the individual patient should be*

the primary factors in any professional judgment concerning the disposition of confidential information received from or about the patient, whether oral, written, or electronic. The standard of nursing practice and the nurse's responsibility to provide quality care require that relevant data be shared with those members of the health care team who have a need to know. Only information pertinent to a patient's treatment and welfare is disclosed, and only to those directly involved with the patient's care. Duties of confidentiality, however, are not absolute and may need to be modified in order to protect the patient, other innocent parties and in circumstances of mandatory disclosure for public health reasons.

The National Association of Social Workers' Code of Ethics § 1.07 (a) provides the following:

Social workers should respect clients' right to privacy. Social workers should not solicit private information from clients unless it is essential to providing services or conducting social work evaluation or research. Once private information is shared, standards of confidentiality apply.

And finally, the American Psychological Association's Ethical Principles of Psychologists and Code of Conduct § 4.01 provides the following:

Psychologists have a primary obligation and take reasonable precautions to respect the confidentiality rights of those with whom they work or consult, recognizing that confidentiality may be established by law, institutional rules, or professional or scientific relationships.

STATE PRACTICE ACTS

Many state professional practice acts impose a duty of confidentiality. For instance, the Illinois Medical Practice Act, 225 ILCS 60/22, provides as follows:

(A) The [state] may revoke, suspend, place on probationary status, or take any other disciplinary action as [it] may deem proper with regard to the license...of any person issued under this Act to practice

DISCUSSION QUESTIONS

1. What are the rationales for imposing on a health, human services, or financial services professional a duty of confidentiality toward patients or clients? Are these rationales valid, in both theory and practice?

2. Do these rationales apply more or less forcefully when older individuals are involved? Why?

3. Why do we impose more demanding confidentiality duties on health care, human services, and financial services professionals than we do on members of other occupations, like hairdressers, electricians, and grocers?

4. Do you agree that unless there is an applicable exception violation of confidentiality should be the basis for professional discipline? Should it be the basis for civil liability in private lawsuits brought by patients or clients? Should the plaintiff be required to demonstrate tangible damage or injury?

5. When older patients waive, to obtain third-party payment of their medical expenses or for other reasons, their rights to have their medical information kept confidential, are they usually really making a voluntary and knowing choice?

6. Do you agree that the older patient's right to confidentiality of medical information needs to yield if the patient's medical condition threatens another person? In such circumstances, should we require health care professionals to come forward and disclose the threat (and, if so, to whom) or should we rely on voluntary reports we encourage health care professionals to make by giving them legal immunity for their good faith disclosures? Should we recognize any exceptions to this exception to the general confidentiality rule? What do you think about the wisdom of requiring, encouraging, or at least permitting (by providing legal immunity) the breach of an older patient's medical privacy not to protect an endangered third party, but rather to protect the older patient himself or herself?

medicine...upon any of the following grounds: (30) Willfully or negligently violating the confidentiality between physician and patient except as required by law.

Exercise

Ms. L is a 79-year-old unmarried woman who has been living in a nursing home for 3 years. She was admitted by her nieces, who stated she could not live alone any longer because of her progressive forgetfulness. She is ambulatory and appears alert but for the past year has been unable to speak. Recently, she seems to have developed a relationship with one of the few male residents, Mr. C. Mr. C is married to a wife who lives in an assisted living facility in a different part of town. Mr. C is alert and without cognitive deficits but needs to ambulate by wheelchair because of a stroke that has left him paralyzed on one side. Ms. L and Mr. C are often observed sitting together in the dining room after meals or in the nursing home common room, and several times she has appeared to be fondling him.

At first, the staff responded by nonchalantly moving Mr. C away from Ms. L. Staff did not confront either resident with what they thought they had observed. A few weeks later, though, they found Ms. L in Mr. C's bed, where they were attempting sexual relations. This bothers the nurse's aide who discovered them, both because Mr. C is married and Ms. L has significant dementia. Ms. L was taken from the room, and a social worker was assigned to speak with Mr. C. Mr. C indicates he does not know how the relationship commenced. Ms. L has sought him out, but he welcomes her advances. He is not bothered by Ms. L's mental deficits or by the fact (which he remembers) that he is still married. However, he states that he does not want his wife told about his trysts with Ms. L.

When the attending physician is informed about this situation, he recalls a conversation he had with Ms. L many years before when he cared for her in the community before she was admitted to the nursing home. In that conversation, he recalls, Ms. L told him she had worked for several years in her youth as a prostitute in Alaska. The physician had decided not to put that information in Ms. L's medical record.

Should the nursing facility permit Ms. L and Mr. C to continue their amorous activities? Should someone notify Mr. C's wife? Why or why not? If she should be notified, who should handle the contact and what should she be told? Should the physician say or do anything regarding Ms. L's (somewhat ancient) history as a prostitute? If so, what should be said and/or done about this information? Answer these questions first from an ethical perspective and then from a risk management perspective.

REPORTING MEDICAL CONDITIONS

Some states impose mandatory reporting requirements that would pertain when an older person's medical condition poses a threat to the health and safety of other persons. For example, a number of states, either by statute or regulation or as a matter of common law, have spoken to the reporting obligations of a physician when a patient's driving abilities have become impaired by neurodegenerative illness or sensory impairment. Some states expressly mandate physicians to report to drivers' licensing authorities any medical condition that might be hazardous to driving. California Health and Safety Code § 103900(a), for example, provides as follows:

> *Every physician and surgeon shall report immediately to the local health officer in writing the name, date of birth, and address of every patient at least 14 years of age and older whom the physician and surgeon has diagnosed as having a case of a disorder*

characterized by lapses in consciousness. However, if a physician and surgeon reasonably and in good faith believes that the reporting of a patient will serve the public interest, he or she may report a patient's condition even if it may not be required under the department's definition of disorders characterized by lapses of consciousness... .

The AMA Code of Medical Ethics § 2.24, Impaired Drivers and Their Physicians, provides the following:

The purpose of this report is to articulate physicians' responsibility to recognize impairments in patients' driving ability that pose a strong threat to public safety and which ultimately may need to be reported to the Department of Motor Vehicles. It does not address the reporting of medical information for the purpose of punishment or criminal prosecution.

1. Physicians should assess patients' physical or mental impairments that might adversely affect driving abilities. Each case must be evaluated individually since not all impairments may give rise to an obligation on the part of the physician. Nor may all physicians be in a position to evaluate the extent or the effect of an impairment (e.g., physicians who treat patients on a short-term basis). In making evaluations, physicians should consider the following factors:

> *a) the physician must be able to identify and document physical or mental impairments that clearly relate to the ability to drive;*
> *b) the driver must pose a clear risk to public safety.*

2. Before reporting, there are a number of initial steps physicians should take. A tactful but candid discussion with the patient and family about the risks of driving is of primary importance. Depending on the patient's medical condition, the physician may suggest to the patient that he or she seek further treatment, such as substance abuse treatment or occupational therapy. Physicians also may encourage the patient and the family to decide on a restricted driving schedule. Efforts made by physicians to inform patients and their families, advise them of their options, and negotiate a workable plan may render reporting unnecessary.

3. Physicians should use their best judgment when determining when to report impairments that could limit a patient's ability to drive safely. In situations where clear evidence of substantial driving impairment implies a strong threat to patient and public safety, and where the physician's advice to discontinue driving privileges is ignored, it is desirable and ethical to notify the Department of Motor Vehicles.

4. The physician's role is to report medical conditions that would impair safe driving as dictated by his or her state's mandatory reporting laws and standards of medical practice. The determination of the inability to drive safely should be made by the state's Department of Motor Vehicles.

5. Physicians should disclose and explain to their patients this responsibility to report.

6. Physicians should protect patient confidentiality by ensuring that only the minimal amount of information is reported and that reasonable security measures are used in handling that information.

7. Physicians should work with their state medical societies to create statutes that uphold the best interests of patients and community, and that safeguard physicians from liability when reporting in good faith.

The AMA and the National Highway Traffic Safety Administration published a *Physician's Guide to Assessing and Counseling Older Drivers* (2003). In the section entitled "Putting It All Together," the *Guide* states the following:

With these competing legal and ethical duties, how can you fulfill them while legally protecting yourself? In this section, we provide recommendations for achieving this balance.

Counsel your patient.

Patients should be advised of medical conditions, procedures and medications that may impair driving performance. (A reference list of medical conditions and medications, with recommendations for each one, can be found [in this Guide]. Recommend driving cessation as needed.

You should recommend that a patient retire from driving if you believe that the patient's driving is unsafe and cannot be made safe by any available medical treatment, adaptive device, or adaptive technique. As always, base your clinical judgment on the patient's function rather than age, race, or gender.

Know and comply with your state's reporting laws.

You must know and comply with your state's reporting laws [listed in the Guide]. If you fail to follow these laws, you may be liable for patient and third-party injuries. If your state has a mandatory medical reporting law [delineating specific medical conditions], report the required medical condition(s) using the DMV's [Department of Motor Vehicle's] official form. If your state has a physician reporting law [requiring the reporting of "unsafe" drivers], submit your report using the DMV's official form and/or any other reporting guidelines. If the DMV's guidelines do not state what patient information must be reported, provide only the minimum of information required to support your case.

Reduce the impact of breaching patient confidentiality.

In adhering to your state's reporting laws, you may find it necessary to breach your patient's confidentiality. However, you can do several things to reduce the impact of breaching confidentiality on the patient-physician relationship. Before reporting your patient to the DMV, tell your patient what you are about to do. Explain that it is your legal responsibility to refer him/her to the state DMV, and describe what kind of follow-up he/she can expect from the DMV. Assure your patient that out of respect for his/her privacy, you will disclose only the minimum of information required and hold all other information confidential. Even in states that offer anonymous reporting, it is a good idea to be open with your patients. When submitting your report, provide only the information required. Consider giving your patient a copy of his/her report. By providing your patients with as much information as possible, you can involve them in the process and give them a greater sense of control. Before contacting your patient's family members and caregivers, request the patient's permission to speak with these parties. If your patient maintains decision-making capacity and denies permission for you to speak with these parties, you must respect the patient's wishes.

Document thoroughly.
Through documentation, you provide evidence of your efforts to assess and maintain your patient's driving safety. In the event of a patient or third-party crash injury, thorough documentation may protect you against a lawsuit. To protect yourself legally, you should document your efforts, conversations, recommendations, and any referrals for further testing in the patient's chart. [Documentation should include the following:]

—Any direct observations of functional deficits, red flags, or crash-related injuries that lead you to believe that your patient may be at risk for medically impaired driving.
—Any counseling specific to driving (e.g., documenting that the patient is aware of the warning signs of hypoglycemia and its effects on driving performance).
—Formal assessment of your patient's function ... .
—Any medical interventions and referrals you have made to improve the patient's function and any repeat testing to measure improvement.
—A copy of the driver rehabilitation specialist (DRS) report, if the patient has undergone driver assessment and/or rehabilitation.
—Your recommendation that the patient continue driving or cease driving. If you recommend that the patient cease driving, include a summary of your interventions (e.g., 'discussed driving retirement with patient and sent letter to reinforce recommendation,' 'discussed transportation options and gave copy of [pertinent literature],' 'contacted family members with patient's permission,' and 'reported patient to DMV with patient's knowledge.'). Include copies of any written correspondence in the chart.
—Follow-up for degree of success in utilizing alternative transportation options and any signs of social isolation and depression. Document any further interventions, including referral to a social worker, geriatric care manager, or mental health professional.

Exercise

Mr. S is a 79-year-old bachelor who is being treated by a family medicine physician for hypertension. Mr. S tolerates the medications without any serious side effects and is in generally good health, except that he has suffered progressive vision loss and been told by his ophthalmologist that he has macular degeneration. His visual acuity is 20/200 in the right eye and 20/80 in the left.

Mr. S lives by himself in a suburban area. A neighbor of Mr. S who is a patient of Mr. S's family physician confided to the physician that she (the neighbor) worries about safety when she sees Mr. S driving down the street. At Mr. S's next regular visit, the physician inquired about the patient's driving. Mr. S expressed no concern about this, stating that he always drove "real careful" and is much more attentive to his driving than all the teenage "whippersnappers" who cruise around his neighborhood.

What legal duties and liabilities, if any, does the physician have regarding Mr. S's driving? Would it make any difference if Mr. S had dementia, alcoholism, syncope, or some other malady rather than macular degeneration? Why is Mr. S so insistent on continuing to drive his car? What kind of compromise plan might be worked out in response to this situation?

Every state has enacted various testimonial privilege statutes. For example, Ohio Rev. Code § 2317.02 provides as follows:

> *The following persons shall not testify [in a legal proceeding] in certain respects:*
> *(A) An attorney, concerning a communication made to the attorney by a client in that relation or the attorney's advice to a client....*
> *(B) A physician or a dentist concerning a communication made to the physician or dentist by a patient in that relation or the physician's or dentist's advice to a patient....*

DISCUSSION QUESTIONS

1. When may a court direct a professional to testify about a patient's/client's communication despite the existence of a testimonial privilege statute in the jurisdiction? When the patient/client has placed issues pertaining to his or her health or care in issue in the litigation? When the communication to the professional was done in the presence of a third party (and therefore made without a reasonable expectation of privacy) or the public welfare need for the information outweighs the individual's right to confidentiality in the particular case?

2. What kinds of safeguards can institutions and agencies put into place to allow for appropriate sharing of patient/client information among involved team members while ensuring that inappropriate release to others does not happen?

(C) A member of the clergy, rabbi, priest, or regularly ordained, accredited, or licensed minister of an established and legally cognizable church, denomination, or sect...concerning a confession made, or any information confidentially communicated, to the member of the clergy, rabbi, priest, or minister for a religious counseling purpose in the member of the clergy's, rabbi's, priest's, or minister's professional character....

FAMILY CAREGIVING AND CONFIDENTIALITY

The question of decision-making authority and family caregiving has parallel ramifications for the handling of access to, and confidentiality of, medical (and other) information concerning the care recipient. Improper disclosure of client-specific information to a third party without either prior authorization by the client (i.e., a waiver of confidentiality rights) or a guardianship/conservatorship order judicially appointing the third party to act as decision maker for the incapacitated client theoretically violates a formal caregiver's common-law confidentiality duties and pertinent professional code of ethics. In a real-world home environment in which the family is intimately involved in providing care, there is no practical way to keep information about the client away from the family caregivers. They can readily monitor and control the flow of communication among the dependent individual, formal caregivers, and the rest of the universe, as well as the release of information about the client to third parties. Families legitimately need adequate information to provide proper care, besides requiring such information to knowledgeably fulfill their role in making or influencing key decisions. Health and human service professionals arguably would be negligent in withholding relevant information from the family if the ignorance thus imposed threatened the family's caregiving performance and hence placed the client at avoidable risk.

Complicating the confidentiality issue is the set of federal regulations (45 Code of Federal Regulations Parts 160 and 164) that became effective on April 14, 2003 to implement the medical privacy provisions of HIPAA. These regulations impose significant restrictions and documentation requirements on health care providers, among others, regarding the release of identifiable medical information to persons or entities other than the patient. The regulations allow limited exceptions when information transmittal is necessary for purposes of treatment coordination, payment, or health care operations. The extent to which the HIPAA regulations affect how health care providers share medical information with family caregivers, absent explicit authorization to do so either from a client capable of making decisions or a court, remains to be seen. The practical parameters of HIPAA will be incrementally developed and delineated through litigation and, perhaps, the promulgation of further regulatory guidance.

ADDITIONAL INFORMATION SOURCES

www.privacyrights.org
www.healthprivacy.org
www.patientprivacyrights.org
www.worldprivacyforum.org

DISCUSSION QUESTIONS

1. Do you agree that "[h]ealth and human service professionals arguably would be negligent in withholding relevant information from the family"? *See* Lynn A. Jansen & Lainie F. Ross, *Patient Confidentiality and the Surrogate's Right to Know*, 28 J. L., Med. & Ethics 137–142 (2000). What is the standard of care regarding confidentiality in the home care setting? How would you finesse this set of issues?

2. Do you believe "the promulgation of further regulatory guidance" in this sphere would be helpful? What would such further regulatory guidance say?

Exercise

Mrs. K is an 82-year-old woman with congestive heart problems and arthritis. She was physically abused by her daughter, with whom she was living, and contacted the local Adult Protective Services (APS) agency for help. The case manager arranged admission to a group home. Mrs. K first needed to undergo an examination by a physician, who noticed her bruises and asked for details. The case manager wanted to contact Mrs. K's known relatives other than the abusive daughter, and a couple of family members contacted the case manager at their own initiative. A local elder advocacy organization was contacted by one of Mrs. K's relatives and wanted to get involved in protecting her. The group home staff noticed all the activity surrounding Mrs. K and wanted information. The different interested parties had differing opinions regarding Mrs. K's decisional capacity.

In doing her job, what privacy considerations must the APS case manager take into account? Whose privacy rights are implicated, and what circumstances would justify infringing on those rights? Does respect for privacy in cases like this one promote or hinder the best interests of older individuals like Mrs. K?

NOTES

Sections of this chapter were originally published in Marshall B. Kapp, Confidentiality, *Encyclopedia of Aging and Public Health* (Sana Loue & Martha Sajatovic, eds.), New York: Springer Science+Business Media (2008), and Marshall B. Kapp, *Family Caregivers' Legal Concerns*, 27(4) Generations 49–55 (Winter 2003–04).

CHAPTER 7

Research Participation and Older Persons

REGULATORY OVERVIEW

The conduct of biomedical and behavioral research involving the use of human beings as participants may be relevant to professionals working in the field of aging in a variety of ways. Gerontologists and geriatricians may act as researchers themselves, as treating professionals of patients or clients who are participants in or candidates for research protocols, or as clinicians who rely on an understanding of the reported results of research to formulate their treatment strategies for particular patients. The extensive system of legal oversight in this sphere may exert important influences on the responsibilities and prerogatives of gerontologists and geriatricians functioning in each of these distinct but overlapping roles.

The historical background leading up to the present state of government command and control regulation of biomedical and behavioral research involving human subjects has been amply recorded elsewhere. Beginning with the Nuremberg Code, adopted in 1947 for use in Nazi war-crimes trials in which defendant physicians tried to justify their atrocities under the guise of scientific experimentation, principles determining the proper conduct of research involving human participants have been formalized into over 30 different international guidelines and ethical codes.

In the United States, Congress in 1974 enacted the National Research Act, establishing the National Commission for the Protection of Human Subjects in Biomedical and Behavioral Research (popularly titled the

Belmont Commission). In 1981, final regulations embodying some of the Commission's recommendations were issued by the federal Department of Health and Human Services (DHHS; at that time, the Department of Health, Education and Welfare).

These regulations originally applied only to research involving human participants that was conducted by the DHHS itself or was funded in whole or in part by DHHS. Most institutions conducting research, however, have now agreed to apply the federal regulations to all of their research protocols regardless of the funding source for a particular study. In addition, other federal agencies have adopted the DHHS regulations as a Common Rule to protect human participants in any research protocol that those agencies sponsor. Research involving the testing of investigational drugs or medical devices is concurrently regulated by the federal Food and Drug Administration (FDA); the Common Rule and FDA requirements overlap considerably but are not identical.

As defined in federal regulations, "research means a systematic investigation...designed to develop or contribute to generalizable knowledge." Thus research is different from usual diagnostic and therapeutic medical practice, which consists of interventions designed solely to enhance the well-being of an individual patient and that have a reasonable expectation of success. Research is also distinguishable from the "off-label" prescribing of a drug for a patient (i.e., prescribing a drug that has been approved by the FDA for one specific purpose for a different, nonapproved purpose) because off-label prescribing is done for the particular patient's benefit rather than to collect data as part of a study.

Research to which the federal Common Rule applies must be reviewed and approved by a local institutional review board (IRB) and is thereafter subject to continuing IRB review. IRB approval is necessary initially and at least annually afterward. An IRB must have at least five members of varying backgrounds; at least one must be from a nonscientific area and at least one must be unaffiliated with the institution sponsoring the IRB.

To approve a protocol, the IRB must determine that each of the following requirements is satisfied:

1. Physical and psychologic risks to subjects are minimized.
2. Physical and psychologic risks to subjects are reasonable in relation to anticipated benefits to those subjects and to the importance of the general knowledge that may reasonably be expected to result.

This is arguably (and intentionally) an exercise in paternalism because the IRB is deciding *for* individuals what is in their best interests.

3. Selection of subjects is equitable.
4. Informed consent will be obtained. Potential participants must be informed of the following:

   a. The purposes of the research, its expected duration, and the experimental procedures
   b. The anticipated risks/discomforts and benefits of participation and the reasonable alternatives to participation in the research protocol
   c. The extent to which research records are confidential
   d. Any compensation and/or treatment for research-related injuries
   e. The right not to participate and the right to discontinue participation at any time without penalty

5. Informed consent will be appropriately documented.
6. When appropriate, the research plan makes adequate provisions for monitoring the data collected to ensure the safety of subjects.
7. When appropriate, there are adequate provisions to protect the privacy of subjects and maintain the confidentiality of data.

The IRB must police the requirement that no human subject is involved in research unless legally effective informed consent has been obtained and "only under circumstances that provide the prospective subject... sufficient opportunity to consider whether or not to participate and that minimize the possibility of coercion or undue influence." The regulatory provisions for informed consent in research are basically a codification and extension of the common law that was developed in the therapeutic setting (see Chapter 2). In both the therapeutic and research contexts, "patients cannot participate in decision making to their desired extent unless they have the right types of information, given in ways optimal for their own level of understanding."

Local IRBs themselves are monitored by the Office for Human Research Protections (formerly the Office of Protection from Research Risks), which is located in the Office of the Secretary, DHHS. The Office for Human Research Protections may award an IRB either a single project assurance, which allows the IRB to review a single study, or a multiple project assurance, which allows the IRB to review any number of studies over a multiple-year period.

In 2001 the Institute of Medicine of the National Academy of Sciences issued a report recommending the establishment of a formal system for accrediting human-research participant protection programs. The Association for the Accreditation of Human Research Protection Programs established and operates such an accreditation system.

Some states have also enacted their own laws concerning conditions for protection of research participants, requiring some manner of prior review and supervision. The precise content of these state statutes varies significantly. In addition, private civil lawsuits may be brought by an individual participant against researchers and protocol sponsors for violation of common-law tort standards of care in the conduct of research involving that participant; in essence, the patient may sue the researchers and sponsors for medical malpractice. Further, federal constitutional protections predicated on an individual's Fourteenth Amendment right to due process and equal protection of the laws and the Eighth Amendment's prohibition against cruel and unusual punishment may be applicable to potential participants in research conducted or sponsored by government agencies.

Participation in many gerontological/geriatric research protocols takes place over a substantial duration of time, during which a participant holds an absolute right to withdraw. The investigator not only owes a legal obligation to ensure that a participant's initial agreement to enroll in the study is valid but also is expected to monitor the continuing voluntariness, knowledge base, and mental capacity of the participant's ongoing (although ordinarily implicit rather than explicit) consent to remain in the study as it progresses. Maintaining the legitimacy of a participant's ongoing consent imposes an obligation on the investigator to provide continual feedback to participants about unfolding positive and negative results of the study and other information as it becomes available that might be material to (i.e., that might affect) a reasonably prudent participant's choice to continue in or to withdraw from the protocol.

Also, because the decisional capacity of a participant in gerontological/ geriatric research may become substantially impaired over the course of time, the researcher is responsible for continually (although usually informally) assessing the participant's present capacity to consent to ongoing participation in the protocol and for looking to a surrogate decision maker when the participant can no longer make legally valid choices. Federal research regulations defer to applicable state laws to delineate the role of surrogate decision makers in the research context; with only a few exceptions, state statutes, regulations, and common law provide little specific guidance on this point. One approach to planning for a decline in the participant's decisional capacity over the course of a research protocol may be for the investigator and/or attending physician to encourage the participant, while still capable, to execute a durable power of attorney, specifically designating some other person to act as the participant's agent in the future regarding decisions about enrollment and continued participation in the research protocol.

Some acute medical conditions, such as cardiac arrest, stroke, or major trauma, may make it impossible for the individual to give informed consent to participation in research aimed at learning more about the treatment of the very emergency condition. Federal law contains special provisions regarding exceptions to informed consent in such emergency research situations. *See* Henry Halperin et al., *Recommendations for Implementation of Community Consultation and Public Disclosure Under the Food and Drug Administration's "Exception from Informed Consent Requirements for Emergency Research,"* 116 Circulation 1855–1863 (2007).

Regulations promulgated by DHHS under the medical privacy provisions of the Health Insurance Portability and Accountability Act (HIPAA) of 1996 impose substantial restraints on the use and disclosure of medical information, even for legitimate research purposes. The rule requires specific written permission (authorization) from a patient to use or disclose "protected health information" about that person for nonroutine purposes such as research. Protected health information is defined as any "individually identifiable health information" transmitted or maintained by a covered entity (e.g., a health plan, data processing firm, or health care provider). One particular form of written authorization is required for clinical trials, whereas a different document is necessary for research involving a person's medical records. The authorization must specify the protected health information to be used or disclosed, who may receive it, how it may be used, and when the authorization expires. In addition, the document must (1) give notice of the patient/subject's right to revoke the authorization and to inspect his or her medical records, (2) indicate whether the covered entity receives compensation for disclosing the information, (3) refer to the entity's detailed notice of practices with respect to privacy (which must be provided on request), and (4) warn that once disclosed for research, the person's medical information may no longer be protected under the HIPAA rule.

DISCUSSION QUESTIONS

1. What are the ethical principles behind the legal regulation of research involving human subjects? See Ezekiel J. Emanuel et al., *What Makes Clinical Research Ethical?* 283(20) J. Am. Med. Ass'n 2701–2711 (2000). Why do we even need to conduct research involving human participants at all? See Steven M. Grunberg & William T. Cefalu, *The Integral Role of Clinical Research in Clinical Care,* 348(14) N. Eng. J. Med. 1386–1388 (2003). If we do need to conduct such research, have we gone overboard in regulating its conduct? *See* Norman Fost & Robert J. Levine, *The Dysregulation of Human Subjects Research,* 298 J. Am. Med. Ass'n 2196–2198 (2007); C. K. Gunsalus, *The Nanny State Meets the Inner Lawyer: Overregulating While Underprotecting Human Participants in Research,* 14(4) Ethics & Behav. 369–382 (2004).

2. FDA guidance recommends that drug sponsors include older persons in clinical drug trials, and FDA regulations require that drug sponsors report clinical drug trial data by age. Agency guidance recommends that drug sponsors avoid excluding persons from research participation on the basis of advanced age. Do you agree with the following rationale?

Assessing whether a drug is safe and effective for use by elderly persons requires that a sufficient number of elderly persons be included in clinical drug trials. As the number of elderly participants in clinical drug trials increases, the ability of drug sponsors to detect responses unique to elderly persons for a given safety or effectiveness outcome also increases. Failing to include sufficient numbers of elderly persons in clinical drug trials may make it less likely that safety concerns and effectiveness outcomes unique to elderly persons will be detected during the clinical drug trials. U.S. Government Accountability Office, Prescription Drugs: FDA Guidance and Regulations Related to Data on Elderly Persons in Clinical Drug Trials, *GAO-07-47R (2007).*

3. How does "research" covered by federal regulations differ from therapy? From "experimentation"? Many individuals do not understand the significant distinctions between research and therapy and therefore—often grasping at any thread of hope—engage in the "therapeutic misconception" that research protocols undertaken to collect data from which generalizable conclusions may be drawn are really primarily treatments intended and expected to therapeutically benefit the particular participants. How can the therapeutic misconception be avoided or at least minimized? Why is this problem important? *See* Gail E. Henderson et al., *Clinical Trials and Medical Care: Defining the Therapeutic Misconception,* 4 Plos Med. 1735–1738 (2007), *available at* www.plosmedicine.org; Paul S. Appelbaum et al., *Therapeutic Misconception in Clinical Research: Frequency and Risk Factors,* 26(2) IRB: Ethics & Hum. Resrch. 1–8 (2004).

4. Despite the regulatory and common law informed consent requirements, is it not true that an older person's treating clinicians usually can convince the individual to enroll in almost any research study? How should we

safeguard against clinicians' proper ability to influence their older patients/clients from becoming undue duress or coercion? *See* Donna T. Chen et al., *Clinical Research and the Physician-Patient Relationship*, 138(8) Annals Intern. Med. 669–672 (2003).

5. What professional or personal backgrounds would make individuals ideal members of an IRB reviewing research protocols involving older persons? What special training should IRBs receive to prepare them to review such protocols?

6. Is it appropriate for an IRB to disapprove a research application because the IRB believes that participation would not be in the best interests of potential human subjects? Is this good or bad paternalism?

7. Does your state have its own specific statutes and/or regulations regarding the protection of human research participants?

8. Do you believe IRBs spend too much time and energy on parsing the wording of written consent forms submitted as part of the research protocols being reviewed? How should IRBs allocate the bulk of their time and energy?

9. Do you believe the HIPAA Privacy Rule is necessary to protect the privacy of human research subjects? Is it adequate? Is it actually counterproductive in the sense of discouraging or impeding the conduct of valuable research? *See* Roberta B. Ness for the Joint Policy Committee, Societies of Epidemiology, *Influence of the HIPAA Privacy Rule on Health Research*, 298 J. Am. Med. Ass'n 2164–2170 (2007); David Shalowitz & David Wendler, *Informed Consent for Research and Authorization Under the Health Insurance Portability and Accountability Act Privacy Rule: An Integrated Approach*, 144(9) Annals Intern. Med. 685–688 (2006). Do you believe older persons value their medical privacy more or less than younger people do?

10. An interesting recent wrinkle is the recent trend of pharmaceutical companies hiring private contract research organizations (CROs) to take over much of academia's traditional role in conducting the clinical trials aspect of drug development. "The nature and extent of regulators' authority over CROs, however, are uncertain, according to the Director of the Office of Critical Path Programs at the FDA. CROs are accountable to the FDA, said [the Director], but 'it's not clear whether their accountability is through the sponsor or directly to us.'" Miriam Shuchman, *Commercializing Clinical Trials—Risks and Benefits of the CRO Boom,* 357 N. Eng. J. Med. 1365 (2007). Is the growing commercialization of clinical trials in the best interests of science, the public, and older human research participants?

DECISIONAL CAPACITY AND RESEARCH PARTICIPATION

Because participation in research protocols, no less than in the diagnostic or therapeutic context, ordinarily requires the voluntary, informed, and competent consent of each participant, there is a general ethical consensus that, whenever feasible, researchers should enroll only those participants who themselves are able to give or deny consent to participation. In other words, individuals with seriously compromised decisional capacity should be considered for recruitment only for those research protocols that are devoted to studying problems specific to the decisionally compromised population.

The disproportionate prevalence of dementias and other severe mental disabilities among the elderly presents a legal and ethical dilemma when research does specifically address the problems of the cognitively and emotionally impaired. On the one hand, progress in developing effective treatments and cures for medical and psychological problems associated with dementia requires that research projects be done in which individuals suffering from the exact problems of interest be the basic units of study. At the same time, paradoxically, those very problems that qualify an individual for eligibility as a subject in such a research project often make it impossible for that person to engage in a rational and autonomous decision-making process about his or her own participation as a research subject. This irony is made more difficult by the fact that research participants generally are more vulnerable to possible exploitation and therefore need even more protection than patients in therapeutic situations because of, among other things, the researchers' potential conflicts of interest.

A number of alternative mechanisms for proxy decision making in the research context are possible. These devices include a durable power of attorney for research participation, reliance on family consent statutes, informal resort to available family members as surrogate decision makers, guardianship with specific authorization for research decisions, explicit prior court orders authorizing the incapacitated subject's participation in research protocols on a case-by-case basis, an independent patient advocate supplied by the organization sponsoring the research or by a government agency, and selection of a surrogate by the IRB or a long-term care facility's resident council.

In making decisions about whether to enroll a decisionally incapacitated elder in a biomedical or behavioral research protocol, a proxy ideally is guided by the substituted judgment standard, which entails knowing or being able to reasonably infer whether the incapacitated person him- or herself would have elected to participate, if that person were now able to make and express his or her own autonomous choice. When applying the substituted judgment standard is not reasonably feasible, because there is no realistic way to know or infer what the incapacitated individual would authentically desire regarding enrollment in a particular research protocol, rather than engaging in unbridled speculation about those desires, the proxy should perform a best interests analysis. In determining the incapacitated person's best interests regarding possible research participation, the proxy should take into account (among other things) the ratio of likely burdens or risks for the research participant versus the possible benefits to that person and others now and in the future emanating from the research findings.

Some have suggested that special procedural safeguards are necessary to protect vulnerable, cognitively impaired human volunteers from injury due to research participation. These safeguards might encompass heightened IRB involvement in the protocol approval process; enhanced IRB activity in the ongoing monitoring and supervision phase of the research, including serving as a forum for appeals and objections by participants or investigators; and requiring individual participant assent (that is, giving participants a veto power) even when informed proxy consent to research participation has been obtained. An important question, especially because the participants of interest are mentally impaired, concerns the definition of assent to be used, namely, whether the failure to actively object to participation in a protocol is enough to be interpreted as an implied form of assent, or whether some more positive manifestation of agreement is necessary.

DISCUSSION QUESTIONS

1. Do the helping professions and the larger society have an ethical obligation to conduct research in which older individuals with compromised decisional capacity are enrolled? Couldn't we avoid many ethical and legal problems by just not doing such research? *See* Rebecca Dresser, *Mentally Disabled Research Subjects: The Enduring Policy Issues,* 276(1) J. Am. Med. Ass'n 67–72 (1996); Jason H.T. Karlawish, *Research Involving Cognitively Impaired Adults,* 348(14) N. Eng. J. Med. 1389–1392 (2003).

2. Does a diagnosis of cognitive and/or emotional impairment *per se* equal decisional incapacity regarding research participation? If not, why not? What other factors ought to be taken into account in determining whether some form of proxy decision making is needed? *See* Bruce J. Winick & Kenneth W. Goodman, *A Therapeutic Jurisprudence Perspective on Participation in Research by Subjects With Reduced Capacity to Consent,* 24(4) Behav.

Sci. & L. 485–494 (2006). How valuable are formal, uniform instruments in assessing decisional capacity for participation in research protocols, in terms of ease of administration and interpretation, internal consistency, interrater reliability, validity, and acceptable sensitivity (not too many false negatives) and specificity (not too many false positives)? *See* Dilip V. Jeste et al., *A New Brief Instrument for Assessing Decisional Capacity for Clinical Research,* 64 Arch. Gen. Psychiatry 966–974 (2007).

3. Should residing in an institutional setting automatically disqualify a person from the right to make choices about participation in research projects? *See* Betty S. Black et al., *Predictors of Providing Informed Consent or Assent for Research Participation in Assisted Living Residents,* 16 Am. J. Geriatr. Psychiatry 83–91 (2008).

4. What do you believe is the best form of proxy decision making regarding research participation for an older person with impaired decisional capacity? Do you believe the idea of creating durable powers of attorney to deal with future decisions about research participation is a realistic one? How would you begin the discussion with an older patient/client about this option? How do you believe most older patients/clients would react to such a discussion? *See* Carol B. Stocking et al., *Empirical Assessment of a Research Advance Directive for Persons with Dementia and Their Proxies,* 55 J. Am. Geriatr. Soc'y 1609–1612 (2007); Rebecca Dresser, *Advance Directives in Dementia Research: Promoting Autonomy and Protecting Subjects,* 23(1) IRB: Ethics & Hum. Resrch. 1–6 (2001).

5. Should limits be set on the decision-making powers of a proxy in the research context? Should the degree of possible risk to the participant in the research make a difference in terms of a proxy's authority? *See* Jeremy Sugarman et al., *Proxies and Consent Discussions for Dementia Research,* 55 J. Am. Geriatr. Soc'y 556–561 (2007); Jason

Karlawish et al., *The Views of Alzheimer Disease Patients and Their Study Partners on Proxy Consent for Clinical Trial Enrollment,* 16(3) Am. J. Geriatr. Psychiatry 240–247 (2008).

6. Should there be special regulations (over and above the generic research regulations delineated above) containing additional procedural safeguards designed specifically to protect vulnerable older individuals? What are the arguments against specifically targeted regulations of that type? Do you agree with the position, stated in the next section, of the Association of American Medical Colleges, expressed in a January 10, 2008 letter to the Office for Human Research Protections?

ARE NEW FEDERAL REGULATIONS NEEDED?

The following Association of American Medical Colleges comments were submitted in response to an Office for Human Research Protections notice, *Request for Information and Comments on Research that Involves Adult Individuals with Impaired Decision-Making Capacity,* 72 Fed. Reg. 50966–50970 (Sept. 5, 2007):

> ...the AAMC [Association of American Medical Colleges] believes that additional regulations or changes to existing regulations are not needed at this time to adequately protect adult individuals with impaired decision-making capacity. Additional regulation could unnecessarily conflict with duly established state or local procedures that already secure the rights of such individuals, and would impede research progress and unnecessarily increase administrative costs and regulatory burdens.

This notice included "a compendium of possible additional protections for subjects with impaired decision-making capacity." What do you think about the desirability of the federal government issuing either formal guidance documents or new regulations in this context regarding any of the following listed items?

- Consent auditor/independent consent monitor
- Sliding scale of capacity (i.e., protections should be proportional to the severity of capacity impairment, or to the magnitude of experimental risk, or both)
- Description of specific tasks to assess capacity
- Independent assessment of decision-making capacity
- Enhancement of IRB expertise such that the IRB includes members or consultants familiar with conditions that may affect decision-making capacity and with the concerns of the population being studied
- Obtaining consent from legally authorized representative
- Obtaining assent from subjects with impaired decision-making capacity (may be limited to objection to inclusion in the research study). This would be in addition to, not in place of, consent from the legally authorized representative.
- Use of advance directive for research where permitted by state/local law
- Use of appropriate waiting periods (after research presented to the subject) before obtaining assent or consent as possible
- Consent enhancements: Interventions to increase the subject's decision-making capacity

STATE REGULATION

Despite the extensive federal presence in regulating research involving human participants, there also exists an important role for the individual states to play in this arena. As stated in a background paper prepared for the National Bioethics Advisory Commission, established by President Bill Clinton: "[S]tate law is hardly irrelevant to the research enterprise. First, to the extent that research is not subject to federal law, pertinent state law (if any) becomes the only legally applicable regulatory regime. Second, federal law, when it does apply to research, expressly preserves any additional state protections." The Common Rule contains the non-preemption language: "This policy does not affect any state or local laws or regulations which may otherwise be applicable and which provide additional protections for human subjects." In addition, it more specifically recognizes additional state requirements for informed consent: "The informed consent requirements in this policy are not intended to preempt any applicable federal, state, or local laws which require additional information to be disclosed in order for informed consent to be legally effective." Identical language appears in the regulations of the FDA.

States have a regulatory interest in health research because they provide tangible economic support to this activity in a variety of direct and indirect ways, such as grant programs to encourage private research on particular topics of concern, tax abatements and other economic development incentives for research enterprises or facilities, and mandated insurance benefit laws that encompass clinical trials or other research interventions. States also facilitate research by allowing cadaver or organ donation for research purposes. State laws regarding the privacy of personal health records influence the conduct of research. Finally, state agencies themselves routinely conduct epidemiologic or other public health research.

Only a few states comprehensively regulate research involving human participants (see examples below). In general, these state statutes reinforce the informed consent, IRB, and confidentiality provisions contained in applicable federal law, and they extend those provisions to all research involving human participants, regardless of sponsor.

Many states restrict the conduct of research involving particular categories of potential participants. For example, many states have codified a nursing home residents' Bill of Rights specifying "the [resident's] right to refuse, with jeopardizing access to appropriate medical care, to serve as a medical research subject." Some states expressly provide similar protections to home health and hospice patients.

The states must review their proper roles regarding the regulation of long-term care research projects involving the participation of vulnerable care recipients. States must consider what additional requirements, if any, ought to be imposed on long-term care researchers to protect potential research participants, while not causing more harm than good by creating or exacerbating unnecessary barriers discouraging the conduct of valuable research, especially involving multisite, multistate collaborative protocols. I recommend a cautious approach to new state regulation regarding the conduct of long-term care research involving human subjects, stressing that any state activity should be thought out to ensure that incremental benefits, in terms of protecting participant rights and well-being, are clearly likely to exceed the financial and nonfinancial costs imposed. At the same time, states should remove certain legal ambiguities in the current long-term care research regulation environment as a way to improve the research climate and facilitate the conduct of more ethically appropriate long-term care research.

Under its *parens patriae* authority to protect persons who are unable to protect themselves against harm, the state has the legal authority to ban outright the conduct of long-term care research activities involving human participants who lack capacity to consent to their own participation. However, as a public policy matter, the state ought not exercise that authority. By permitting research to take place by enrolling individuals without decisional capacity, the state is making the proper value judgment that, in particular research projects, the potential long-range benefits to society may outweigh the immediate risks to individual study participants. Having made that judgment, policymakers may consider what requirements should be imposed on long-term care researchers to protect the interests of potential and actual participants while permitting legitimate research.

DISCUSSION QUESTIONS

1. What statutes and regulations does your own state have concerning the conduct of biomedical and behavioral research involving human participants? Does your state have particular laws regarding the conduct of long-term care research? If your state does not have specific laws pertaining to human subject research, should it enact such laws? What should those laws say? If your state already has such laws, do they need to be amended? In what way?

2. In your own profession, have any private organizations published guidelines for the conduct of ethically and legally responsible research, especially involving human participants with impaired decisional capacity?

Exercise

Dr. T is meeting with the IRB at the medical center where she works. She has designed a research protocol to study a promising new drug for the treatment of Alzheimer's disease (AD). She must now explain to the IRB how the protocol will be conducted and how patient safety will be ensured.

In the research protocol, Dr. T indicated that this will be a double-blinded clinical trial in which half of the participants will receive a placebo and the others will receive the study drug. Based on preliminary studies of this drug, Dr. T knows that participants—especially individuals who are in the early to middle stages of AD—may experience improvements in memory and other cognitive functioning, although not without some risk. The drug may exacerbate hypertension in those already prone to the condition, and if doses even modestly exceed clinically effective levels, severe kidney damage may result. Dr. T plans to recruit participants through AD support groups and advertisements placed in the local newspaper. Prospective volunteers will be interviewed to make certain they fit the desired participant profile. The interview will consist of a series of questions designed to assess the extent of the prospective participant's impairment and sense of orientation to the environment. Persons selected to participate in this clinical drug trial will be paid $300 for their time and trouble.

As an IRB member reviewing this protocol, what explanations do you expect from the investigator about how she will evaluate the capacity of prospective participants to understand the objectives, risks, and benefits of the study? How will Dr. T deal with the situation of a participant who has sufficient decisional capacity at the time of initial enrollment in the study but whose mental status later during the life of the protocol deteriorates significantly? Does the investigator intend to rely on proxy consent if the participant lacks decisional capacity? Should proxy consent be permitted? How should it be monitored? What does Dr. T intend to do about the family member who wants to enroll a loved one in the study but does not want the real purpose of the study spelled out to the loved one? How will the investigator ensure that participation in the study is truly voluntary, particularly when desperate family members are pushing their afflicted loved ones to enroll? Is the $300 payment such a large incentive that it destroys the element of voluntariness; if the payment is disallowed, how will the investigator be able to recruit enough participants to do the study properly?

NOTES

Sections of this chapter were originally published in Marshall B. Kapp, *Regulating Hematology/Oncology Research Involving Human Participants,* 16(6) Hem./Oncol. Clinics N. Am. 1449–1461 (2002); Marshall B. Kapp, Ethics and Medical Decision Making, *Encyclopedia of Gerontology* (2nd ed., Vol. 1, pp. 526–532) (James E. Birren, ed.), Copyright © Elsevier 2007; and Marshall B. Kapp, *Protecting Human Participants in Long-Term Care Research: The Role of State Law and Policy,* 16 J. Aging & Soc. Pol'y 13–33 (2004).

CHAPTER 8

Family Law Issues and Older Persons

FAMILY CAREGIVERS' LEGAL CONCERNS

Family caregivers are the backbone of the long-term care system (to the extent it really is a system) in the United States. They provide about 80% of the care for people who need assistance with activities of daily living, such as bathing and dressing, taking medications, and paying bills. "Caregiving has become an issue that affects the quality of life for millions of individuals and demands attention from every community." Ronda C. Talley & John E. Crews, *Framing the Public Health of Caregiving*, 97 Am. J. Pub. Health 224–228 (2007). For good historical background on family caregiving, see Karen Buhler-Wilkerson, *Care of the Chronically Ill at Home: An Unresolved Dilemma in Health Policy for the United States*, 85 Milbank Q. 611–639 (2007).

A Duty to Care?

A basic issue for many family members confronted with the long-term care needs of an ill or disabled relative is whether there exists a legally enforceable obligation on their part to provide caregiving assistance to the individual, especially when active family involvement is essential to implementation of the individual's desired care plan (for instance, the individual prefers to remain in his or her own home rather than entering a nursing home). The short answer is this: Although strong arguments may support a moral duty in this situation, no law compels family members to personally provide direct, hands-on care to dependent relatives.

Family members, thus, are people who have "volunteered" for this role in the sense that they legally could have declined. Voluntariness in this context may be much more complex, though, from a psychological perspective. In many cases the amount of subtle or direct "persuasion" exerted on family members by health and human service professionals, other family members, or the care recipient may be considerable.

Once a family member has chosen—more or less willingly—to undertake the caregiver role, then every state has a statute that makes it illegal as a form of elder mistreatment (discussed below) for the caregiver to willfully ignore the basic needs of, or otherwise through acts or omissions endanger, the dependent person. However, legitimate (that is, driven either by the client's own wishes or by a consideration of the client's best interests) decisions by a caregiver to limit medical or other types of intervention for an individual on the basis of a good-faith effort to weigh the burdens versus the benefits should not be considered mistreatment.

Elder mistreatment laws thus apply only once a caregiving relationship has been established and do not require any family member to enter into such a relationship in the first place. Even when such a relationship has been established, the family may fulfill its obligation to refrain from neglect by securing formal caregiving—institutional or community based—for the dependent person rather than providing the services itself.

When a family member agrees (more or less voluntarily) to undertake the caregiving role, both the caretaker and the client have certain expectations about the implementation of their relationship. Because each party makes at least implied (and in some cases express) promises about his or her own end of the bargain, their relationship may be characterized as a contract. It is unlikely that a court would legally enforce the terms of such a contract, and certainly not by ordering specific performance of implied promises, but nonetheless it behooves both the caregiver and client to reach as clear an understanding as possible, as early as possible, about their mutual expectations and commitments. This understanding may be altered continually, of course, as the needs and capacities of the respective parties evolve over time.

Although the law does not impose direct caregiving responsibilities on families, approximately 30 states (as well as several other countries, including Italy, Israel, Japan, and Singapore) still have in effect family or filial responsibility statutes enacted more than half a century ago imposing a duty on adult children, if they are able, to provide financial assistance to indigent parents. The courts have tended to uphold the validity of these statutes against the claims (among others) that they violate the U.S. Constitution's Fourteenth Amendment mandate of equal protection of the law and the Constitution's prohibition against government taking of property without just compensation. As a practical matter, though, these laws are very rarely enforced; almost a dozen states' filial responsibility statutes have never been invoked against any nonsupporting adult child.

Ohio Revised Code § 2919.21 provides that no person "shall abandon, or fail to provide adequate support to...[t]he person's spouse, as required by law;...[t]he persons aged or infirm parent,...who from the lack of ability and means is unable to provide adequately for the parent's own support." It is a defense that an accused person "was unable to provide adequate support or the established support but did provide the support that was within the accused's ability and means."

Similar laws exist in a number of other nations. In 2007, for example, the Indian Parliament enacted legislation providing for imposition of 3 months of imprisonment and a stiff monetary fine, with no right of appeal, on adult children who fail to provide "maintenance" (i.e., food, clothing, residence, and medical care) for their parents. For discussions of the cultural aspects of filial responsibility, *see* Andrea Rickles-Jordan, *Filial Responsibility: A Survey Across Time and Oceans,* 9 Marquette Elder's Advisor 183–204 (2007), and John W. Traphagan, *Power, Family, and Filial Responsibility Related to Elder Care in Rural Japan,* 7 Care Management J: J. Long Term Home Health Care 205–212 (2006).

The financial status of adult children regarding the formal care of disabled parents needs to be distinguished from the obligations of spouses of people receiving paid long-term care services. Under the traditional legal doctrine of "necessaries," each spouse has been held equally (jointly and severally) liable for debts incurred by the other spouse for "necessary" goods and services. A number of states lately have modified the apportionment of financial responsibility for necessaries between the two spouses by holding the spouse who incurred the necessary expense primarily liable for payment, with the other spouse becoming secondarily liable when the spouse who incurred the expense does not have sufficient assets or income to satisfy the debt.

The other side of the coin may appear when a family insists on participating in caregiving for a disabled or ill relative but that person objects. Families have neither a duty *nor a right* to be involved, as long as those individuals who object to the family providing direct services to them are capable of making and expressing their own autonomous decisions.

Do I Need a Professional License?

The question often arises as to whether the family caregiver must be licensed to provide particular services. In theory, professional licensure laws may act as a complicating factor concerning informal caregiving. Physician orders (in an increasing number of jurisdictions nurses also have prescribing authority, albeit under physician supervision) for prescription or over-the-counter medications or for other forms of therapy normally are directed at other health care professionals for their implementation. However, when willing and able family members are available, it is typical and broadly accepted practice for home health agencies and hospital or nursing facility discharge planners to train those relatives to provide certain personal care and homemaker services for the disabled individual.

Most state nurse practice acts explicitly exempt from their restrictions health-related services provided by family (and, in most cases, by friends too) to care recipients in their homes. Research reveals no reported findings of liability against either a family member, supervising home health agency, or primary physician for negligence by the family member in the performance of health-related services provided within the individual's home.

No state explicitly empowers family caregivers to administer medications or other medical treatments. Neither do most states expressly disallow this practice. It is common for family members to help relatives take over-the-counter medications. The legal authority of family members to administer prescription drugs without technically violating nurse practice acts is, theoretically, more problematic. As a practical matter, relatives help care recipients to take medications thousands of times per day without any reported criminal prosecutions for practicing nursing without a license. The legal situation becomes murkier still in the case of more complicated medical interventions, such as the operation of sophisticated machines.

What If the Care Recipient Injures Someone?

Another common question is whether the caregiver can be held legally liable if the care recipient injures someone else. Individuals for whom family caregivers are caring may injure third parties through their actions. For example, a mentally impaired care recipient might physically abuse and hurt a formal caregiver who comes into the home to provide services or assault a delivery person whom the care recipient mistakes for an intruder. The extent to which a family member who has voluntarily undertaken the care of that individual may be held legally responsible for the individual's injury-producing wrongful behavior is a matter of potential concern and uncertainty, and one with substantial public policy implications.

Family members probably could not successfully argue as an affirmative defense to a civil action brought by an injured formal caregiver that the formal caregiver had assumed the risk of possible injury by a mentally impaired client as part of his or her job. At the same time, it is equally unlikely that a court would hold a severely mentally impaired recipient or that person's family caregivers liable for the injurious acts of the mentally impaired person in the first place. People who were injured in their work capacity would have at least partial redress available through state-administered worker's compensation systems, which are no-fault in nature and funded through mandatory premiums paid by employers and which operate as an alternative to civil lawsuits.

There are, though, two main exceptions to tort law's general reticence to hold informal caregivers directly liable for the injuries that a person under their care inflicts on others: (1) when the caregiver is on notice of the dangerous propensities of his or her charge and has assumed control of the person's actions and (2) when the caregiver assumes the duty by trying to prevent the dangerous activity but fails. On one hand, these exceptions, permitting injured third parties to seek redress (that is, monetary damages) from informal caregivers in the civil justice system, might have the salutary effect of encouraging informal caregivers to more tightly control the actions of mentally impaired individuals for whom they have voluntarily assumed care responsibilities, thereby preventing some injuries from occurring. On the other hand, however, frightening informal caregivers with the specter of being exposed to personal liability for the acts of their care recipients may have negative consequences. First, anxiety about legal repercussions may discourage some family members who otherwise would have been willing to voluntarily enter into or continue the caregiving role from doing so. Second, apprehensions may raise the level of sacrifice for family caregivers, by compelling them to pay premiums to purchase insurance (even assuming that such an insurance product were available in the marketplace) to protect themselves against the financial risks associated with legal exposure for negligent caregiving. Perhaps most important, expanded liability exposure of family caregivers could encourage them to exercise control efforts that would severely impinge on the freedom enjoyed by care recipients. For instance, it is questionable whether advocates for older and disabled people would consider as positive developments such family caregiver conduct as physically or chemically restraining people to keep them from acting out or initiating or consenting to other restrictive behavioral strategies.

What About Legal Protections and Benefits?

Besides being financially compensated for their services under some limited circumstances, family caregivers are entitled to certain legal protections and benefits by virtue of their caregiving activities. For example, the dependent care tax credit may be available to assist with the costs of providing care for a disabled spouse or parent. Moreover, an individual who serves as the primary caregiver for a disabled family member in the home is protected against discrimination under the Americans With Disabilities Act, which provides that "a public accommodation shall not exclude or otherwise deny equal goods, services, facilities, privileges, advantages, accommodations, or other opportunities to an individual or entity because of the known disability of an individual with whom the individual or entity is known to have a relationship or association." Some commentators have suggested that the federal or state governments, in recognition of the benefit of family caregiving services and as an incentive for families to continue providing those services, should extend some type of disability and workers' compensation insurance coverage to family caregivers who are at high risk of being injured in the course of their caregiving activities.

Family caregiving and the question of decision-making authority has parallel ramifications for the handling of access to, and confidentiality of, medical and other information concerning the care recipient. These privacy rights concerns are addressed in Chapter 6.

DISCUSSION QUESTIONS

1. Should there be a legal duty imposed on family members to provide care for their disabled relatives? How would we delineate the extent and limits of that duty? What exceptions should we recognize? Upon which specific family members should such a duty be imposed? What penalty should be meted out for violation of this duty? What procedural protections (e.g., right to jury trial, right to legal representation, right to appeal) should be provided before a penalty may be imposed on the neglectful family member(s)?

2. Do you agree that a good faith decision by the caregiver to withhold life-prolonging medical intervention (such as feeding tubes or antibiotics) from a person based on a benefits versus burdens calculation ought to be exempted from characterization as elder mistreatment?

3. Do you believe most family members or friends consider their agreement to help care for a dependent loved one as constituting a "contract" when they make that agreement? If not, how do family members and friends characterize such agreements? Do most family members or friends put such agreements into words, or do they imply a promise to care through their actions? Does the situation change if the older dependent person is financially compensating a relative to act as caregiver? *See* Rachel E. Silverman, *Who Will Mind Mom? Check Her Contract,* Wall St. J., Sept. 7, 2006, at D1.

4. Do you believe the doctrine of "necessaries," which holds one spouse liable for the debts incurred by the other spouse to purchase medical or long-term care, is fair? If not the spouse, then who should pay those debts?

5. Should family members and friends be allowed to help their loved one in a home care environment by performing activities that normally could only be performed

by licensed health care professionals? What justifies an exception to the usual licensure requirements?

6. There is a limited trend in many states to pay family members to provide care to their dependent relatives in the home environment. Do you agree with this development? What family-provided services should be eligible for public dollars? What safeguards or limits should be placed on state programs to compensate family caregivers? To what extent should federal tax policy encourage families to provide care for older adults? *See* Richard L. Kaplan, *Federal Tax Policy and Family-Provided Care for Older Adults,* 25 Virginia Tax Review 509–562 (2005).

7. Should family caregivers be held legally responsible for the actions of care recipients that cause harm to innocent third parties? Why or why not?

8. Should family members be provided with disability and workers' compensation insurance coverage for their caregiving activities? Who should pay the premiums for this insurance?

FAMILY AND MEDICAL LEAVE ACT

Family members who need to take time off from work to attend to caregiving responsibilities may be entitled to job protections under the federal Family and Medical Leave Act of 1993, 29 U.S.C. §§2601–2654, with implementing regulations at 29 C.F.R. pt. 825. *See* Michael J. Ossip & Robert M. Hale, eds., *The Family and Medical Leave Act,* Washington, DC: American Bar Association Section of Labor and Employment Law (2006). The Family and Medical Leave Act imposes on private employers with 50 or more employees, as well as most public agencies, an obligation (among other things) to provide workers with unpaid leaves of absence totaling up to 12 weeks during a 12-month period to care for, among other family members, a spouse or parent with a serious health condition. In 2008, the U.S. Department of Labor indicated an intent to revise the

Family and Medical Leave Act regulations and called for public comment on those revisions. 73 Fed. Reg. 7876–8001 (Feb. 11, 2008). For a 50-state survey of state legislation authorizing the use of paid time off for care of an adult family member, *see* http://lawprofessors.typepad.com/elder_law/2008/03/center-for-elde.html.

Additional Information Sources

National Family Caregivers Association, www.thefamilycaregiver.org
Family Caregiver Alliance, www.caregiver.org
National Alliance for Caregiving, www.caregiving.org

Exercise

Case 1

Mrs. J is a 69-year-old widow with chronic obstructive pulmonary disease based on a lifetime of smoking cigarettes. She also has osteoarthritis and mild dementia but is still capable of making and expressing many decisions about her life. Her main relative is a daughter who lives far away and has visited Mrs. J a few times a year. Mrs. J was admitted to a hospital for treatment of pneumonia. The daughter told the hospital discharge planner that she would like the discharge planner's assistance locating an assisted living facility near the daughter where Mrs. J could be admitted. The discharge planner has serious doubts concerning the daughter's sincerity about wanting Mrs. J closer to her, the daughter's likely level of attentiveness in looking after Mrs. J, and the daughter's general ability to oversee Mrs. J's well-being given that the daughter already struggles with her own daily life challenges and vicissitudes. The discharge planner also believes that the hospital's geographical area, where Mrs. J has lived most of her adult life, has several fine assisted living facilities, including one owned by the hospital system by which the discharge planner is employed.

What are the obligations of the discharge planner here to Mrs. J as her advocate, to the daughter, and to the discharge planner's own employer? What options are available to the discharge planner if the daughter insists on a plan of action that the discharge planner believes is not in Mrs. J's best interests? Does the discharge planner have a conflict of interest? If so, how should that conflict be handled? How should Mrs. J herself be involved in the decision-making process?

Case 2

Mrs. K is an 81-year-old widow who lives alone, financially secure between Social Security and her pension earned as a former school teacher, in her own house. She has four adult children, all living locally and doing well financially, who generally have little contact with their mother except for her birthday, Mother's Day, and major holidays.

Mrs. K takes a taxi to the emergency department of the community hospital every few weeks complaining of various aches and pains. Each time she visits the emergency department, she is given a thorough diagnostic workup (mainly an exercise in defensive medicine by the physician). Sometimes her complaints have a physiological explanation (stemming, for example, from her diabetes and hypertension), but on most occasions no physiological cause can be identified.

Mrs. K is a very nice person toward whom the emergency department personnel feel fondly. She is appreciative of the care she receives and always brings in cookies and candy on various holidays. She always patiently waits her turn in the emergency department without complaining. The emergency department staff, however, has become concerned that Mrs. K's repeated medically unnecessary visits are not really in her best interests (or those of the Medicare program, which pays for her care).

What can the hospital social worker do to deal with this situation? Can the adult children be forced to take on more responsibility for Mrs. K? What form(s) would such coerced responsibility take? How would such responsibility be enforced? Is it true that "we cannot legislate love"? What role should the emergency department physician and nurses play in this kind of scenario?

ELDER MISTREATMENT

Definitions

Elder abuse is "the infliction upon an adult by self or others of injury, unreasonable confinement, intimidation, or cruel punishment with resulting physical harm, pain, or mental anguish." Physical harm includes any "bodily pain, injury, impairment, or disease suffered by an adult." Elder neglect is "the failure of an adult to provide for self the goods or services necessary to avoid physical harm, mental anguish, or mental illness, or the failure of a caretaker to provide such goods or services." Exploitation is "the unlawful or improper act of a caretaker using an adult or an adult's

DISCUSSION QUESTIONS

1. Do you agree with these definitions? Are they too broad to be useful? Do they leave anything out that should be included? How would you improve these definitions?
2. To what extent (if any) should cultural differences be taken into account in deciding whether elder mistreatment is occurring within a particular family? *See* Toshio Tatara ed., *Understanding Elder Abuse in Minority Populations,* Philadelphia: Brunner/Mazel (1999).

resources for monetary or personal benefit, profit, or gain." Ohio Revised Code § 5101.60.

Within the last several decades, health care, human services, and legal professionals in the United States involved in serving older persons have discovered what is generally described as the widespread social phenomenon of elder mistreatment. Other terms that have been applied to this phenomenon include granny battering or bashing, battered elder syndrome, elder mistreatment, old age abuse, and miscare. Elder mistreatment may be inflicted through a wide range of acts (abuse or exploitation) or omissions (neglect) on the part of others, and it may occur in institutional or community-based locations (including the home). It may arise from varied etiologies representing a panoply of risk factors. As used in the recent report of the National Research Council, "elder mistreatment":

> *[R]efers to (a) intentional actions that cause harm or create a serious risk of harm (whether or not harm is intended) to a vulnerable elder by a caregiver or other person who stands in a trusted relationship to the elder or (b) failure by a caregiver to satisfy the elder's basic needs or to protect the elder from harm. The term "mistreatment" is meant to exclude cases of so-called self-neglect—failure of an older person to satisfy his or her own basic needs and to protect him or herself from harm—and also cases involving victimization of elders by strangers.*

DISCUSSION QUESTIONS

1. "Elders neglecting themselves usually live alone. They display such behaviors as piling garbage inside the home, ignoring serious medical issues, and even lying in their own excrement." Carmel B. Dyer et al., *Vulnerable Elders: When It Is No Longer Safe to Live Alone*, 298 J. Am. Med. Ass'n 1448–1450 (2007). Do you agree with

the National Research Council that an older person's self-neglect should be excluded from the definition of "elder mistreatment"? Why or why not?

2. What do you believe are the most important reasons that elder mistreatment occurs?

3. The number of reported cases of elder mistreatment is rising. Do you interpret this rise as an indication that the amount of elder mistreatment is increasing, or that people are more likely to report instances of elder mistreatment than previously?

4. Is it financial exploitation if a person or business, without making any fraudulent or untruthful representations or promises, convinces an older person to enter into a financial transaction that turns out to be very disadvantageous to the older person? Should an older person be allowed to undo bad financial deals or be compensated for losses just because of the person's age? Should older persons be relieved of some of the responsibility for their choices? What practical consequences might accompany adoption of such an approach to financial responsibility? *See* Charles Duhigg, *Shielding Money Clashes With Elders' Free Will,* N.Y. Times, Dec. 24, 2007, *available at* www.nytimes.com/2007/12/24/business/24golden .html?th=

ACKNOWLEDGMENT OF, AND RESPONSES TO, ELDER MISTREATMENT

Concerned gerontological professionals in academic, social service, legal, and public policy settings have spawned an enormous amount of literature on this subject. They also have sought to share with government officials their concern about this problem and have organized to lobby legislators into vigorous lawmaking action, for instance, through the Older Americans Act (OAA).

Congressmen and senators have garnered favorable media fanfare for years by publicly, repeatedly investigating the problem. A bipartisan Elder Justice Act has been introduced in Congress repeatedly since 2002. Proceeding on the theory that where there exists any social problem, massive government involvement must be the best (and usually the only desirable) solution, this bill would establish new, dual Offices of Elder Justice at the federal Department of Justice and Department of Health and Human Services (DHHS) to coordinate federal, state, and local elder mistreatment prevention efforts, while also housing policy experts and coordinating programs to study, detect, treat, prosecute, and prevent abuse, neglect, and exploitation of older citizens living independently and in residential care facilities. The bill additionally would establish new programs to assist victims and provide grants for education and training of law enforcement personnel and prosecutors while developing more forensic expertise. It would enhance incentives for the reporting of crimes in institutional settings and require Federal Bureau of Investigation criminal background checks for staff members employed by long-term care providers.

The OAA, originally enacted in 1965 at the recommendation of a White House Conference on Aging, is the major vehicle for the organization and delivery of supportive and nutritional services to older persons. This statute and other legislative initiatives of the Great Society grew out of a concern that many older persons at the time were impoverished and needed federal assistance. Although older persons already were eligible to receive some services under preexisting federal programs, the OAA was the first major federal legislation to organize and deliver community-based social services exclusively to the older population. The OAA authorizes a wide array of service programs (including Adult Protective Services [APS]) through a nationwide network of approximately 57 State Units on Aging and approximately 650 Area Agencies on Aging. At the federal level, the OAA is administered by the Administration on Aging, which is part of DHHS.

However, most of the legal activity in the elder mistreatment sphere thus far has taken place at the state level (see Table 8.1). Every state has spun a wide web of laws dealing with this subject. Some states rely on generic APS laws to address elder mistreatment, whereas others have enacted specific statutes on this matter. Additional relevant provisions are found in state criminal or penal codes, domestic violence laws, and

DISCUSSION QUESTIONS

Is enactment of a comprehensive federal statute setting up a large, new federal bureaucracy necessary and the optimal strategy to deal with the elder mistreatment situation? What are the possible shortcomings of this approach? Is the problem of elder mistreatment one that is better dealt with on the level of local communities? *See* Donna Schuyler & Bryan A. Liang, *Reconceptualizing Elder Abuse: Treating the Disease of Senior Community Exclusion,* 15 Annals of Health Law 275–305 (2006); Arlene D. Luu & Bryan A. Liang, *Clinical Case Management: A Strategy to Coordinate Detection, Reporting, and Prosecution of Elder Abuse,* 15 Cornell Journal of Law and Public Policy 165–196 (2005).

Table 8.1   State Statutory Approaches to Elder Mistreatment

Where to look to find a particular state's laws on this subject:
- Generic APS statutes and/or specific elder mistreatment statutes
- Provisions in criminal or penal codes classifying elder mistreatment as
  - A misdemeanor (e.g., Utah)
  - A felony (e.g., Nevada)
  - Unspecified punishment (e.g., Alaska)
- Generic criminal statutes
  - Assault
  - Battery
  - Theft
  - Fraud
- Provisions in domestic violence statutes
- Provisions in probate statutes
- Lump together both institutional and noninstitutional caregivers or
  - Handle institutional elder mistreatment separately
- Protect all "vulnerable," "disabled," or "incapacitated" adults or
  - Limit protection to persons over a specified age
- Mandatory reporting of suspected elder mistreatment by
  - Designated professionals or
  - Any person or
  - Voluntary (encouraged) reporting of suspected elder mistreatment

probate statutes. Most states include self-neglect in their respective statutes as a discrete category of elder mistreatment, and indeed it is allegations of self-neglect that now comprise the overwhelming majority of cases of elder mistreatment reported to authorities.

STATE APPROACHES TO ELDER MISTREATMENT

Although policymakers continue to be routinely chastised for not going far enough in this regard, almost every state explicitly imposes criminal liability for willful acts or omissions amounting to elder mistreatment. Some states make elder treatment a misdemeanor, others classify this conduct more seriously as a felony, whereas a few statutes do not specifically deal with the question of punishment for violations. The criminal statutes ordinarily apply to the older person's "caregiver" and others. A number of states explicitly lump together institutional and noninstitutional caregiver mistreatment in the same statutes, whereas other jurisdictions handle these two categories distinctly, at least for legislative (if not programmatic) purposes. Mistreatment of older persons also may violate generic assault and battery criminal statutes in every jurisdiction. When the caregiver who is responsible for mistreatment is a licensed health or human service professional, proof of the mistreatment may be grounds for discipline of that professional by the applicable state licensing board.

State mistreatment statutes differ in their respective specifications of the class of individuals who may qualify for legal protection. In some states, all "vulnerable," "disabled," or "incapacitated" adults (persons over 18 years old) are protected. Elsewhere, only persons over a designated higher age—usually 60 or 65—are covered.

Over 40 states have enacted statutes mandating a wide variety of helping professionals to report known or reasonably protected cases of elder mistreatment to designated public bodies, usually local APS agencies or law enforcement offices, for further investigation. Several of these statutes extend the duty to report to "any person." These mandatory reporting statutes make noncompliance punishable as a criminal offense. Some commentators argue that physicians and other health care professionals also should be exposed to professional disciplinary action by the relevant state licensing board and civil malpractice lawsuits initiated by or on behalf of individual mistreatment victims for failure to timely report mistreatment that was or should have been reasonably suspected. Some states already explicitly create a civil cause of action for negligent or intentional failure to report mistreatment of a protected adult, but use of this remedy by older mistreatment victims has been rare. A few states encourage but do not require the reporting of suspected elder mistreatment, by keeping reporters' identities confidential and immunizing reporters against any form of legal liability if they voluntarily make good faith reports.

DISCUSSION QUESTIONS

1. Why do you believe it is that "allegations of self-neglect ...now comprise the overwhelming majority of cases of elder mistreatment reported to authorities"? Is this fact good or bad in terms of the goal of protecting vulnerable adults? *See* Maria P. Pavlou & Mark S. Lachs, *Could Self-Neglect in Older Adults Be a Geriatric Syndrome?* 54(5) J. Am. Geriatr. Soc'y 831–842 (2006). If APS and others were more aggressive in seeking out and treating self-neglecters, would those efforts "unleash an avalanche of healthcare costs"? *See* Mark Lachs, *What Does "Self-Neglect" in Older Adults Really Cost?* 56(4) J. Am. Geriatr. Soc'y 757 (2008).

2. How should we distinguish between an older person who competently chooses to live in squalor versus a situation in which frailty and isolation make the older person so vulnerable and decisionally impaired that competent choices are impossible? *See* Aanand D. Naik et al., *Assessing Capacity in the Setting of Self-Neglect: Development of a Novel Screening Tool for Decision-Making Capacity,* 18 J. Elder Abuse & Neglect 79–91 (2006).

3. Is the phenomenon of elder mistreatment best treated as a matter of criminal law? Should it be classified as a misdemeanor (usually punishable by up to one year of incarceration) or a felony (carrying a heavier penalty)? Are prosecutors, judges, other court personnel, and correctional

officials well-qualified to address this multifaceted social problem? Does the criminal justice system have adequate financial and human resources to deal effectively with this problem? What are some alternative approaches, both legal and nonlegal, to this problem? *See, e.g.,* www.apa.org/pi/aging/eldabuse.html (describing elder mistreatment as primarily a psychological issue).

4. Should mistreatment statutes explicitly protect all adults at risk, regardless of age, or should statutory protections be targeted to those over a specified age? If the latter, what specific age should trigger statutory protections?

5. At least 14 states have statutes pertaining to nursing home licensure with text specifically addressing the topic of abuse reports and investigation in nursing homes. *See* Jeanette M. Daly & Gerald J. Jogerst, *Nursing Home Abuse Report and Investigation,* 19 J. Elder Abuse & Neglect 119–131 (2007). What are the advantages and disadvantages of states enacting separate elder mistreatment statutes pertaining to nursing home residents? In addition, the Omnibus Budget Reconciliation Act of 1987 requires the states to provide timely review of complaints and to investigate allegations of neglect, abuse, and misappropriation of resident property in nursing homes. The performance of the states is monitored by the Centers for Medicare and Medicaid Services, the agency within the federal DHHS responsible for oversight of Medicare and Medicaid. Moreover, the DHHS Office of Inspector General has authority to investigate cases of significant abuse and neglect and take appropriate administrative action. *See* Testimony of Gregory E. Demske, Office of Counsel to the Inspector General, before the United States Senate Special Committee on Aging, July 18, 2007, *available at* http://aging.senate.gov/hearing_detail.cfm?id=279115&

6. Should states mandate reporting of suspected elder mistreatment, or instead encourage voluntary reporting?

Whom (just certain designated professionals or everybody) should be required or encouraged to report? For a chart on current mandatory and voluntary reporting laws, *see* www.abanet.org/aging/about/elderabuse.shmtl.

7. Is the reporter's having "reasonable cause to suspect" that a vulnerable adult has been or is being abused, neglected, or exploited a sufficient trigger for mandatory or voluntary reporting, or should actual knowledge of abuse, neglect, or exploitation be required before the reporting provisions (including legal immunity for the reporter) are triggered?

8. Should a health care or human service professional report suspected (or known) elder mistreatment to authorities if the client asks the professional not to report it, perhaps because the client fears being taken out of the home environment and admitted to an institutional environment or the client does not want to get family members into legal trouble? In the elder mistreatment context, how should the professional balance the ethical principles of client autonomy (self-determination), nonmaleficence (preventing harm), and beneficence (doing good)? How should the professional handle the tension between ethical and legal duties regarding elder mistreatment reporting?

9. Should a health care or human service professional's failure to report a case of elder abuse be the basis for civil liability if the victim suffers further mistreatment because the authorities were not alerted in time to intervene and protect the victim? How about if the professional did not actually suspect the mistreatment but "reasonably should have" suspected it? Is exposing professionals to personal legal liability for nonreporting likely to be an effective remedy for mistreated older persons or an effective way to encourage reporting by professionals? Is it likely to encourage *over*-reporting (i.e., too many false positive reports)?

Exercises

Case 1

Mrs. N is a 75-year-old widow with no children. The person closest to her is an 80-year-old neighbor. APS received a report from Mrs. N's mailman alleging medical and physical self-neglect. APS did an initial investigation and determined that Mrs. N had multiple dogs and that her house smelled badly and was infested with fleas. There was food in the pantry and the utilities were turned on. Mrs. N was poorly groomed and her clothes were dirty. She responded to the investigator's questioning about her health history that she had hypertension and diabetes and that she frequently forgot to take her medication or have her prescriptions refilled. She also reported an earlier minor stroke.

The APS worker documented that Mrs. N was oriented to person and place but not to time. She had memory deficits but knew unambiguously that she wanted to remain in her own home. The APS worker returned a few days later with a geriatrician, who confirmed the APS worker's earlier findings. Mrs. N denied depression. Halfway through the interview, Mrs. N asked the geriatrician, "Hi. Who are you again?" The geriatrician and APS worker convinced Mrs. N to come into the hospital clinic for a more complete workup, at which Mrs. N was found to have uncontrolled hypertension and diabetes, flea infestation, and possible Alzheimer's disease with vitamin B_{12} deficiency.

Was the mailman correct to report Mrs. N to APS, or was he a "buttinsky," acting too paternalistically? Is this a case of self-neglect or an idiosyncratic lifestyle? How should this set of circumstances be handled by APS? What happens if APS disagrees with the clinic staff? How much room is there here for negotiation? Who needs to be involved in any negotiation and what topics should be subject to such a negotiation? What are the risks if Mrs. N is sent back home to live on her own?

Case 2

Mr. P is a 74-year-old hospitalized person with one brother. Mr. P is legally blind because of poorly controlled diabetes, with severe retinopathy with neuropathy and hypertension. He was admitted because of a rapid change in mental status and what initially appeared to be some temporary ambulation problems stemming from a small stroke that had occurred several days before hospital admission. The home health aide who had brought Mr. P to the hospital emergency department indicated that Mr. P had earlier resisted going to the hospital.

In the hospital, Mr. P suffered a second stroke. He subsequently received rehabilitation in the subacute unit of the hospital, and his diabetes was stabilized. The physician tried to change from injectable insulin to an oral agent despite the patient's history of insulin dependence. After a lengthy time period, a combination of the oral agent and diabetes education appeared to be effective.

Before his hospital admission, Mr. P had a long history of neglecting his medical needs. He was treated for his diabetes but frequently failed to have his prescriptions refilled and would go for months at a time without his insulin. He would not admit anyone into his dilapidated house, including his brother whom he distrusted, except for one home health aide who was paid for under a Medicaid waiver program in operation in his jurisdiction. When he was admitted to the hospital, Mr. P admitted that he could not read his insulin bottle or see the level of insulin in his needle. His injection practice was inadequate. He acknowledged that he was a diabetic but otherwise denied that he had any other medical problems. He wishes to be discharged back to his house to live by himself.

If the hospital discharges Mr. P back to his house to live alone under these circumstances, will it be condoning self-neglect? Would the hospital be aiding and abetting neglect?

What will be the likely practical consequence if the hospital notifies APS? Are there compromise resolutions possible to balance Mr. P's autonomy, on one side, and his need for proper medical care, on the other? How can Mr. P's brother be brought into the discussion?

Case 3

Mrs. C is an 84-year-old widow with insulin-dependent diabetes, hypertension, vascular dementia, a prior stroke with left-sided weakness, angina, and a history of falls. She has prescriptions for many medications that are supposed to be taken according to a complicated schedule. She lives in her own very run-down, old house with her one daughter, who has limited intellectual capacity and works at marginal employment, her chronically unemployed and heavily drinking son-in-law, and her surly teenage grandson. Mrs. C has fallen numerous times during the last year in the home.

As a result of her most recent fall, Mrs. C was treated for a concussion and multiple abrasions and was hospitalized for observation. Mrs. C is adamant to the discharge planner that she wants to go back to the preexisting living arrangement. Medication reviews and blood glucose levels indicate poor compliance with her medication regimen. The home care team suspects that some of her falls may be related to both her noncompliance and the horrible condition of her house, which she refuses to get repaired. Although Mrs. C is able to perform many activities of daily living independently, she needs help with many others (for example, shopping, cleaning, money management, medication management, meal preparation, and transportation). The son-in-law is home alone with Mrs. C during the day while his wife works and his son is in school. All the falls have taken place while the wife is at work.

What should the discharge planner do? If sent home, would Mrs. C be released back into an abusive environment?

What realistic alternatives exist? Should APS be called? Who might be exposed to legal liability in this situation? If Mrs. C had a large untapped bank account available, how would that affect the range of possible solutions?

Regarding protections for people who report instances of known or suspected elder abuse, neglect, or exploitation, Fla. Stat. § 415.1036 is typical:

Any person who participates in making a report under [the law] or who participates in a judicial proceeding resulting therefrom is presumed to be acting in good faith and, unless lack of good faith is shown by clear and convincing evidence, is immune from any liability, civil or criminal, that otherwise might be incurred or imposed.

DISCUSSION QUESTIONS

1. Is providing legal immunity for persons reporting known or suspected abuse, neglect, or exploitation a good idea? Is such a provision necessary to induce people to file reports? Do you believe the existence or absence of such an immunity provision would actually encourage or discourage the filing of reports?
2. Here are citations to state elder mistreatment reporting statutes; find your own state statute and discuss it. Ala. Code § 38-9-8; Alaska State. §§ 47.24.010-.900; Ariz. Rev. Stat. Ann. §§ 46-451-456; Ark. Code Ann. § 5-28-101-306; Cal. Welf. & Inst. Code §§ 15630-15632; Colo. Rev. Stat. § 26-3.1-102; Conn. Gen. Stat. Ann. § 17b-451; Del. Code Ann. tit. 31, § 3910; D.C.

Code Ann. § 7-1903; Fla. Stat. Ann. § 415.1034; Ga. Code Ann. § 30-5-4; Haw. Rev. Stat. § 346-0224; Idaho Code § 39-5303; 320 Ill. Comp. Stat. Ann. 20/1-13.5; Ind. Code Ann. § 12-10-3-9; Iowa Code § 235B.3; Kan. Stat. Ann. § 39-1402; Ky. Rev. Stat. Ann. § 209.030; La. Rev. Stat. Ann. § 14:403.2; Me. Rev. Stat. Ann. tit. 22 §§ 3477-49; Md. Code Ann., Fam. Law §§ 14-302; Mass. Gen. Laws ch. 19A, § 15; Mich. Comp. Laws Ann. § 400.11a; Minn. Stat. § 626.557; Miss. Code Ann. § 43-47-7; Mo. Ann. Stat. § 660.255; Mont. Code Ann. § 52-3-811; Neb. Rev. Stat. § 28-372; Nev. Rev. Stat. Ann. 200.5093-.50935; N.H. Rev. Stat. Ann. § 161-F:46; N.J. Stat. Ann. § 30:1A-3; N.M. Stat. Ann. § 27-7-30; N.Y. Soc. Serv. Law § 473b; N.C. Gen. Stat. § 108A-102; N.D. Cent. Code § 50-25.2-03; Ohio Rev. Code. Ann. § 5101.61; Okla. Stat. tit. 43a, § 10-104; Or. Rev. Stat. § 411-021-0010; 6 Penn. Admin. Code § 15.21; R.I. Gen. Laws § 42-66-8; S.C. Code Ann. § 43-35-25; S.D. Codified Laws § 34-12-51; Tenn. Code Ann. § 71-6-103; Tex. Hum. Res. Code Ann. § 48.051; Utah Code Ann. § 62A-3-305; Vt. Code Ann. tit. 33 § 6903; Va. Code Ann. § 63.2-1606; Wash. Rev. Code Ann. § 74.34.035; W. Va. Code § 9-6-9; Wis. Stat. Ann. § 46.90; Wyo. Stat. Ann. § 35-20-103.

Additional Information Sources

Pamela B. Teaster et al., *Elder Abuse and Neglect,* 3(1) Aging Health 115–128 (2007), *available at* www.futuremedicine .com (excellent review of the literature since 2001 on the following aspects of elder abuse and neglect: definitional issues; screening and assessment instruments; scope of the problem; sexual abuse; risk factors; outcomes; studies of APS; multidisciplinary teams; interventions by medical, criminal justice, and policy communities; long-term care facilities; and theoretical perspectives).

National Center on Elder Abuse (part of federal Administration on Aging), www.ncea.aoa.gov

National Adult Protective Services Association, http://apsnetwork.org

National Committee for the Prevention of Elder Abuse, www.preventelderabuse.org

National Research Council, *Elder Mistreatment: Abuse, Neglect, and Exploitation in an Aging America* (2003).

Journal of Elder Abuse and Neglect, www.haworthpressinc.com

Georgia J. Anetzberger, ed., *The Clinical Management of Elder Abuse,* Binghamton, NY: Haworth Press (2005).

American Society of Adult Abuse Professionals and Survivors, www.asaaps.org

GRANDPARENTS' RIGHTS

Grandparents' Visitation Rights

Every state has a statute that provides for grandparent visitation of minor grandchildren in some form. The state legislatures' authority to enact these statutes is included within the *parens patriae* power of the states, in appropriate circumstances, to regulate "the family itself...in the public interest." *Prince v. Massachusetts,* 321 U.S. 158, 166 (1944).

The states' authority in this arena is not unlimited. In *Troxel v. Granville,* 530 U.S. 57 (2000), the U.S. Supreme Court dealt with the validity of Washington State's grandparent visitation statute in the context of a dispute between the paternal grandparents and the minor children's mother. The Court held as follows:

> *The Fourteenth Amendment provides that no State shall "deprive any person of life, liberty, or property without due process of law"....*
> *The liberty interest at issue in this case—the interest of parents in the care, custody, and control of their children—is perhaps the oldest of the fundamental liberty interests recognized by this Court.*

DISCUSSION QUESTIONS

Even if states have the legal authority to intervene in the area of grandparents' visitation rights, why should a state legislature exercise that power? What are the policy justifications for a state to legislatively intervene in this arena? *See* Rebecca J. O'Neill, *Grandparents Raising Grandchildren in Illinois—Establishing a Right to a Continuing Relationship Through Visitation, Custody, and Guardianship*, 38 Loy. U. Chi. L.J. 733 (2007).

Section 26.10.160(3) [of Washington Statutes], as applied to Granville and her family in this case, unconstitutionally infringes on that fundamental parental right. The Washington nonparental visitation statute is breathtakingly broad. According to the statute's text, "[a]ny person *may petition the court for visitation rights at* any time, *and the court may grant such visitation rights whenever visitation may serve* the best interests of the child."

As we have explained, the Due Process Clause does not permit a State to infringe on the fundamental right of parents to make child-rearing decisions simply because a state judge believes a "better" decision could be made. Neither the Washington nonparental visitation statute generally—which places no limits on either the persons who may petition for visitation or the circumstances in which such a petition may be granted—nor the Superior Court in this specific case required anything more. Accordingly, we hold that § 26.10.160(3), as applied in this case, is unconstitutional.

Because we rest our decision on the sweeping breadth of § 26.10.160(3) and the application of that broad, unlimited power in this case, we do not consider the primary constitutional question passed on by the Washington Supreme Court—whether the Due Process Clause requires all nonparental visitation statutes to include a showing of harm or potential harm to the child as a condition precedent to granting visitation. We do not, and need not, define today the precise scope of the parental due process right in the visitation context. In this respect, we agree...that the constitutionality of any standard for awarding visitation turns on the specific manner in which that standard is applied and that the constitutional protections in this area are best elaborated with care.

Grandparents' Legal Authority

The Supreme Court observed the following in the *Troxel* case:

The demographic changes of the past century make it difficult to speak of an average American family. The composition of families varies greatly from household to household. While many children may have two married parents and grandparents who visit regularly, many other children are raised in single-parent households. In 1996, children living with only one parent accounted

DISCUSSION QUESTIONS

1. Do you agree that a parent's right to control who has visits with his or her child ought to be treated as a "fundamental liberty interest" under the Constitution, thereby requiring the state to prove it has a "compelling interest" before it may infringe upon that right? Where, specifically, is this right enumerated in the Constitution? *See* the dissenting opinions of Justices Thomas and Scalia in *Troxel.*

2. The majority opinion in *Troxel* found fault with the broadness of the Washington statute. Examine your own state's statute on grandparents' visitation rights and analyze whether it, too, is written in overly broad language that could not now pass constitutional muster. Could your state's statute be interpreted more narrowly, such that it might be constitutionally acceptable?

*for 28 percent of all children under age 18 in the United States....
Understandably, in these single-parent households, persons outside
the nuclear family are called upon with increasing frequency to
assist in the everyday tasks of child rearing. In many cases, grandparents play an important role.*

One aspect of assisting in the everyday tasks of child-rearing is making
decisions about the child's medical care. Several states explicitly give
grandparents the authority, under certain circumstances, to make medical
decisions on behalf of their minor grandchildren even when the grandparents
have not been appointed guardian for their grandchildren by a court. For
example, California Family Code § 6550 provides the following:

*(a) A caregiver's authorization affidavit that meets the require-
ments of this part authorizes a caregiver 18 years of age or older
who completes items 1–4 of the affidavit...and signs the affidavit to enroll a minor in school and consent to school-related
medical care on behalf of the minor. A caregiver who is a relative and who completes items 1–8 of the affidavit provided in
Section 6552 and signs the affidavit shall have the same rights*

DISCUSSION QUESTIONS

1. Are statutes empowering grandparents to make medical decisions for their grandchildren advisable? What are
   some of the dangers raised by such laws? How can those
   dangers be averted or minimized?
2. Some statutes empowering grandparents as medical
   decision makers for their grandchildren, such as D.C.
   Code § 16-4901, depend on the parent signing a form
   giving the grandparents that decision-making authority; in other statutes, parental consent is not required.
   Which approach is better, and why?

to authorize medical care and dental care for the minor that are given to guardians under...the Probate Code. The medical care authorized by this caregiver who is a relative may include mental health treatment....

Florida Statutes § 743.0645 provides the following:

(2) Any of the following persons, in order of priority listed, may consent to the medical care or treatment of a minor...when, after a reasonable attempt, a person who has the power to consent as otherwise provided by law cannot be contacted by the treatment provider and actual notice to the contrary has not been given to the provider by that person:
   (c) The grandparent of the minor.

KINSHIP CARE

In the United States (and internationally) growing numbers of children are being raised by their grandparents. In 2007, more than 6 million American children were being raised in households headed by grandparents and other relatives, 2.5 million children were in grandparent-headed households without any parents present, and 2.4 million grandparents were responsible for their grandchildren living with them. A variety of factors pertaining to the parents contributes to this grandparent-reliant kinship care phenomenon: drug and alcohol problems, mental illness, incarceration, death, poverty, divorce, child abuse and neglect, teen pregnancy, HIV/AIDS, domestic violence, and military deployment, among other things. *See* Amy Goyer, *Intergenerational Relationships: Grandparents Raising Grandchildren,* AARP Foundation Grandparent Information Center (Feb. 2006), *available at* www.Aarp.org/research/international/perspectives/nov_05_grandparents.html; *A Fact Sheet for Grandparents and Other Relatives Raising Children,* AARP Foundation (Oct. 2007), *available at* www.Aarp.org/families/grandparents/gic/gic_pubs.html.

The legal options available to define a kinship caregiver's rights and responsibilities depend on the family's individual circumstances and applicable state law. In general, these options for delineating the grandparent's rights and responsibilities concerning the grandchild are as follows:

- Delegation of authority from the parents to the grandparent to do such specified things as enrolling the child in school, consenting to medical care, and applying on the child's behalf for available public benefit programs such as Medicaid, all subject to the authority being revoked by the parent
- Foster care
- Legal custody
- Adoption
- Guardianship
- Standby custody

DISCUSSION QUESTIONS

Which of these types of legal relationships would you recommend to a grandparent? Why?

There are several sources of financial support for grandparents who are heading "grandfamilies":

- Temporary Assistance for Needy Families, created by the Personal Responsibility and Work Opportunity Reconciliation Act of 1996 (PRA), Pub. L. No. 104-193, 110 Stat. 2105, codified in 42 U.S.C. § 601 et seq.
- Foster care payments, if the child is in state custody and the grandparent meets foster care licensing requirements, including a basic payment plus supplemental payments for clothing, school expenses, or the care of special needs children
- If income is low enough, housing subsidies
- If income is low enough, additional food stamps
- Medicaid coverage for the child

- Subsidized guardianship programs, providing financial assistance in over half the states for a grandparent who becomes the legal guardian of the grandchild. *See* Fact Sheet, *Grandfamilies: Subsidized Guardianship Programs,* Washington, DC: Generations United (6th Rev. Printing 2006), *available at* www.gu.org.

NOTES

Sections of this chapter were originally published in Marshall B. Kapp, *Family Caregivers' Legal Concerns,* XXVII(4) Generations 49–55 (Winter 2003–04), and Marshall B. Kapp, *Book Review, Elder Mistreatment: Abuse, Neglect, and Exploitation in an Aging America,* 5 Marquette Elder's Advisor 121–128 (Fall 2003).

CHAPTER 9

Protection of Older Consumers

THE REGULATORY LANDSCAPE

To ensure that older individuals' personal and financial choices truly are autonomous (i.e., voluntary, informed, and capable), American society has established a substantial web of laws designed to protect consumers against the potential excesses of a completely laissez faire, caveat emptor (buyer beware) environment. Frequently, consumer protection laws explicitly identify older persons as especially vulnerable and therefore needing special protection in the marketplace. For example, statutes may include enhanced criminal penalties for committing certain fraudulent conduct when the victim is older than a specified chronological age.

Many older persons entrust their life savings to salesmen with such titles as "certified senior advisor," "chartered senior financial planner,"

DISCUSSION QUESTIONS

Are laws that impose enhanced criminal penalties for defrauding older persons good public policy? Isn't there a danger that such laws will unfairly stigmatize older persons by labeling them as being especially vulnerable?

or "certified financial gerontologist." Some of these salesmen are very knowledgeable, such as those who have been through the training provided by the American Institute of Financial Gerontology (*available at* www.aifg.org). Others, though, have little if any real training. In response to the problem of older individuals receiving deficient, and sometimes outright fraudulent, financial investment advice, some states have begun to limit the use of particular professional designations. Missouri, for example, in 2008 announced through its Attorney General's Office a rule that would allow only securities brokers and investment sales agents to use titles that are specifically approved both by the state and a recognized accrediting agency. Under this rule, groups or individual sales people who are found to mislead older persons with exaggerated designations could face the suspension or revocation of their licenses to deal in securities.

DISCUSSION QUESTIONS

1. Are older persons particularly susceptible to being mislead about financial investments? Why?
2. Do older people as a group really need this kind of governmental protection? Should government be involved in this normally private kind of activity? Doesn't this form of governmental intrusion amount to paternalism that stigmatizes older individuals as especially helpless?

Case Study: Home Screening Tests

Many older individuals live in dread of one day becoming a victim of Alzheimer's disease or some other form of dementia. Especially for those who believe they are experiencing what they understand to be early symptoms of this devastating condition, the psychological appeal of products that may offer even a scintilla of useful information about the person's actual medical disease is strong. There is now a "do-it-yourself" gross screening tool that is being marketed directly to potential consumers for home use. Critics have raised a number of scientific and ethical misgivings regarding the public availability and use of this product at the present time. The advent of the Early Alert Alzheimer's Home Screening Test (AHST) also implicates a panoply of potential legal issues. For instance, what are the legal responsibilities (and the possible liability exposures for a breach of those responsibilities), in terms of appropriate diagnostic and therapeutic follow-up, of the physician who is presented with the results of an AHST that a patient has self-administered? What are the confidentiality obligations of health care providers whose patients give them their self-administered AHST results, especially in light of the medical privacy regime ushered in by regulations implementing the Health Insurance Portability and Accountability Act (see Chapter 6)? What are the legal ramifications of misuse of AHST results by insurers, employers, or others for discriminatory purposes (see Chapter 10)? What are the legal parameters shaping the health care provider's permissible response to a patient's request for advice regarding, or help in performing, an AHST? There is also the question of whether (and, if so, how) the federal government ought to be regulating the marketing and availability of the AHST to a consumer public that, because of apprehension about the ravages of dementia, may be described as vulnerable bordering on desperate.

Most aspects of the modern American health care industry are extensively regulated. To understand why the AHST's entry into the consumer marketplace is essentially unconstrained by the current regulatory structure, it is useful to distinguish AHST from other kinds of products and activities. First, the federal Food and Drug Administration

(FDA) imposes detailed premarketing approval require-ments, in terms of demonstrated safety and efficacy, on drugs and medical devices. The Food, Drug, and Cosmetic Act (FDCA) (21 U.S.C. § 321) defines a *drug* as "articles intended for use in the diagnosis, cure, mitigation, treat-ment, or prevention of disease"; a *device* "means an instru-ment, apparatus, implement, machine, contrivance, implant, in vitro reagent, or other similar or related article, includ-ing any component, part, or accessory, which is intended for use in the diagnosis of disease or other conditions, or in the cure, mitigation, treatment, or prevention of disease." The FDA does not have authority to regulate the AHST as a drug or device or as a *biological product* used for "the prevention, treatment or cure of a disease or condition of human beings" (21 C.F.R. pt. 600). Unlike, for example, home-testing kits used for identifying genetic mutations or defects and thereby predicting (with more or less cer-tainty) the particular consumer's medical future, AHST is designed and sold only as a gross screening instrument rather than as a diagnostic device. Although many patients fail to appreciate the difference between screening and diag-nostic testing, the fact that AHST falls in the screening test classification is crucial in its effect of putting it outside of the FDA's jurisdiction.

Second, because the AHST is a screening test intended exclusively for home use, it falls outside of the provisions of the FDCA and the Clinical Laboratories Improvement Act (CLIA) (42 U.S.C. § 1201 et seq.) pertaining to test kits manufactured for use in *laboratories*. A laboratory is defined in CLIA as "a facility for the biological, microbio-logical, serological, biophysical, cytological, pathological, or other examination of materials derived from the human body for the purpose of providing information for the diag-nosis, prevention, or treatment of any disease or impair-ment of, or the assessment of the health of, human beings."

For the same reason, AHST cannot be regulated under the various state law counterparts to CLIA.

Third, even though at this time its use is still very much a matter of clinical innovation rather than scientifically proven or accepted professional practice, the advertised intended purpose of the AHST is to provide some benefit to the specific consumer who is taking the test. The AHST is *not* undertaken by any consumer as part of a scientifically designed research protocol being conducted to gather data from which generalized conclusions may be drawn to benefit unknown other persons in the future. Thus the substantial body of federal regulation that protects the rights and safety of human beings who are asked to enroll as participants in research studies is inapplicable to the AHST context.

In regards to the availability of an AHST marketed directly to, and used in the home by, members of the general public, should health care professionals' and older persons advocates' reaction be, "There ought to be a law against, or at least setting certain limitations regarding, such a thing"? The answer, I believe, is both yes and no.

At the least, consumers need more and better information to assist them in deciding whether to purchase, use, and rely on the results of this product. On packaging or other materials that are readily readable without first buying and opening the kit, the manufacturer would be required to clearly state for lay persons that (1) the product is a gross screening tool rather than a diagnostic test, (2) it has certain limitations (which should be listed), and (3) the consumer should consult with a physician regardless of the test results. This information also ought to be mandated for inclusion in any advertising done for this product. Because the manufacture, marketing, and sale of the AHST are a matter of interstate commerce, the Federal Trade Commission could impose such informational admonitions on manufacturers under its authority to study and regulate "unfair or deceptive" acts or practices. State Federal Trade Commission counterparts have matching authority exercisable within their own respective borders. Government regulation of commercial speech, including compelling business entities to provide specified information to the public, is an important and legitimate strategy to safeguard consumer health and safety.

Beyond strategies aimed at empowering consumers to make informed, voluntary choices, however, health professionals should be cautious about advocating any broad new regulatory initiatives, such as expanding the reach of the FDCA or CLIA to encompass home screening tests like AHST. Decisions about the use of even well-validated screening tools for early detection of disease in older adults must be made on a very individualized basis, "reflecting the primacy of individual choice." "Let the buyer beware" is no longer a completely adequate response to an increasingly complex health care marketplace, but to deprive or unduly restrict the opportunity for consumers to choose to avail themselves of a product that they may believe, even in light of full and honest disclosure regarding the product's limitations, offers them the possibility of sufficient benefit (defined according to their own set and prioritization of values) to justify its use would be an exercise of governmental paternalism that disrespects the autonomy interests of competent adults. Although the ethical propriety of selling a product that preys on the (often overblown and misinformed) anxieties of a vulnerable population may be questioned, health professionals should be wary about enlarging the role of government qua protective nanny when that means excessively impinging on the prerogative of older adults to make informed, albeit perhaps ill-advised, decisions about the most personal aspects of their lives.

DISCUSSION QUESTIONS

1. How paternalistic should government be in protecting vulnerable older persons from the sales pitches of products aimed at them? What is the proper role of government in controlling the marketing and sale of goods and services that appeal particularly to vulnerable older adults? What form, if any, should regulation take?

2. If a patient/client asks for your professional advice about using the AHST or a similar home screening test, what would your advice be? What about if the home screening test was used for detecting some condition other than Alzheimer's disease?

Fraud Laws and Quality Control in Nursing Home Care

Federal prosecutors, working in collaboration with the Department of Health and Human Services' Office of Inspector General (OIG), have secured criminal indictments against nursing homes based on the theory that a nursing home that bills the Medicare or Medicaid programs for payments when the care provided was substandard has attempted to defraud the government and hence violated the False Claims Act. The submission of fraudulent claims through the mail or electronic transfers allows the government to additionally invoke the Mail and Wire Fraud Acts, which are considered predicate offenses under the Racketeer Influenced and Corrupt Organizations Act. In addition to criminal penalties, nursing homes may be exposed to remedies for violation of the civil False Claims Act, including a fine of between $5,000 and $10,000 per false claim submitted plus treble damages.

The OIG devotes an increasing amount of attention under its Operation Restore Trust initiative to assessing the quality of care in nursing homes. Quality of care studies have included evaluations of the role of the nursing home medical director, family experience with nursing home care, quality assurance committees in nursing homes, nurse aide training, and survey and certification consistency and reliability. This flurry of OIG activity adds to the sense of besiegement felt by the industry, especially when combined with a previous U.S. Attorney General's vehement public endorsement of the use of fraud and abuse prosecutions to punish nursing homes for "inadequate care." Most states have enacted their own counterparts to the federal False Claims Act, making it illegal to fraudulently bill their respective state Medicaid programs.

Although the propriety of the government's use of the False Claims Act as a mechanism to try to enforce quality standards in nursing homes is highly debatable, the threat of prosecution persists and encourages nursing home personnel to conceal rather than disclose errors with which they might be associated. This threat and its consequences are magnified by the ability of private citizens, for between 25% and 35% of the eventual monetary recovery, to act as "private Attorneys General" or "relators" and bring their own civil False Claims Act qui tam (whistleblower) actions against nursing homes. If the government elects to bring a criminal prosecution using the relator's evidence, then the relator receives between 15% and 25% of the eventual recovery. The federal Administration on

DISCUSSION QUESTIONS

1. Is the use of the federal and/or state False Claims Acts to impose criminal and/or civil penalties a proper mechanism to try to enforce quality standards in nursing homes? Why or why not?

2. What are the other possible legal remedies available to consumers or the government for substandard care by nursing homes? What are the advantages and disadvantages of pursuing those remedies as opposed to pursuing government prosecution under a fraud theory?

3. What do you think about the law creating financial incentives to encourage private whistleblowers to initiate fraud cases against nursing homes? Is it in the best interests of residents for the legal system to give nursing home staff one more reason to be continually looking over their own shoulders?

Aging has provided grants for senior Medicare patrol projects "to train retired persons to serve in their communities as volunteer expert witnesses and educators in combating health care error, fraud, and abuse," thereby giving nursing home staff one more reason to be continually looking over their own shoulders.

On March 16, 2000 the federal Department of Health and Human Services OIG published, at 65 Fed. Reg. 14289–14306 (Mar. 16, 2000), a compliance program guidance (CPG) for nursing facilities. (On January 24, 2008 OIG published at 73 Fed. Reg. 4248–49 a Solicitation of Information and Recommendations for Revising the Compliance Program Guidance for Nursing Facilities.) The original CPG stated the following:

> *The creation of compliance program guidances is a major initiative of the OIG in its effort to engage the private health care community in combating fraud and abuse [in Medicare, Medicaid, and other federal health programs]. The development of these types of compliance program guidances is based on our belief that a health care provider can use internal controls to more efficiently monitor adherence to applicable statutes, regulations and program requirements.*

The CPG for nursing facilities set forth "seven elements that the OIG has determined to be fundamental to an effective compliance program." These elements are contained in Table 9.1. The CPG also identified several

Table 9.1 Elements of OIG CPG for Nursing Facilities

Written policies, procedures, and standards of conduct
Designated compliance officer and compliance committee
Conduct of effective education and training
Development of effective lines of communication
Standards enforced through well-publicized disciplinary guidelines
Conduct of internal monitoring and audit
Prompt response to detected offenses and development of corrective action

Adapted from Compliance Program Guidance (CPG) for Nursing Facilities, DHHS OIG at 65 Fed. Reg. 14289–14306 (Mar. 16, 2000).

Table 9.2   OIG CPG for Nursing Facilities: Risk Areas

Quality of care
Residents' rights
Employee screening
Vendor relationships (kickbacks, inducements, and self-referrals)
Billing and cost reporting
Record keeping and documentation (creation and detention)

Adapted from Compliance Program Guidance (CPG) for Nursing Facilities, DHHS OIG at 65 Fed. Reg. 14289–14306 (Mar. 16, 2000).

specific risk areas where nursing facilities may encounter compliance problems. This list is contained in Table 9.2.

Fraud Targeting Older Persons Residing in the Community

Fraud targeting older individuals who reside in the community occurs in many forms: telemarketing fraud, Internet fraud, pyramid schemes, and "get rich quick" schemes, among others. Older individuals may be scammed into bad investments, buying goods and services they do not need, or donating money to phony organizations. In 2005, 22% of telemarketing fraud victims were over the age of 70, for a total loss of $5 million and an average loss of almost $3,000.

DISCUSSION QUESTIONS

1. Do you agree with the OIG's "belief that a health care provider can use internal controls to more efficiently monitor adherence to applicable statutes, regulations and program requirements"? Do you trust health care providers to carry out the compliance monitoring task using internal controls?

2. Do you agree with the lists of elements of a compliance program (see Table 9.1) and risk areas (see Table 9.2) compiled by the OIG? What particular items would you add to or subtract from these lists?

Every state has unfair and deceptive acts and practices statutes that outlaw a range of activities, including common law fraud, taking unfair advantage of a consumer by using superior knowledge or bargaining position, and coercive or misleading sales practices. These laws may be enforced through criminal prosecutions brought by the state and private civil lawsuits brought by or on behalf of the victimized consumer. Criminal prosecutions may result in imprisonment and/or monetary fines; civil remedies may include compensatory damages, punitive damages if intentional violations can be proved, equitable relief ordering the wrongdoer to do or refrain from doing specific actions, court costs, and recovery of the plaintiff's attorneys fees.

DISCUSSION QUESTIONS

1. Why are older persons often the most inviting target for scam artists?
2. Why are most older individuals reluctant to report financial abuse to law enforcement agencies, human services providers, their own families, their friends, or others?
3. What can health care, human services, and legitimate business professionals do to prevent older patients/clients from becoming victims of consumer fraud? What can family members do?
4. How should we balance our need to protect older persons against harm, on the one hand, and our need to respect the autonomy of older persons (including the right to make bad choices), on the other?

NOTES

Sections of this chapter were originally published in Marshall B. Kapp, *Should Home Screening Tests for Alzheimer's Disease Be Regulated?* 43(3) Gerontologist 292–294 (2003), and Marshall B. Kapp, *Resident Safety and Medical Errors in Nursing Homes: Reporting and Disclosure in a Culture of Mutual Distrust,* 24(1) J. Legal Med. 51–76 (March 2003).

CHAPTER 10

Age Discrimination and the Law

WHAT IS THE RELEVANCE OF A PERSON'S AGE?

One fundamental issue is how, if at all, the law's content ought to reflect the phenomenon of age. In shaping and enforcing laws, to what extent is age *material,* that is, potentially making a meaningful difference in the outcome? To what extent may we object that age is irrelevant? The answer to that question about the proper relevance of age in shaping law's content turns on society's generally schizophrenic attitudes toward aging and older persons. Sometimes we believe, and our laws reflect, embody, and shape this concept, that age and aging are irrelevant and that older persons are robust and self-reliant just like the rest of the population. Therefore the law's content should focus on ensuring older individuals equal treatment and protection against unfair discrimination. This philosophy results in the enunciation of liberty or negative rights; that is, the right of the independent, autonomous older individual to be protected against unwanted and external interference or unequal treatment. Conversely, sometimes we think of older persons as an identifiable group that is unique in some pertinent manner that justifies special or preferential treatment as compared with everyone else. The outcome of this position is the legislative creation or judicial recognition of entitlements, or claims for the provision of specific benefits that may be enforced by an individual—solely by virtue of his or her membership in a specific age category—against public officials or private actors. At times, advocates for older persons have made,

DISCUSSION QUESTIONS

How would you resolve society's schizophrenic attitude about the legal relevance of a person's chronological age? Is age irrelevant, such that the law should protect people against discrimination based on age? Or, is age so central a consideration that the law ought to provide special protections and benefits for people over a specified age? Or, does the significance of age depend on the particular issue under consideration?

and lawmakers have responded to, both sorts of arguments depending on the particular issue under consideration.

The principle of equality, dictating nondiscriminatory treatment that judges each person as an individual, is reflected in many civil rights laws that affect various facets of older persons' lives. Prominent examples of these laws include the Age Discrimination Act, Age Discrimination in Employment Act, Americans With Disabilities Act (ADA), Fair Housing Act Amendments, the state and local counterparts to these federal statutes, federal and state constitutional provisions that prohibit health care rationing schemes based on age, and the removal of references to age in most state guardianship statutes as automatic grounds for finding persons incompetent to make their own personal and financial decisions.

The 1975 Age Discrimination Act (42 U.S.C. §§ 6101–6107) is the most straightforward illustration of a law in this category. This Act provides that "no person in the United States shall, on the basis of age, be excluded from participation in, be denied the benefits of, or be subjected to discrimination under any program or activity receiving federal financial assistance."

AGE DISCRIMINATION IN EMPLOYMENT

Building on the focus of racial equality in the 1964 Civil Rights Act (42 U.S.C. § 2000a), Congress enacted the Age Discrimination in Employment Act (ADEA) (29 U.S.C. §§ 621–634) in 1967 to protect people over age 40 against discrimination in the workplace based exclusively on their age. The ADEA, as subsequently amended several times, imposes on most private employers, employment agencies, and labor unions nondiscrimination obligations, that is, the responsibility to treat everyone equally regardless of age concerning hiring, termination, promotion, training, and other terms and conditions of employment or retirement. Older persons who have been unfairly discriminated against may have their rights enforced through a complaint to the Equal Employment Opportunity Commission (EEOC) and, ultimately, through a civil lawsuit for monetary damages and equitable relief, such as job reinstatement, in federal court.

In 2004 the U.S. Supreme Court cleared up any ambiguity about who the ADEA is intended to protect. In *General Dynamics Land Systems v. Cline* (540 U.S. 581 [2004]), a group of present and former employees between the ages of 40 and 49 years sued the employer under the ADEA. They alleged that a collective bargaining agreement between the employer and the union, which eliminated the employer's retiree benefits health insurance coverage for workers then under age 50, impermissibly discriminated against *younger* workers. The Supreme Court held that the employer, by eliminating health insurance benefits for workers under 50 years of age but retaining coverage for workers over 50 years of age, did *not* violate the ADEA because discrimination against the relatively young is outside the ADEA's protection. The majority opinion, in examining the issue of legislative intent, held as follows:

> *Congress used the phrase "discrimina[tion]...because of [an] individual's age" the same way that ordinary people in common usage might speak of age discrimination any day of the week. One commonplace conception of American society in recent decades is its character as a "youth culture," and in a world where younger is better, talk about discrimination because of age is naturally understood to refer to discrimination against the* older.

This same, idiomatic sense of the statutory phrase is confirmed by the statute's restriction of the protected class to those 40 and above. If Congress had been worrying about protecting the younger against the older, it would not likely have ignored everyone under 40. The youthful deficiencies of inexperience and unsteadiness invite stereotypical and discriminatory thinking about those a lot younger than 40, and prejudice suffered by a 40-year-old is not typically owing to youth, as 40-year-olds sadly tend to find out. The enemy of 40 is 30, not 50.

The Supreme Court had sounded a very different note 4 years earlier in its analysis of workplace ageism. In *Kimel v. Florida Board of Regents* (528 U.S. 62 [2000]), the issue presented was whether the nondiscrimination provisions of the ADEA applied to state and local public sector employers. The precise, complicated legal issue concerned the authority of Congress under the Fourteenth Amendment's Equal Protection clause to enact an exception to the Eleventh Amendment's prohibition of lawsuits being initiated against the states by private citizens. In essence, the outcome of the case revolved around proof of the extent older persons in this country *historically* had or had not been subjected to workplace discrimination by states and localities. In finding that the historical record of age discrimination by public sector employers was *not* sufficient to justify abrogating the Eleventh Amendment's sovereign immunity protections, the Court held as follows:

Age classifications, unlike governmental conduct based on race or gender, cannot be characterized as "so seldom relevant to the achievement of any legitimate state interest that laws grounded in such considerations are deemed to reflect prejudice and antipathy." Older persons, again, unlike those who suffer discrimination on the basis of race or gender, have not been subjected to a "history of purposeful unequal treatment." Old age does not define a discrete and insular minority because all persons, if they live out their normal life spans, will experience it.

Since the ADEA regulates the actions of employers, employment agencies, and labor organizations that are engaged in various kinds of businesses, the authority of Congress to enact the ADEA is found in the United States Constitution, Article 1, Section 8: "The Congress shall have the power to regulate commerce with foreign nations, and among the several states..." During most periods in American history, the courts have interpreted Congress' commerce power very broadly. The authority of individual states to pass parallel anti-discrimination statutes pertaining to employment stems from the states' inherent police power to act to protect and promote the general health, safety, welfare, and morals of the community.

In terms of legal process, the *Kimel* case illustrates the doctrine of judicial review. Under this doctrine a court may invalidate on constitutional grounds a statute enacted by a legislature and signed by the jurisdiction's chief executive. For example, in that case the Supreme Court overturned a provision of the ADEA because Congress lacked authority under the U.S. Constitution (the Eleventh Amendment) to enact that particular provision. Besides examining statutes in light of compliance with the federal Constitution, a court also may invalidate a state statute on the grounds that it violates the pertinent state constitution.

DISCUSSION QUESTIONS

1. At what age do you believe the law ought to begin protecting individuals against discrimination in the various facets of employment? Is 40, as used in the ADEA, the proper trigger for protection? Do 40-year-olds need to be protected against discrimination taking place in the workplace in favor of older—as well as younger—workers?

2. Do you agree with the Supreme Court's holding in *Kimel* that older persons in the United States have not traditionally been targeted for purposeful unequal treatment? In American history, has there been less age discrimination than discrimination on the basis of race and gender? Should older persons be entitled to less legal

protection regarding employment than members of particular racial groups or women?

3. Typical of the way that many statutes and regulations are written, the obligations imposed on employers, employment agencies, and labor organizations by the ADEA are phrased in negative terms, as "Thou Shalt Not" commandments. Should the law go further than just prohibiting age discrimination in employment? Should the law impose some sort of positive affirmative action requirements on employers, employment agencies, and labor organizations regarding older employees, the way the ADA imposes affirmative obligations regarding "reasonable accommodations" for mentally and physically disabled persons?

4. One of the purposes of the ADEA is to prohibit (with limited exceptions for owners or partners of a business, highly paid executives, firefighters, and law enforcement officers) mandatory retirement policies based on age. Despite this prohibition, the actual retirement age of American workers continues to decrease. Should we enact laws intended to encourage (i.e., provide incentives for) individuals to take more advantage of the ADEA and stay in the workplace longer?

5. Should age discrimination be characterized primarily as an economic equity issue or as a human rights issue? What practical difference would it make?

The actual retirement age of American workers continues to decrease largely because more employers are offering early retirement plans to entice older workers to leave their employment voluntarily. In return for the benefits provided by the early retirement plan (usually a cash payout or credit for additional years in the pension calculation), the retiring worker ordinarily is required to sign a document waiving, or giving up, any potential ADEA claims he or she might otherwise be entitled to bring

---

Table 10.1 Requirements for a Valid Early Retirement Waiver of ADEA Rights

---

To be legally enforceable, the waiver must
- Be written in understandable language
- Explicitly mention rights or claims under the ADEA
- Exclude rights or claims arising after the waiver is signed
- Provide the employee additional consideration (something of value) in return for signing the waiver
- Advise the employee to consult an attorney before agreeing to the waiver
- Give the employee at least 21 days to consider the agreement or at least 45 days if the waiver is part of an exit incentive or employment termination program
- Give the employee a "cooling off" period of at least 7 days after signing, during which the employee may revoke the waiver
- If the waiver is part of an employment termination program, give employees details as to whom the program applies

---

Data from ADEA, 29 U.S.C. § 626(f)

---

against the employer. The ADEA, 29 U.S.C. § 626(f), provides that only "knowing and voluntary" waivers are enforceable and lists nine factors that must be met for the waiver to so qualify (see Table 10.1).

DISCUSSION QUESTIONS

What is/are the purpose(s) of these requirements? Are these requirements really necessary, or are they just formalistic overkill? Are these requirements fair to employers?

Several defenses may be asserted against an accusation that one has committed an ADEA violation. 29 U.S.C. § 623(f) provides as follows:

> *It shall* not *be unlawful for an employer, employment agency, or labor organization—*
> *(1) to take any action otherwise prohibited [by the ADEA] where age is a* bona fide occupational qualification *reasonably*

necessary to the normal operation of the particular business, or where the differentiation is based on reasonable factors other than age, *or where such practices involve an employee in a workplace in a* foreign country *and compliance with [the ADEA] would cause such employer, or a corporation controlled by such employer, to violate the laws of the country in which such workforce is located;*

(2) to take any action otherwise prohibited under [the ADEA]—

> *(A) to observe the terms of* a bona fide seniority system *that is not intended to evade the purposes of [the ADEA], except that no such seniority system shall require or permit the* involuntary retirement *of any individual [age 40 or above] because of the age of such individual; or*
>
> *(B) to observe the terms of a* bona fide employee benefit plan—
>
>> *(i) where, for each benefit or benefit package, the actual amount of payment made or cost incurred on behalf of an older worker is no less than that made or incurred on behalf of a younger worker; or*
>>
>> *(ii) that is a* voluntary early retirement incentive plan *consistent with the relevant purpose [of the ADEA]; or*
>
> *(3) to discharge or otherwise discipline an individual for* good cause.

DISCUSSION QUESTIONS

1. Would it be unlawful under the ADEA for a company, during a plant closing and downsizing, to give younger workers more severance pay than older coworkers?
2. Would it be unlawful under the ADEA for an employer to offer its Medicare-eligible (i.e, most people over age 65) retirees health insurance coverage that is less complete

than coverage offered to retired employees who are not eligible for Medicare (i.e., people under 65)? The court said no in *Erie County Retirees Association v. County of Erie,* 220 F.3d 193 (3d Cir. 2000), but the United States EEOC said yes in a final regulation published at 72 Fed. Reg. 72938-45 (Dec. 26, 2007), and the federal courts have upheld the reasonableness of this regulation, *AARP v. Equal Employment Opportunity Commission,* 489 F.3d 558 (3rd Cir. 2007), *cert. denied,* 128 S.Ct. 1733 (2008).

3. Would it be unlawful under the ADEA for a health plan to pay more to physician-recruits who are in their early years of practice than to those who have been practicing longer?

4. What roles might be played by health care, human services, and business professionals in helping to determine whether a valid defense to an ADEA claim exists in a particular case? What particular kinds of expertise and experience might such professionals bring to this inquiry?

Exercise

Flatbelly's, a chain of health clubs whose target client demographic is the young professional crowd, wants to hire some new aerobics instructors. How can it legally advertise for those positions in a way likely to obtain applications from attractive, fit applicants in their 20s rather than from retirees in their 50s and 60s who may have substantial aerobics experience garnered from participation in the local hospital's active seniors program? If Flatbelly's does not hire an older applicant and is sued for age discrimination, what defense(s) might be available?

What is the burden of proof in an ADEA case? In *Reeves v. Sanderson Plumbling Products, Inc.,* 530 U.S. 133 (2000), the Supreme Court held that a plaintiff asserting an ADEA claim need not prove by direct evidence (i.e., the proverbial "smoking gun") illegal intent on the part of the employer:

> *("[W]hen all legitimate reasons for rejecting an applicant have been eliminated as possible reasons for the employer's actions, it is more likely than not the employer, who we generally assume acts with some reason, based his decision on an impermissible consideration"). Thus, a plaintiff's prima facie case, combined with sufficient evidence to find that the employer's asserted justification is false, may permit the trier of fact to conclude that the employer unlawfully discriminated.*
>
> *This is not to say that such a showing by the plaintiff will always be adequate to sustain a jury's finding of liability. Certainly there will be instances where, although the plaintiff has established a prima facie case and set forth sufficient evidence to reject the defendant's explanation, no rational factfinder could conclude that the action was discriminatory. For instance, an employer would be entitled to judgment as a matter of law if the record conclusively revealed some other, nondiscriminatory reason for the employer's decision, or if the plaintiff created only a weak issue of fact as to whether the employer's reason was untrue and there was abundant and uncontroverted independent evidence that no discrimination had occurred.*
>
> *Whether judgment as a matter of law is appropriate in any particular case will depend on a number of factors. Those include the strength of the plaintiff's prima facie case, the probative value of the proof that the employer's explanation is false, and any other evidence that supports the employer's case and that properly may be considered on a motion for judgment as a matter of law.*

The ADEA provides persons who have been illegally discriminated against in the employment arena because of their age with various remedies. An individual alleging unlawful discrimination under the ADEA must first file a charge with the federal EEOC (www.eeoc.gov),

DISCUSSION QUESTIONS

1. Do you agree with the *Reeves* decision? Does it unfairly expose employers to liability based on circumstantial or inferential, rather than direct, evidence? On the other hand, would requiring production of direct evidence of the employer's intent to discriminate based on age impose an impossible hurdle for plaintiffs?

2. How can a plaintiff in an ADEA lawsuit establish the "prima facie" (on its face) case of discrimination required by *Reeves*? It is undisputed that the petitioner satisfied this burden here: (1) at the time he was fired, he was a member of the class protected by the ADEA ("individuals who are at least 40 years of age"), (2) he was otherwise qualified for the position of Hinge Room supervisor, (3) he was discharged by respondent, and (4) respondent successfully hired three persons in their 30s to fill petitioner's position.

which decides whether or not to bring a civil action in federal district court on the individual's behalf. If the EEOC declines to bring a lawsuit, "Any person aggrieved may bring a civil action in any [federal] court of competent jurisdiction for such legal or equitable relief as will effectuate the purposes of [the ADEA]." 29 U.S.C. § 626(c) (1). Legal relief could include money damages for back pay (e.g., lost wages after an illegal firing or failure to hire) or front pay (e.g., anticipated future lost wages due to an illegal firing). When money damages are sought, the plaintiff has a right to a jury trial on any factual issues. When a jury finds that the discriminatory actions of the employer, employment agency, or labor organization were *willful, McGinty v. State of New York,* 193 F.3d 64 (2d Cir. 1999), it may impose double the actual amount of damages. Equitable relief could include court orders (injunctions) directing the defendant to take some action other than paying money damages (e.g., to promote or reinstate) to the aggrieved individual.

DISCUSSION QUESTIONS

Why do you believe age discrimination is a global problem that is prevalent in a number of very otherwise dissimilar countries? What is the common element? Is the American legal response likely to be effective globally?

Legal representation of individuals alleging unlawful age discrimination ordinarily is by private attorneys, especially because a court has authority to award reasonable attorneys' fees to a prevailing plaintiff's attorney at the expense of the losing defendant. Regarding the availability of legal services relating to age discrimination, see www.aoa.dhhs.gov/prof/ aoaprog/elder_rights/legal_services.asp.

Every state has enacted its own counterpart to the ADEA. Even individuals, such as state employees under *Kimel v. Florida Board of Regents,* 528 U.S. 62 (2000), who are precluded from suing for age discrimination under the ADEA in the federal courts may try to vindicate their rights in state court under their own state statute. Additionally, some state age discrimination statutes impose broader protections for the employee than does the ADEA.

Beyond U.S. borders, age discrimination is a global problem. A recent report from the International Federation on Ageing compiled and compared the current legal responses in eight different nations (Argentina, Australia, Canada, Jamaica, Japan, South Africa, the United Kingdom, and the United States) to this phenomenon. *See* Stephen Charters, *Age Related Policies: A Global Review on Age Discrimination Legislation,* International Federation on Ageing (Jan. 2008), *available at* www.ifa-fiv .org/en/accueil1.aspx.

DISABILITY DISCRIMINATION

The ADA (Public Law No. 101-336, codified at 42 U.S.C. §§ 12101 et seq.) was enacted in 1990. Building on § 504 of the Rehabilitation Act of 1974 (29 U.S.C. § 794), which prohibits discrimination based on disability in all programs or activities operated by recipients of federal financial assistance, such as Medicare, Medicaid, or Department of Housing and Urban Development grants, the ADA prohibits employers, plus providers of goods and services to the public, from discriminating in their relationships with potential or actual employees, students, or customers on the basis of an individual's mental or physical disability as long as the individual is "otherwise qualified" to participate in such a relationship and enjoy its benefits. Individuals are protected against discriminatory treatment if they have diseases or defects that significantly interfere with one or more major life functions, if they have a history of such a disability, or if others (correctly or mistakenly) perceive them as having such a disability. Financial and equitable (i.e., orders to others to do things other than pay money) remedies are available to aggrieved parties through complaints to the EEOC and private federal lawsuits.

Of importance, however, the ADA goes further than simply prohibiting discrimination against "otherwise qualified" disabled persons. It imposes on employers and the providers of goods and services the affirmative or positive duty to make "reasonable accommodations," short of "undue hardship," when those reasonable accommodations will make the difference between a disabled person's participation in or exclusion from an activity. An example is building a wheelchair ramp to allow a wheelchair-bound person to enter a building to purchase goods or services or to work. Older persons often benefit from such affirmative accommodations.

Even though the ADA is not on its face targeted directly to the elderly, its coverage enables many older persons to benefit from its antidiscrimination and reasonable accommodations provisions. For instance, the Supreme Court's analysis of Title 2 of the ADA in the case of *Olmstead v. L.C.* (527 U.S. 581 [1999]), interpreting the ADA to require the states to provide publicly funded services to the disabled in the most integrated, least restrictive setting possible, has given a major boost to the development of home and community-based alternatives to nursing home placement. Every state has enacted its own counterpart to the federal ADA.

In *Olmstead,* the state of Georgia was sued by two women whose disabilities included mental retardation and mental illness. Both women lived in state-owned and -operated institutions, despite the fact that their treatment professionals had determined they could be appropriately served in a community setting. The plaintiffs asserted that their continued institutionalization was a violation of their legal right under the ADA, 28

C.F.R. § 35.130(d), to live "in the most integrated setting appropriate to the needs of qualified individuals with disabilities." The Supreme Court found that "Unjustified isolation...is properly regarded as discrimination based on disability." It observed that "institutional placement of persons who can handle and benefit from community settings perpetuates unwarranted assumptions that persons so isolated are incapable or unworthy of participating in community life" and "confinement in an institution severely diminishes the everyday life activities of individuals, including family relations, social contacts, work options, economic independence, educational advancement, and cultural enrichment."

DISCUSSION QUESTIONS

1. How well does the *Olmstead v. L.C.* reasoning apply to frail, debilitated older individuals? Is living and receiving services in the home always really less restrictive, segregated, and isolated for such individuals than living in a long-term care facility surrounded by other people? Is a frail elder living at home, ambulating poorly, really "participating in community life" more than he or she would be in a long-term care facility with planned group activities?

2. Has the *Olmstead v. L.C.* decision made a noticeable difference in your jurisdiction, in terms of discouraging nursing home placement and encouraging home and community-based long term care for older persons with impaired ability to carry out activities of daily living? If so, has the effect of *Olmstead*, in your opinion, been a positive development? *See* Julia G. Gaughan, *Institutionalization as Discrimination: How Medicaid Waivers, the ADA, and Section 1983 Fail*, 56 U. Kan. L. Rev. 405–438 (2008). What are some of the dangers of "deinstitutionalizing" long-term care?

HOUSING

The housing rights of persons with disabilities, including older Americans, are covered by Title II (public services) and Title III (public accommodations and services rendered by private entities) of the ADA, as well as by § 504 of the Rehabilitation Act, 29 U.S.C. § 794. In addition, many states and localities have enacted statutes and ordinances that prohibit discrimination in the sale or rental of housing based on the potential buyer's or tenant's age.

On the federal level, Congress has enacted the Fair Housing Amendments Act (FHAA), Public Law No. 100–430, codified at 42 U.S.C. § 3604, implemented at 24 C.F.R. pt 100. The FHAA prohibits discrimination based on race, color, religion, sex, national origin, disability, or familial status (living with children under the age of 18) in most housing and housing-related transactions. The FHA applies to almost all housing activities or transactions, whether in the public or the private sector; the provision of services connected with a dwelling and zoning, land use, or health and safety regulations. These federal, state, and local laws are intended to protect older persons from being involuntarily segregated away from desired housing opportunities.

DISCUSSION QUESTIONS

1. If someone owns private property, should the federal government have authority to restrict what the property owner can do (in terms of sale or rental) with that property? Should government have the authority to impose affirmative accommodation requirements on the property owner to make the property suitable for older renters or buyers?

2. Assuming (accurately) that the federal and state governments both have the authority to set conditions on the sale or rental of property, is it wise policy to prohibit discrimination against the disabled in this regard? For

antidiscrimination purposes in the housing context, should a handicap be treated the same way we treat race, color, religion, sex, familial status, and national origin?

3. Should frailty (a common condition among the aged) be considered a "disability" for purposes of the FHAA?

4. How can you help older individuals choose from among the array of residential options that may be available to them? *See* Lawrence A. Frolik, *Residence Options for Older and Disabled Clients,* Washington, DC: ABA Press (2008).

The reason the FHAA restricts one's right to live in adults-only housing is to prevent discrimination in the housing marketplace against families with children. The FHAA provides an exception (in other words, it does permit adults-only housing), however, in the case of "housing for older people," which is defined in three alternate ways:

1. Housing provided by federal or state programs that the Secretary of the Department of Housing and Urban Development identifies as designed for older persons

2. Housing intended for, and solely occupied by, persons age 62 and over

3. Housing "intended and operated for occupancy by at least one person age 55 or over per unit," provided

   a. Eighty percent of the units must be occupied by someone age 55 or over

   b. Management must publish and follow policies that demonstrate intent to provide housing for persons age 55 and over.

In the Housing for Older Persons Act of 1995, 42 U.S.C. § 3607(b)(2) (c), Congress set out a four-prong, fact-based test to be used when making a determination about whether a housing complex is legitimately exempt from the FHAA under the "housing for older persons" exemption.

DISCUSSION QUESTIONS

1. Do you agree that adults-only housing should be permitted if one of the three enumerated conditions is met? Should we permit adults-only housing even if those conditions are not satisfied, that is, should we repeal the FHAA prohibitions against age-segregated housing?
2. Why should we permit age-segregated housing under any circumstances, when the law does not permit segregated housing on the basis of race, religion, or national origin?

Municipalities generally welcome senior housing. However, sometimes there is opposition to senior housing from local officials or neighboring property owners and residents. Although both federal and state laws regulate and largely prohibit private discriminatory housing practices, very little impedes municipalities from using their zoning power to effectively exclude or limit senior housing.

DISCUSSION QUESTIONS

Do you believe municipalities should ever exercise their zoning authority to exclude or limit senior housing projects within a municipality's boundaries?

HEALTH CARE RATIONING

Another area in which older persons are at risk of discrimination on the basis of their age is in the distribution of health care resources. There is a growing, albeit reluctant, recognition in American society and within the health care enterprise that money often influences both the process and the ultimate content of health care decisions. Consideration of this reality inevitably raises the specter of the dreaded "R" word—rationing of health care. This topic, particularly as it affects older persons, is discussed in Marshall B. Kapp, *Health Care Rationing Affecting Older Persons: Rejected in Principle But Implemented in Fact,* 14 J. Aging & Soc. Pol'y 27–42 (2002):

> *Health care resources in the United States are abundant, but like everywhere else, finite. Demands for health services [including LSMTs] are infinite, and consequently will inevitably exceed the available supply. This has always been the case in modern times. The reality of limits is especially exacerbated today as health care costs in the United States continue, after a brief respite of relative tranquility in the mid-1990s, to rise substantially in absolute dollars, percentage of the Gross Domestic Product, and as compared to other countries. There are multiple reasons for the constant escalation of demands—by both consumers and providers for health services and the accompanying cost of satisfying those demands. Advances in technology and the aging of the population arguably both play important parts in this dynamic.*

We are victims of our own success in continually improving the quality of health care and enabling many more people to live longer lives, albeit often with chronic and disabling conditions that require management via expensive medical interventions. The growing disequilibrium between demand and supply makes it increasingly impossible to avoid the hard choices of deciding under what circumstances potentially beneficial health services will not be made available to particular individuals. Even if health resources were themselves somehow unlimited, the total sum of resources available to address all of society's needs remains finite. To try to evade the need to budget society's resources in the public interest, which is to say make rationing choices that may disadvantage specific individuals, is Pollyannish and ultimately socially counterproductive.

Against this backdrop, several criteria or methods for rationing scarce health resources in the United States have been proposed over the past decades. For example, we have been urged officially to adopt approaches based on treating health care as a pure economic good, with access based exclusively on personal ability to purchase; a lottery system; prioritization based on first come, first served (i.e., when the budget for the year runs out, shut the doors); utilitarian social worth calculations taking into account such factors as a patient's productivity potential and family responsibilities; and rationing by prioritizing the value of specific services so that more individuals can be included but for more limited coverage, in contrast to our present approach of excluding some individuals from coverage for any services.

The most controversial rationing proposals have suggested the use of a potential patient's chronological age as a categorical criterion for determining whether public programs, most notably Medicare, should pay for particular health services. These proposals have a certain superficial appeal because the aged make a convenient scapegoat for some of our major national social problems, including those pertaining to the costs and financing of health care in the United States. First, because the elderly as a group are heavy users of health services, focusing on them as a potential source of large savings makes sense, much as Willie Sutton explained that he chose to rob banks because "that's where they keep the money." Second, older persons are highly dependent on public programs, especially Medicare, to finance the bulk of their extensive health care usage. A person over the age of 65 who has paid FICA (i.e., Federal Insurance Contribution Act) taxes for at least 40 quarters receives Medicare benefits; a younger, nondisabled person who has similarly paid 40 quarters of FICA taxes receives no Medicare benefits. This preferential treatment afforded by the Medicare program to eligible beneficiaries because of their age acts as a double-edged sword. What can be given can also be taken away. Although there is general agreement that singling out the elderly for health benefits may have made sense in 1965 when the Medicare legislation was originally enacted, their special treatment may breed resentment and backlash today. Indeed, perhaps the existence of Medicare has taken political pressure off federal and state lawmakers to adopt some form of universal health coverage. That possibility, in turn, may feed into the claims of generational equity proponents that the financing of social goods is a zero-sum affair in which a dollar spent on an older person's respirator is a dollar therefore unavailable to educate a youngster properly.

Since the late 1990s or so, calls for formal, official, age-based rationing have essentially receded in the face of a slew of practical and ethical objections that have been raised against them. Age-based rationing proposals have been vigorously attacked on the grounds, among others, that they, by considering persons as group members, ignore relevant individual differences in health, productivity potential, contribution to family and society, and need; show disrespect for the personhood of older persons, thereby setting a negative example for younger generations; set a precedent for the devaluation of and discrimination against older persons that could lead from health care to other areas of policy and practice; and give insufficient weight to the value of intergenerational interdependence. Whatever the merit of these objections may be, the political reality is that the United States is extremely unlikely to enact as official public policy anything resembling health care financing mechanisms that explicitly ration access to potentially beneficial services categorically on the basis of consumers' age.

The absence of an affirmative government response to earlier proposals for official policies that ration health resources categorically according to patient age does not mean that the issue of health care rationing and its implications for older persons have disappeared. On the contrary, rationing practices that affect, or threaten to affect, the elderly are already widespread in the United States but are being implemented *de facto* rather than *de jure* and, frequently, without open acknowledgment that they even entail resource rationing. This stands in contrast to the honesty with which Europeans admit to their own implicit age-based rationing practices. In significant ways, proponents of age-based rationing in the United States may have lost their public intellectual and political battles, but ultimately they are seeing the fundamental thrust of their proposals effectuated in action nonetheless.

There are four current forms of *de facto* health care rationing that carry real but largely hidden ramifications for older persons: third-party payer behaviors, physician practice patterns, the spread of evidence-based clinical practice parameters or guidelines in medicine, and the shift toward greater consumer choice in selecting health plans.

In terms of third-party payer behaviors, governmental (i.e., Medicare) and private third-party payers indirectly but effectively limit the access of older persons to potentially beneficial health care interventions in several ways. Access limitations may be precipitated by payers limiting or reducing the amount of payments made to health care providers for serving older patients. Providers are legally precluded from discriminating against patients on the basis of age by explicitly turning away older patients. Nonetheless, a provider can make itself less attractive to older patients or otherwise subtly discourage them from seeking care from that provider by, for example, manipulating its hours, location, or advertising emphasis. Access for older persons also might be impeded when they are forced to increase their own out-of-pocket expenditures for health care, as a result of rising premiums under Medicare B (or Part C private insurance options), increased deductible amounts and coinsurance contributions for that coverage (and for Medicare Part A coverage), and the escalating costs of essential but uncovered items. The result frequently might be that older persons do without (i.e., ration for themselves) some potentially beneficial aspects of health care. The same result may occur when the administrative hassle factor that must be overcome to secure Medicare or private payment for a particular service wears down the patient and/or provider to the point of submission.

Physician practice patterns constitute another form of discrimination against older persons in terms of resource allocation. In the United States, the public, policymakers, and health care providers have taken great pride in rejecting suggestions for explicit, categorical rationing schemes based on chronological age. We often tout our moral superiority in this regard over places like the United Kingdom. There, the practice of physicians in limiting various forms of medical treatment for their patients—from dialysis to coronary care unit admission, hypertension medication, and proper cancer treatment—based on patient age has been one of the world's best known "secrets." The reality, however, is that in the United States, too, physicians routinely engage in the practice of consciously but covertly making clinical compromises that result in some potentially beneficial interventions being withheld from their older patients.

It is certainly true that many older patients or their decision-making surrogates, using their personal benefit-to-burden calculation, select less intrusive alternatives to intensive therapy in certain situations, when presented with a choice. However, there is evidence that expensive but possibly helpful forms of medical care are often unilaterally withheld in the absence of the older person's or surrogate's own informed participation in the decision.

This practice may take place, for instance, when patient age is silently factored into individual clinicians' decisions about whether or not to admit patients to the hospital, provide intensive care, terminate therapy, or initiate vigorous treatment. The health sciences literature amply establishes that particular decisions carried out at the bedside about the distribution of health resources are made, not infrequently, by clinicians on the basis of the patient's advanced age, even when potential confounding variables such as prognosis and severity of illness have been controlled for in the analysis. Cancer is often screened for and treated less aggressively in older patients, both male and female, solely because of the age factor. Older patients are more likely than their younger counterparts to be designated "do not resuscitate" (DNR), even when all other conditions are equal. When attempted resuscitation is initiated for cardiopulmonary arrest, the elderly frequently receive shorter trials of advanced cardiac life support before death is pronounced. Advanced age has been identified as a separate risk factor for discontinuation of dialysis, undertreatment of acute heart attacks, underdiagnosis and undertreatment of asthma, and poor representation in clinical drug trials. Physicians may be less likely to offer an older patient a diagnostic workup for a gastrointestinal bleed or to pursue vigorously treatment of certain mental health problems in the aged.

Limits are placed on aggressive care in nursing facilities, where the resident population is predominantly elderly, in tacit and often poorly understood ways. *De facto* age discrimination appears to be most pronounced in the case of the oldest old. Less is spent per hospital admission on persons over age 80 than on younger elderly patients, perhaps because the oldest old patients, solely because of their advanced age, are not offered aggressive care.

There are a variety of plausible explanations for covert rationing by physicians on the basis of patient age. Physicians may be well intentioned but misjudge the likely outcome of medical intervention with older patients. Physicians may be uncertain about the likely clinical value of a specific medical intervention with older patients. Or, rationing by age at the individual bedside may derive from physicians' own often unconscious biases regarding the elderly, which are ubiquitously evident at the earliest stages of professional socialization. Such medical ageism may act alone or in combination with therapeutic miscalculations, uncertainties, and other factors such as the physician's personal financial incentives to conserve resources. Whatever the explanation, the practice of covert bedside rationing of potentially beneficial medical interventions on the basis of patient age is undeniable.

Leaders in health care acknowledge that a substantial amount of everyday medical practice consuming significant resources is predicated more on custom and habit than solid empirical evidence regarding clinical efficacy and effectiveness. In response to this realization, professional organizations, specialty societies, governmental agencies led by the federal Agency for Healthcare Research and Quality, and individual institutions and agencies in the United States and elsewhere have engaged in an ambitious, continuous effort to develop, collect, and disseminate to practicing clinicians a panoply of evidence-based clinical practice guidelines or parameters. These are intended to inform practitioners about what diagnostic and therapeutic interventions have actually been shown, as opposed to merely being assumed, to produce benefits for patients. Although there remains debate about how often clinical guidelines promulgated thus far actually accomplish their quality improvement aim, ideally this effort provides a scientific means for individual physicians to supplement their professional intuition (i.e., the "art" of medicine) in particular cases with advice validated by scientific data as interpreted through a process of expert consensus building.

In theory, clinical practice parameters are supposed to reflect consensus based only on scientific evidence, without considering cost ramifications. The explanation of proponents is that some parameters may increase health care expenditures by encouraging more, or more intensive, interventions in certain circumstances but that other parameters will contribute to cost reductions by convincing physicians to eliminate or reduce the use of interventions that have been identified as conveying little or no value to all or certain groups of patients.

However, a number of physicians and others harbor suspicions that practice parameters will ultimately be used more as instruments for cost control than for quality assurance purposes, especially when their development has been initiated by purchasers or providers of health care insurance. Some ethicists share the same qualms. Even with the best of intentions present, there is a danger that the evidentiary basis for particular practice parameters may be faulty or lacking or that available evidence will be misinterpreted or misapplied to the detriment of some patients. In applying population-based research findings to any particular patient's bedside, value judgments are unavoidable. According to one set of authors, "Consequently, although crude applications of [research] trial results may on average do more good than harm, they may nonetheless disadvantage some patients [including the elderly]" (I. Kerridge, M. Lowe, and D. Henry, *Ethics and Evidence Based Medicine*, 316 British Medical Journal 1151–1153 [1998]). At the same time, rationing decisions implemented at the bedside may be acceptable if the practice parameters on which they are based were developed through fair and open procedures in which the legitimate interests of older patients are accurately and sufficiently considered.

Proponents of age-based health care rationing contend that an officially adopted public policy of rationing, based categorically on patients' chronological age, is ethically preferable to widespread *de facto* rationing that is real but tacit. Whatever the arguments in favor of this position, for primarily political reasons the *de jure* approach is highly unlikely in the foreseeable future in the United States, whereas *de facto* rationing is very much happening. To the extent that we embrace, or at least tolerate, *de facto* rationing, though, we must remain attentive to the important implications for older persons' well-being and their legitimate interests in a fair and just society.

To that end, I propose the following starting principles against which any form of *de facto* health care rationing ought to be ethically evaluated:

1. Every person should have reasonable access to a decent minimum level of good quality health services appropriate to his or her individual needs.
2. The first priority of the U.S. health care delivery and financing system should be the elimination or reduction of wasteful and/ or unnecessary medical treatments that improperly consume finite resources.
3. Every individual should have access to accurate, comprehensive, timely information about the health care options financially and logistically available to, and medically appropriate for, that individual.
4. The interests of decisionally incapacitated persons should be protected through the empowerment of surrogate decision makers and advocates.
5. Decisions and actions concerning the medical care of individuals should result from informed, honest, "real-time" negotiations

between the particular patient (or proxy) and health care provider(s) taking place within the constraints of whatever health care delivery and financing system applies to that patient.

6. All these principles should be implemented without regard for the patient's chronological age or other personal characteristics, unless age or other personal characteristics are directly, independently relevant to specific health care options or decisions.

DISCUSSION QUESTIONS

1. Do you agree that health care rationing of some sort is necessary in the United States today? Why or why not?

2. If you answered yes to the previous question, what process ought to be used to make rationing decisions, and according to what criteria? Should the necessary rationing be conducted officially and openly (i.e., *de jure*) or unofficially and tacitly (i.e., *de facto*)?

3. What role should the chronological age of individual consumers play in decisions about the distribution of limited health care resources?

4. Do you agree with the preceding section that health care rationing that discriminates against older persons actually does take place in practice? Can you give examples from your own experience? Does this type of discrimination upset you? Why? What potential legal objections might you raise against such discrimination? *See* Marshall B. Kapp, *De Facto Health Care Rationing by Age: The Law Has No Remedy,* 19 J. Legal Med. 323–349 (1998).

5. What do you believe about the recommendations made in the preceding section? Are they desirable? Are they realistic? How could they be expanded upon or improved?

Exercise

Mr. M, a 69-year-old married man, is morbidly obese and has several chronic conditions, including chronic obstructive pulmonary disease from a history of smoking, congestive heart failure, diabetes, and arthritis. While on various medications for these problems, he recently had a spontaneous hip fracture. Mr. M has had multiple hospital admissions over the past few years. He is quite uncooperative generally with his plan of care and refuses to get up and out of bed even when assisted. After hospitalization for the hip fracture, he was admitted to a nursing home for short-term physical and occupational therapy. While Mr. M was there, a psychiatric consultant diagnosed him as passive-aggressive with self-destructive behavior. He was discharged home from the nursing home under the supervision of his wife, who herself has many physical limitations. Mr. M's frequent hospitalizations may fairly be attributed to his noncompliance with taking medications and sticking to his physician-recommended diet.

Mr. M's long-time primary care physician believes that Mr. M's medical problems could be controlled and hospitalizations could be reduced or even eliminated if Mr. M were more compliant with instructions. The physician believes that Mr. M is wasting the physician's time and also exposing the physician to potential risk of liability for Mr. M's inevitable bad outcomes. Mr. M receives comprehensive health care coverage from a preferred provider organization (PPO) that enrolls Medicare Advantage-eligible people in that geographical area.

Can the physician legally discontinue Mr. M as a patient because of Mr. M's noncompliance in his own medical affairs? If so, what specific steps must the physician engage in to sever the physician–patient relationship without exposing the physician to negative legal repercussions? Is noncompliance an ethically valid reason for a physician to unilaterally terminate her relationship with Mr. M? May the PPO drop Mr. M as a customer because Mr. M's noncompliance results in much higher medical expenses than necessary? May the PPO decline to renew Mr. M's policy when the current contract expires? Could the PPO have refused to insure Mr. M in the first place based on his weight and medical history?

VOTING

Another arena in which *de facto* age discrimination may occur, even when the laws themselves appear on the surface to be neutral about age, is that of voting. Voting is a fundamental right protected by the federal and state constitutions. A "legal survey informs us that all but twelve state constitutions bar people with various kinds of mental impairment from voting—for example, those who are *non compos mentis,* admitted to a mental institution, under guardianship, incapacitated, or mentally ill. The categories are sweeping and imprecise. State election law concerning voter eligibility on cognitive grounds does not necessarily track the state constitutional provisions, using different terminology in all but fourteen states...." Charles P. Sabatino & Edward D. Spurgeon, *Facilitating Voting as People Age: Implications of Cognitive Impairment,* 38(4) McGeorge L. Rev. 843, 850 (2007). These laws may have the practical effect of disproportionately discouraging or eliminating older individuals from exercising their right to vote.

DISCRIMINATION IN FAVOR OF OLDER PERSONS

At the very same time that laws against nondiscrimination aimed at individuals on the basis of age or age-related disability have been proliferating, the elderly, as members of a group, also have been perceived as significantly different from, and presumptively more dependent and vulnerable than,

DISCUSSION QUESTIONS

1. Do you agree with the following consensus recommendations made by national experts meeting by invitation at a 2007 conference convened on this topic, reported at *Recommendations of the Symposium*, 38(4) McGeorge L. Rev. 861 (2007):

   Goal 1: Prevent unfair or unlawful exclusion from voting.

   > *A. In those states with voting eligibility limits based on lack of capacity, every person should be presumed to have the capacity to vote absent a constitutionally adequate adjudication to the contrary.*
   > *B. It is inappropriate for any population to be screened for decisional capacity to vote based on age, disability, diagnosis, place of residence, guardianship status, or other characteristic.*

   What are some of the practical problems likely to be encountered in trying to implement these noble ideals?

2. What can health care and human services professionals and institutions do to ensure that older people are able to exercise their right to vote without jeopardizing the integrity of the electoral process? *See* Nina A. Kohn, *Preserving Voting Rights in Long-Term Care Institutions: Facilitating Resident Voting While Maintaining Election Integrity*, 38(4) McGeorge L. Rev. 1066–1111 (2007); Jason H. T. Karlawish et al., *Identifying the Barriers and Challenges to Voting by Residents in Nursing Homes and Assisted Living Settings*, 20(1) J. Aging & Soc. Pol'y 65–79 (2008).

their younger counterparts. Under this sensitive or paternalistic conceptu-alization of the aged as real or potential victims of neglect or exploitation, the creation of laws has been pushed that provide special, preferential ben-efits to persons eligible solely, or at least in large part, by virtue of having stayed alive for a set chronological period of time.

One form of state-sponsored discrimination in favor of older persons *qua* older persons is the legal creation of public benefit programs that use chronological age as the criterion, or at least one very important criterion, for eligibility predicated on the presumption of unique needs due to old age. The legislative and regulatory adoption of age as at least a partial proxy for demonstrated need, and therefore program entitlement, may be seen in such government programs as the Social Security retirement system and other public pension programs, Medicare, Supplemental Security Income, services under the Older Americans Act, and public housing subsidies for the elderly. Other forms of preference provided by the law are predicated on a perception that all or most older persons automatically belong to a group characterized by particular vulnerability and an inability of its members to protect themselves. A number of jurisdictions include these forms of preference: expedited hearings, such as

DISCUSSION QUESTIONS

1. Do you agree with the practice of state-sponsored dis-crimination in favor of older persons in the form of public benefit programs that use age as a very important criterion for program eligibility? When, if ever, is age a reliable proxy for need? Is needing public help the same thing as deserving such help?

2. Should older persons be given preferences such as prior-ity in scheduling hearings in civil litigation to which the older persons are parties? On what basis? What about the risk of stigmatizing the elderly as not self-reliant? What are some other potential drawbacks to showing older persons preference based solely on age?

priority scheduling for older parties in civil litigation; increased penalties for criminals whose victims have exceeded a specified chronological age threshold; alternatives, such as closed-circuit television, in place of live testimony for older witnesses in criminal trials; reduced sentences or early release for older convicted criminals; and adult protective services statutes classifying the acts or omissions of formal caregivers, family members, and others as forms of elder mistreatment (abuse or neglect) solely on the basis of a victim's age.

NOTES

Sections of this chapter were originally published in Marshall B. Kapp, *Social Values and Older Persons: The Role of the Law,* 7(1) Marquette Elder's Advisor 69–81 (2005), and Marshall B. Kapp, Aging and the Law, *Handbook of Aging and the Social Sciences* (6th ed., pp. 419–435) (Robert Binstock et al., eds.), Burlington, MA: Academic Press (2006).

Index

I

DATE DUE

DISCARDED

Printed
in USA